Arthurian Poets

JOHN MASEFIELD

At the end of the nineteenth century, a homeless runaway teenager in New York found a job in a bar and discovered Malory. So began the lifelong interest of the future Poet Laureate, John Masefield (1878–1967), in the story of King Arthur. After becoming a popular, successful narrative poet and playwright, Masefield turned to the Arthurian material in earnest, producing the verse drama *Tristan and Isolt* in 1927 and *Midsummer Night*, with its Arthurian cycle, a year later.

All twenty-eight of Masefield's previously published Arthurian poems, from the *Ballad of Sir Bors* (1903) to *Caer Ocvran* (1966), are collected here, along with the play *Tristan and Isolt*. This edition also presents a number of works never before published, including the full-length tragi-comedy *When Good King Arthur*, and prose notes which, together with nine new poems, reveal Masefield undertaking an ambitious retelling of the Arthurian myth.

In this collected edition, readers may enjoy the grim humour, vivid description and narrative inventiveness of this exceptional story-teller and poet.

DAVID LLEWELLYN DODDS, A.M., was a Rhodes Scholar and Richard Weaver Fellow at Merton College, Oxford. He has lectured in English at Harlaxton College, worked at the Houghton and Regenstein Libraries, and acted as Curator of C.S. Lewis's house. His previous work includes the Charles Williams volume in this Arthurian Poets series.

T0366963

Arthurian Poets

MATTHEW ARNOLD AND WILLIAM MORRIS
Introduced by James P. Carley
ALGERNON CHARLES SWINBURNE
Introduced by James P. Carley
EDWIN ARLINGTON ROBINSON
Introduced by James P. Carley
CHARLES WILLIAMS
Edited and introduced by David Llewellyn Dodds

The hardback edition of this volume
is published as
ARTHURIAN STUDIES XXXII
(ISSN 0261–9814)

Details of previous volumes of Arthurian Studies
are printed at the back of this volume

Arthurian Poets

JOHN MASEFIELD

Edited and introduced by
DAVID LLEWELLYN DODDS

THE BOYDELL PRESS

Editorial matter © 1994 David Llewellyn Dodds
Previously unpublished John Masefield poems, plays and prose © 1994
The Estate of John Masefield
Ballads © 1903 John Masefield
Midsummer Night and other Tales in Verse © 1928 John Masefield
Minnie Maylow's Story and other Tales and Scenes © 1931 John Masefield
On the Hill © 1949 John Masefield
My Library: Volume One © 1950 John Masefield
In Glad Thanksgiving © 1966/7 John Masefield
Tristan and Isolt: A play in Verse © 1927 John Masefield

First published 1994
The Boydell Press

Transferred to digital printing

ISBN 978-0-85115-363-6

The Boydell Press is an imprint of Boydell & Brewer Ltd
PO Box 9, Woodbridge, Suffolk IP12 3DF, UK
and of Boydell & Brewer Inc.
668 Mt Hope Avenue, Rochester, NY 14620, USA
website: www.boydellandbrewer.com

A CiP catalogue record for this book is available
from the British Library

This publication is printed on acid-free paper

PART IV. UNPUBLISHED PROSE

INTRODUCTION

When Masefield was chosen as Poet Laureate, in May 1930, he was a 'popular' writer in every sense: the first English edition of his *Collected Poems* (1923) sold some 80,000 copies, and some of his novels did almost as well.[1] It is not easy to say how Masefield is best known at the moment: perhaps as a 'sea poet', perhaps for his novel *The Midnight Folk* (1927), which Jennifer Goodman has suggested may be a 'prolific author's best work' and a source of 'Masefield's most entrancing and influential contributions to twentieth-century Arthurian literature'.[2] However, if Masefield remains justly famous for that significantly Arthurian fantasy, one may not immediately think of him as an Arthurian poet.

In fact, he is responsible for the fullest and most ambitious retelling of the Arthurian story in verse of any English poet between Tennyson and Charles Williams – as previously unpublished works presented in this volume make clear for the first time. He also wrote Arthurian poetry which was not a part of this retelling – among which the full-length play, *When Good King Arthur*, also published here for the first time, should probably be classified. That Masefield's Arthurian poetry is not only significant but enjoyable, the reader may readily discover by sampling two such different poems from *Midsummer Night* as 'On the Coming of Arthur' and 'The Old Tale of the Breaking of the Links'.

John Masefield (1878–1967) always considered himself primarily a story-teller – whether in prose or verse. 'From the first, I delighted in stories,' he wrote, and these included poems, many of which were 'known by heart long before I could read, though I learned to read easily, and early' – and read broadly indeed. Notably absent from his reading, however, was

1

anything Arthurian. While Tennyson's 'The Dying Swan' had been one of the earliest poems to delight Masefield, he had tried, later in childhood, to read some of Tennyson's Arthurian poems 'without any success'[3]: 'the time was unpropitious,' he later wrote, 'I had never read one right through'.[4]

Already, as a child, Masefield had what might be called a mystical apprehension of the world – and more:

> All that I looked upon was beautiful, and known by me to be beautiful, but also known by me to be, as it were, only the shadow of something much more beautiful, very, very near, and almost to be reached[.]

And then, when he was 'a little more than five years old', he 'entered that greater life'.[5]

Within a year-and-a-half after this, his mother died; five years later, his father had broken down completely, and his uncle and aunt took on the guardianship of John and his two sisters and three brothers. John was sent to the school-ship, HMS Conway, in Liverpool. Here, he read yet more widely in the ship's library (though still nothing Arthurian), and he loved to listen to one of his instructors, Wally Blair, 'a born story-teller, delighting all hearers'.

Masefield recalled that in unformed, wild dreams, 'I had hoped to be a writer', 'to know a great many books, to know a great deal of knowledge, and to tell all sorts of stories in all sorts of ways', but was perplexed because these longings 'seemed absurd even to people in whose wisdom I had some belief': everyone 'told me to put "this writing-rubbish" (that was the chosen phrase) right out of my head.'[6]

A month after his schooling for the merchant marine ended, in April 1894, Masefield set sail, as apprentice, on a voyage round Cape Horn to Chile. In August, too ill for the return voyage, he was discharged. Then, after a winter recuperating at home, he was nagged back into service, and in March 1895, went by steamship to New York, where he was to join his ship, bound for Japan.

Instead, he deserted, and disappeared. Unable to find work,

he became one of the homeless, drifting about, doing odd jobs, nearly starving. Then, reading the job advertisements in a newspaper in the bar of Luke O'Connor's Columbian Hotel (at the junction of Greenwich Avenue, Christopher Street, and old Sixth Avenue), he was surprised to be offered a job there, by the proprietor.[7] With this new start in life, Masefield determined to begin reading and learning as he longed to. His first step in this direction led to his discovery of Malory.

Masefield celebrated this event, which kindled his life-long interest in the Arthurian material, several times in print – perhaps most strikingly in 'My Library: Volume One' (1950) reprinted below. In the Sixth Avenue bookstore of Mr Pratt, an Englishman, the seventeen-year-old Masefield saw a row of books in the Camelot Classics series, and among them, the first volume of Malory's Morte d'Arthur. He had read about this as being the original of some of Tennyson's poems; 'Now I felt stirred to buy the Malory.' Reading it, he found it 'genuine, and Tennyson's Poems seemed lifeless when set beside it.'[8] 'I was at once enchanted by Malory', Masefield wrote later, 'All the story-telling instinct in me was thrilled as I read.'[9] After working in O'Connor's bar until 2.00 or 2.30 a.m., Masefield would go up to his garret, 'where I read the "Morte d'Arthur", my only book, until I fell asleep.'[10]

In September 1895, Masefield moved to Yonkers, to take a job with better pay and more leisure time – in the cutting shop of a carpet factory – and Malory went with him: 'I continued to read in it, especially the tales of Merlin and of Balin and Balan.'[11] He kept it for the rest of his life – and always had a copy of Malory among the favourite books by his bed.[12]

When he 'had been at Yonkers for a few weeks', Masefield wrote, he found 'an illustrated article on the Arthurian legend' which delighted him 'both for what it told and what it suggested.' Hoping to master what 'little was or could be known' about Arthur, Masefield wrote to a New York bookseller, 'asking if they could tell me what books were published' on the Arthurian material. 'The firm replied with a charming letter and a bibliography of 200 titles which they had then in stock,

3

adding that if their stock did not hold what I wanted, they would be delighted to search further for me.' Masefield, 'somewhat dashed', 'ordered a complete Malory and a copy of a translation of the Mabinogion', reading 'Malory straight through, with growing pleasure. The last book enchanted me'. He 'liked the Mabinogion much less, but as I believed then that the tales were ancient, possibly contemporary with Arthur, I gave them due respect. That Arthur had lived, I did not then doubt.'[13]

In what appears to be a set of rough lecture notes, written around 1965, Masefield reveals another influence on his early Arthurian studies. He says his reading of Malory

> turned me to the study of King Arthur in books and magazines for some months, when it was my fortune to meet every day a young Welsh chemist who knew another kind of Arthurian history [–] the memory of the Welsh for whatever had occurred in Wales since Rome ceased to be a power here. He knew; as the Welsh [seemed] to know instinctively what king had ruled in each small throne.
>
> From this man I learned this Arthur was not a king, only a clever soldier employed by allied kings against marauding pirates, and that at some time in his career he had won a great victory over the pirates at a place called Badon Hill.
>
> After this victory, he said, the war ceased, for a full generation, and Britain knew a little quiet.
>
> This was my first hearing of Badon Hill[.][14]

It was probably also around this time that Masefield became acquainted with the works of Thomas Love Peacock, including his brilliant (and scholarly) interweaving of the stories of Taliesin and of the abduction of Queen Gwenyfar, *The Misfortunes of Elphin* (1829) – another enduring pleasure.[15]

Masefield wrote that in 'a little more than a year after my buying of the Malory, I gave up this prose-reading for the study of poetry.' His discoveries here included, among poets he loved 'for their power of telling tales', Chaucer and D.G. Rossetti.

Rossetti led him to the Pre-Raphaelites and Burne-Jones – an interest he fed, after returning to England in 1897, both in Liverpool and London, and one which further nurtured his Arthurian interests, particularly through his discovery of William Morris.[16] In 1930, Masefield wrote to a friend, after a visit to Morris's grave and Kelmscott Manor, 'It makes one wonder: what would my life have been without him?'[17] Years later, he wrote to 'Reyna' in similar terms, mentioning *The Defence of Guenevere*, and told her

> I often went to his grave at Kelmscott to say what was said over Lancelot's grave.
> 'Now there thou rest, that never wast matched by mortal man.'[18]

Masefield's Arthurian interests not only grew in 1895–97, to endure throughout his life, but bore immediate fruit – though not publicly. In *So Long to Learn* (p. 91), Masefield says 'I will spare the reader an account of the wild Arthurian tales that were in my imagination for the next few months' after his discovery of Malory. And around 1898, he gave his cousins, the Parkers, a notebook which included, in the words of his biographer,

> a long romantic saga in six parts, 'The Tale of Elphin', based largely upon William Morris's *Earthly Paradise*, and written in poetic prose with an Arthurian flavour.[19]

Public evidence of Masefield's Arthurian interests came only with his second book, *Ballads* (October 1903), which had as its first poem 'The Ballad of Sir Bors'. This is unique among Masefield's Arthurian works in its attention to the Quest for the Holy Grail (presented with imagery reminiscent of the 'Celtic Twilight'[20]). The ballad is not, so far as we know, part of any more extended retelling, and this can leave uncertainties about its possible context: for example, does it look forward to the events of Malory XVII, 2–23, or might it presuppose them, and amplify or vary those of XXI, 10–13, with Bors questing to the end of his life? In any case, it imagines with some success the realities both of Bors's experience and endurance, and of the difficulties and strain entailed.

More that twenty-three years elapsed before Masefield's next Arthurian work appeared before the public, with the first performance of *Tristan and Isolt* on 21 February 1927. There was, however, public evidence of Masefield's continuing interest in the material. For example, the Grail appears in a significant simile in *Dauber* (1913), IV, stanza 5. And, in the twelve-sonnet sequence, *Animula* (1920), the speaker investigates a love-triangle in which the wife and her lover 'both were saints: elopement could not be': she is later discovered drowned in the ocean, and the speaker says, 'haply' she 'runs like light', 'One with the blue sea's pureness of delight', while the lover, a scholar and poet, is effectively likened to Arthur:

> He died in that lone cottage near the sea.
> In the grey morning when the tide was turning
> The wards of life slipt back and set him free
> From cares of meat and dress, from joys and yearning.
> Then like an old man gathering strength, he strayed
> Over the beach, and strength came into him,
> Beauty that never threatened nor betrayed
> Made bright the eyes that sorrow had made dim;
> So that upon that stretch of barren sand
> He knew his dreams; he saw her beauty run
> With Sorrowful Beauty, laughing, hand in hand;
> He heard the trumpets blow in Avalon.[21]

Masefield's 'Introduction' (dated 10 June 1913) for R.C. Phillimore's *Poems* – a volume including 'Sir Breuse Sans Pitie' and 'The Betraying of Guinever' – provides more prominent evidence. Masefield singles out for notice Phillimore's

> interesting metrical retelling of some of the Arthurian story. Against the Arthurian story it may be objected that Malory has told it finally in a fitting form, and that since we have it in prose we should therewith be content. Similar objections were raised, no doubt, when Shakespeare made free with Holinshed. The two or three

great English stories should be a quarrying ground for the imaginations of our poets[.]

While praising Phillimore's 'Guinever', he says, 'It is more an opening than a completed poem,' yet the force of narrative makes 'one hope that Mr Phillimore will do more poems like it.'[22] There may or may not be a hint in this that Masefield himself hoped to attempt a more satisfactory 'metrical retelling' of some, or all, of the Arthurian story. There is no doubt that, in the event, 'Sir Breuse' became a significant character in Masefield's retelling, and that we are now able to see something of his process of working on the matter of 'The Betraying of Guinever' and its context (Malory XX, 1–10), which yielded 'The Fight on the Wall', 'The Breaking of the Links', and 'The Old Tale of the Breaking of Links' in *Midsummer Night* – and more than one poem published here for the first time – of which we will say more below.

Between 'The Ballad of Sir Bors' and *Tristan and Isolt*, Masefield had published nine long narrative poems and three verse dramas, as well as a number of other plays in prose (and eight novels).[23] In 1966 Masefield wrote to Corliss Lamont, 'I am a story-writer, and am always drawn to narrative, seldom to drama or to pure thought.' And Judith Masefield reported, 'He said that the dramatic form was never one that he could master.'[24] Nonetheless, he was keenly interested in drama, and in promoting the popularization of drama, especially in verse; and his contribution to the beginnings of the Canterbury Festival in 1928[25] was perhaps the most notable of his many aids to the revival of English verse drama.

While *Tristan and Isolt: A Play in Verse* is Masefield's first major published Arthurian work, it is not sufficient to say that, and no more. We are now able to see something of the complexity of the situation, though it is not possible to supply dates, or even to establish the relative chronology certainly, for all the items involved.[26]

Let us begin, however, with some reflections, and a call, which Masefield made in 1952:

William Morris is said to have hoped that his countrymen might some day reckon the *Morte d'Arthur* as a holy book. Why not? [. . .]

Has not the time come for a re-making and re-issue of the epic by a body of good scholars and writers? Is not the time ripe for an Authorized Version using old poems and fables little used by or unknown to Malory, and rejecting (or putting in some condemned Apocrypha) the late, inferior tales that have no place in any credible tradition? [. . .] Malory's work may be less read than in my youth; it must be more critically studied. Much shrewd and precious work has been done upon some early forms of the tales, with a consequent lessening of liking for some of the versions he includes. Men have delved a little into our pre-history, and have striven to lighten our Dark Age, with some success.

It is our English epic; we ought to make more use of it than we do. Its wonderful last book is unmatched in our language; it is one of our great contributions to the world; it will be in the world, as epic, drama, opera and ballet, for a thousand years to come.

The time is ripe for it. The scholars and writers are here, waiting for a word of encouragement; the land is Arthur's land, and her people need more than ever the exaltation that a great national fable alone can give. A few learned and gifted men, working on tales already shaped by love and genius, would soon complete a version. Would we not all rather have it than not have it? Would not some say: 'How strange that no-one did this long ago'?

Certainly, the Arthurian cycle or body of fables offers subjects in plenty for the English playwright, epic poet, and maker of opera.[27]

There seem to be two strands here, easily, if not necessarily, contradictory. Earlier in the same work, Masefield states one of these: 'The foundation of part of the epic must be British. What a foundation it is, for the imagination to work upon, for the story-teller to invent upon' (p. 91). In this strand, the

Arthurian material is seen as a source for things to be used, altered, varied. In the other strand, what is sought seems to be a final, perfected, authoritative version of the Arthurian story, involving, perhaps, a consideration of historical as well as artistic factors.

Looking at Masefield's published Arthurian work, our immediate inclination might be to see his practice as lying overwhelmingly with the first strand – with a varying, altering, inventing, and multiplying which is quite luxuriant – whether we think of his three (or four?) different versions of the story of Tristan and Isolt (particularly the 1949 poem), or, for example, his inclusion in *Midsummer Night* of an adaptation of the story of 'The Ring Given to Venus' which makes Arthur the giver. It seems simply paradoxical for such a practitioner to call for a comprehensive, polished, version of the whole story.

If, however, there is finally something paradoxical here, it is not so simple and straightforward as it first appears. Both strands seem, in fact, to be present in the quotations from Masefield's 1913 'Introduction' given above. And if we turn to the published verse, some explicit indications may be found of a greater unity than is immediately apparent. For example, when in *Midsummer Night*, reference is made to 'Bedwyr, the Cornish Knight, whom Tristan fooled',[28] this surely refers to the comic subplot of *Tristan and Isolt* – and so indicates that the Arthurian cycle in the later book in some way presupposes the events of the play, and that both are parts of a greater whole.

The items, both in prose and verse, published here for the first time (and assigned titles for convenience of reference), clarify the situation immensely, though many details remain uncertain. *Notes 1* and *2* show that at some time Masefield began gathering materials for a retelling of the Arthurian story, whether with any particular work or works in mind or not. The material in *Notes 1* is entirely Welsh, while *Notes 2* draw on Malory as well. I have not attempted to identify Masefield's immediate source(s) – much of the information occurs in Lady Charlotte Guest's notes to her translation of the *Mabinogion*, but there are too many differences in detail for this simply to be the source. A good example of this is the treatment of Iddawc, called 'Iudoc' in *Notes 1*, where 'The Dream of Rhonabwy' and some triads must be the ultimate sources, but Guest's translation and notes are surely not Masefield's direct source. While *Notes 1* are quite miscellaneous, *Notes 2* show an ordering of their materials, though they are full of specific alternatives and do not constitute a plot-sketch. The *Prospectus* represents a further stage, proposing a retelling, cast in the form of a play (I know of no evidence that more was written, beyond this outline).

The *Sketch* is presumably later, and certainly more ambitious, giving a detailed, circumstantial outline of a retelling of Arthur's story, and, by several specific dates and ages, showing that Masefield has now given a fair degree of attention to the chronology of the story, at least in its earlier parts. The expression 'We suggest . . .' may indicate that the *Sketch* is a kind of proposal, but, if so, it is not clear what work or works may be proposed. We know neither when Masefield wrote the *Sketch* nor when he began writing the poems of his Arthurian cycle. However, it is possible that the poem published in *Midsummer Night* as 'The Okd Tale of the Begetting' dates from the same time as the *Sketch*: it is certainly consonant with the beginning of the *Sketch*, where Masefield has not yet abandoned the version of the story fournd in Malory (I, 2). And an earlier version of the poem, without any title or introductory couplet, survives in typescript.[29] 'The Begetting of Modred' may also date from this time, or at least from this stage of retelling: the most obvious sense of the final lines – 'And the father, the uncle, / Had a nephew for son' – is that Morgause is at least Arthur's 'half-sister', as in the *Sketch*, rather than his aunt, as in 'The Begetting of Arthur'.[30] It may also be noted that the descriptions in *Tristan and Isolt* of Arthur as 'Captain of the Romano-British Host' and as 'Lord' or 'Sir Arthur' (rather than 'King Arthur') are in keeping with the details of the *Sketch*.

Tristan and Isolt reveals as much careful concern for ages and dates as the *Sketch*. And the *Chronology*, while it revises the dates of the *Sketch*, corresponds with the play in all the details relative to Marc, Kolbein, Tallorc, and Olwen.[31]

A letter to Florence Lamont shows Masefield intent on finishing *Tristan and Isolt*, in September 1926 if possible. Another, from April 1927, includes his comments on its production by the Lena Ashwell Players, and shows that his own seasoned amateur troupe, the Hill Players, were contemplating a production of it that autumn: 'The poetical theatre', he observes, 'needs a technique of its own, which we, who only play verse, begin to know now.'[32] For whatever reason, the first major Arthurian work which Masefield published is concerned with what he elsewhere calls the 'tale of Tristan' in apparent distinction from the 'Arthur stories'.[33] Presumably, this 'tale' was originally independent of the Arthurian story, and has certainly been treated as such – notably by Thomas, who makes Mark King of England, and by Gottfried von Strassburg who follows him in this. Masefield, however, has thoroughly, and essentially, integrated it into the Arthurian story in *Tristan and Isolt*. While Masefield did not specify any examples when he later wrote, with respect to Malory,

> Much shrewd and precious work has been done upon some early forms of the tales, with a consequent lessening of liking for some of the versions he includes

he might well have been thinking of the 'tale of Tristan', and even of Joseph Bédier's reconstruction *Le Roman de Tristan par Thomas* (whether in the original or in Hilaire Belloc's translation). In fact, we do not know Masefield's immediate sources, but *Tristan and Isolt* would serve as a good example of what he later called for: remaking the story 'using old poems and fables little used by or unknown to Malory'. He clearly takes the story as found in Thomas or Gottfried as his starting point, rather than Malory, combining it with Welsh sources, and historical speculation. Thus, Tristan is the son of the Northern king, Tallorc, who was on Arthur's 'staff in the Pentland war', and is named after his grandfather King Tristan, rather than with any deliberate reference to *triste*.

11

Masefield compresses and streamlines the action, with the main events apparently taking place between spring and late summer of one year. This may be partly because he chose to write a play, but Masefield clearly has deeper reasons as well. For example, the Irish king and his champion are replaced by one figure, Kolbein Blood-axe, and the periodic tributes exacted, by Kolbein's effective usurpation of Cornwall. But more than this: Kolbein also replaces Duke Morgan as the slayer of Tristan's father, and is made the slayer of Marc's father, and – in one of the many surprises which ate characteristic of Masefield's retelling – is revealed to be Isolts's 'father' only by virtue of having killed her actual father the day before her birth, and made her mother his queen. Thus, Marc, Tristan, and Isolt, have suffered identically, and are given strong grounds for mutual sympathy, Marc and Isolt more particularly as each has long been effectively 'a slave to Kolbein' – as Isolt's mother, Thurid, says, and Tristan knows.

Here we meet a major theme of the play, slavery and the release from slavery. By defeating Kolbein, Tristan frees Marc and Cornwall – and Thurid and Isolt – from 'slavery'. Arthur, analogously, is raising men to fight a war to preserve, or extend, freedom from the Saxons. The theme contributes to the seriousness in Masefield's reworking, as a comic subplot, of the story from the triads explaining why Tristan is called one of the three powerful swineherds of Britain. Tristan, to guarantee that the swineherd and his family will gain their freedom, humbly and conscientiously undertakes to guard the swine so that Hog may go as his messenger to warn Isolt of a trap. Though the attempts, then, by Kai and Bedwyr to steal the swine, are wildly sportful, the trap, the intention to discredit and drive out Tristan, and the slaves' freedom, are all thoroughly serious matters. As elsewhere in the play, Arthur's interventions are made decisive to the course of events. Here, he gives Tristan a hint, before seeming to join Kai and Bedwyr in their raid. In the process, Arthur gently encourages Tristan to return to the realm he has inherited.

In Thomas's and Gottfried's versions, Tristan easily gives his own land, and all the cares of its government, to his Marshal, and goes to live in Cornwall. Masefield allows no such option: Tristan neglects his political and moral responsibilities. While he admirably keeps faith with the swineherd to assure his freedom by defending the swine with his life, Tristan allows his own subjects, and friends, to be slaughtered, answering the request 'for our King to lend our host to the war', with 'War is an unreal thing to a man who has love.' By contrast, Marc, who never cast off Kolbein's yoke, once freed by Tristan goes as king to lead his men, including the apparently unlikely Kai and Bedwyr, to fight beside Arthur at Badon – and to die there.

The 'tale of Tristan' is thus essentially integrated into the Arthurian story, with Arthur made a crucial character. All his generosity to the lovers may evoke our recollection of the parallel story of Gwenivere and Lancelot – never mentioned in the play – and the question, what shall this Arthur do, when his turn comes?

Two notebooks survive which include drafts of some, but not all, of the poems published in the *Midsummer Night* cycle, and of others that, for whatever reason, were never finished or published (all without titles). The first notebook begins with a draft of 'Arthur and his Ring', started on 4 March 1927[34] – while *Tristan and Isolt* was in the second week of its run.

'The Hunt is Up' is the next Arthurian poem in this notebook, with the date 'June 25. 1927' opposite its first line – five days before *Tristan and Isolt* was published. It is followed by 'Modred the Messenger'. The last stanza of that is varied and succeeded by the drafts of what was published in *Midsummer Night* as 'The Old Tale of the Breaking of the Links', with '12 Oct. 1927' opposite the first line of the full draft and 'Oct 27. 1927' written after the end of the poem. This is followed in turn by 'Gareth's Wake', with 'Nov 14' near the beginning and 'Nov 17 1927' near the end. Here we see Masefield trying his hand at the subject of Phillimore's 'The Betraying of Guinever' and its surrounding matter in Malory XX, 1–10. It is quite clear that when all of these were drafted, there was no question of their relating to an 'Old Tale': they were simply Masefield's version of the story. 'The Old Tale of the Breaking of the Links' must likewise have succeeded the draft as the current version, with the much more circumstantial poem, 'The Fight on the Wall', replacing 'The Hunt is Up' – perhaps at an early stage: at any rate, 'The Fight' is compatible with the draft, as well as the final, version of 'The Old Tale'. Thus, the question as to what the compassionate Arthur of *Tristan and Isolt* will do when his turn comes, has very different answers at different times. Perhaps the desire for consistency with that characterisation was among the things which motivated Masefield finally to abandon the trial of Gwenivere and her rescue by Lancelot – and with it, the killing of Gareth.[35]

His letters to Florence Lamont show Masefield, between drafting 'The Hunt is Up' and 'The Old Tale', 'going to beyond Severn' in order 'to see the Roman remains, just as good King Arthur left them 1400 years ago', including the ruins at Viroconium, which he 'had not seen for 20 years', and on the way back having 'a good view of Buttington, which I believe to be the Mons Badonicus of Arthur's victory.'[36]

Whether 'Badon Hill' was written thereafter, we do not know, and the questions of how far the geographical references and vivid details in that, and other poems, indicate that Masefield has decided upon, and described, particular sites, await further investigation.

Neither do we know exactly when 'The Old Tale of the Begetting' became 'The Old Tale'. But this must have occurred by 23 January 1928, when Masefield began 'Brother Lot' (which follows 'Gareth's Wake' in the first notebook), for it presupposes at least the plot of 'The Begetting of Arthur' in some form. The *Chronology* also assumes essential details found in 'The Begetting'.

A version of the *Chronology* with no very significant differences from the one printed here (except that it lacks the three final entries – apparently brief summarizing entries of years given in the main sequence, unless they represent an antecedent to the full *Chronology*), is pasted into the beginning of the second notebook. At first glance, this notebook seems to

14

present something of a mystery. For, opposite 'Before the Darkness Came' is written 'Sunset. Feb 21. between Luxor + Edfu', and on the next page, opposite the 'Sailing of Hell Race' outline, is 'Feb 22', while at the end of the first draft of 'The Sailing of Hell Race' which follows, is written '5.56. Feb 25. Sat^y. 1927. 1 hour after sailing N from Abu Simbel in Upper Egypt' But Agnes Lauchlin vividly remembered Masefield being present at the first performance of *Tristan and Isolt* on 21 February 1927.[37] And in 1927, 25 February fell on a Friday: it fell on a Saturday in 1928. The solution is surely that Masefield has unconsciously written the old year, '1927' – even as he did in the first notebook, where, in the date opposite the beginning of 'Brother Lot', 'Mon. Jan 23' 28', the '8' has been written over an original '7', while at the end of the poem is written '26 Jan 5.16 eve of departure' – presumably, the departure on the trip which included the Nile cruise.

While the *Chronology*, 'Brother Lot', and the outline and drafts in the second notebook for 'The Aftermath', are all closely related, we do not certainly know the order in which they were written. Together, they show how carefully Masefield has worked out the familial relations between Arthur, Marc, Lancelot, and Tristan. And, while there are variations between the *Chronology* and the 'Aftermath' drafts, he is clearly trying to work out the dates with comparable care.

From the combined evidence of *Tristan and Isolt*, the *Chronology*, the notebooks, other surviving drafts, and *Midsummer Night*, it is clear that the published works are manifestations and parts of a fuller reworking of the Arthurian story. When Masefieldd decided upon a reworking on the scale he did, is not known. That he had done so by the beginning of 1928 is inescapable. We know neither how he came to publish *Mdsummer Night*, with just the contents it has, nor why he prepared no more of his retelling for publication.

Anne Ridler has noted a problem which arose in the course of Charles Williams's work on his Arthurian retelling: 'the poet came to presuppose a certain knowledge in the reader which has nowhere been conveyed'.[38] Something similar may be said of Masefield. For example, when in 'The Fight on the Beach', Masefield says of Lancelot's brother, Maximin, 'Dead fell that youngling of the golden queen', we have to go to such an unpublished source as the *Chronology* or 'The Aftermath' to discover that 'the golden queen' is Ygern's younger sister, Elaine, who features so prominently in 'The Begetting of Arthur'.

We have seen examples of how Masefield's reworking of the story underwent major alterations and developments in the process of the writing, and one example – 'The Begetting of Modred' – where something from an earlier stage seems to have escaped revision, or assignment to an appendix of 'Old Tales'. We may now note a rather different case.

The *Chronology* gives the earliest evidence of Masefield's intending to include something analogous to the events of the *Preiddau Annwfn* in his retelling – assigning this voyage 'to the underworld' to A.D. 525. When he turned to the actual writing, on 'Feb 22' [1928], Masefield, sensibly enough, in keeping with the content he had decided upon, set the action at an earlier time. Just when, is not clear: in the outline for 'The Sailing of Hell Race' of that date in the second notebook, Masefield sets it after 'the Pentland war' and before 'the great invasion' and makes it end with the first meeting of Arthur and Gwenivere. In *Tristan and Isolt*, 'the Pentland war' must have taken place before A.D. 497 – which would accord with Arthur meeting Gwenivere in 498, as in the *Chronology*. The first draft of 'The Sailing of Hell Race' begins 'So having fought the Pentland war'. But a later draft, begun 12 March 1928 in the first notebook, changes this to 'When Arthur came from warring'. So the poem reads in *Midsummer Night*, but there it comes after 'Badon Hill'. If this also implies that the events occurred in that order – that Arthur met Gwenivere after the battle of Badon (which Masefield, following one of the interpretations of the *Annales Cambriae*, dates to 518 in both *Sketch* and *Chronology*) – then acute problems follow from this major alteration. For, in 'Midsummer Night' we learn of Modred's coming to court, not long after the heir to

16

the throne, Lacheu, was killed 'riding to Wales' (together with another major innovation: that Lacheu was in fact Lancelot's bastard). While the combination of a late date for the marriage of Arthur and Gwenivere with a son old enough to ride to Wales need not present any problems for a retelling as such, some further major revisions would seem to be required in Masefield's carefully constructed Chronology in order to accom-modate these facts.[39]

Nonetheless, there are many things in either the Chronology or in the previously unpublished drafts which may well be assumed to remain part of the retelling in its latest form. For example, 'Arthur's Youth' might be allowed to stand as it is – together with some version of 'Brother Lot' and 'The After-math'.[40] But there can be problems – often very enjoyable problems – of what, and how, to decide in particular cases. Should we assume, for instance, that behind Modred's words in 'Midsummer Night' about Lacheu – 'Then your son's killing happened' – lies the fact which Modred reveals in one of the drafts: that he told the pirate Kol 'hour and day / Of Lacheu's riding, so that he might slay'? Similarly, should we assume that Iddoc helps to administer 'Uther's kingdom in trust for Arthur' (as in the Chronology) and yet ends up playing 'at a triple game' as he says in a 'Midsummer Night' draft – and that Iddoc's apparent difficulties in 'The Breaking of the Links' are in fact part of this game? And may we imagine that the 'Breuse' op-posing Arthur in 'The Fight on the Beach' is the now grizzled 'Breuse the Heartless' who helped kill Uther? Or must we here accept the Chronology or 'The Aftermath', that Ban killed 'baron Breuse', making this another of that name?[41]

Whatever we may decide in such cases, it remains clear that Masefield, in the 1920s, had himself attempted something like what he was calling for in 1952: 'a re-making and re-issue of the epic'. One is repeatedly impressed by Masefield's humility. When, at eighty-six, he accepted an award for his latest vol-ume of poetry, he said, 'I am still writing and hope to write better some day', and also referred to the majesty of 'those fables that still await retelling.'[42] Perhaps he numbered the

17

'Arthur stories' among these, as he had done in 1944, when, speaking of 'great bodies of our fable', he said, 'We have a wealth and a wonder there, not yet touched with undying life such as brought Macbeth and Lear from the dull lines in Holinshed.'[43] Such later references clearly suggest that Masefield had no pretensions that he had achieved the kind of retelling he wished might be. But he had made his own attempt in that direction – and had made it in verse.

'Brevity', says the villainous poet in *When Good King Arthur*, 'is the soul of poetry.' The writing of long poems, and narrative poetry, has been problematical ever since the critical stress on lyric intensity gave rise to the notion that something could not be both long or narrative and 'poetry'. Arthurian poets from Tennyson on, have had to face this fact, and have worked out their various solutions. Masefield was a champion of narrative poetry, and by 1926, the very successful author of nine long narrative poems. As Fraser Drew has noted, three of these are in rime royal,[44] while *The Everlasting Mercy* and *Reynard the Fox* are in octosyllabic couplets, and *Rosas* is in stanzas of six ten-syllabled lines. In *King Cole*, Masefield uses both rime royal and decasyllabic couplets. The metrical components of *Enslaved* and *Right Royal* are more varied and adventurous – which might also be said of *Philip the King* and the short sequence *Lollingdon Downs* (1917). If these last-mentioned works point forward to his Arthurian solution, it is still noteworthy that Masefield has, in part, elected upon a cycle, rather than a single poem – and a cycle which not only includes, for example, poems in ten-syllable couplets, and various ballad forms, but also displays an astonishing fertility in the invention of new narrative stanzas. More striking still, is the fact that his single retelling has been embodied in more that one medium: in a play as well as a cycle.

Tristan and Isolt is emphatically no closet drama; it is designed for performance. It may be that the poems of the Arthurian cycle (and 'South and East', the other tale in *Midsummer Night* which is Arthurian – by virtue of its setting) were, in fact, so designed as well, though in a different sense.

For, after judging a verse-speaking competition in 1922, Masefield organized, under University auspices, the Oxford Recitations (1923–29), becoming ever more concerned with the idea that poetry should be communicated by – and written for – the living voice. The poetry in *Minnie Maylow's Story and Other Tales and Scenes* (1931), which includes three more Arthurian poems, was certainly so designed: it was written for performance during three years of small non-competitive festivals which followed the University Recitations.[45] Looking back on the whole period, Masefield wrote that, 'for some years', he was able to make 'certain experiments in narrative'. These 'were in methods of story-telling: in taking an event known to have involved certain persons, and devising means for letting each person tell his or her share in the experience.' He adds that, in a variation on this method, he made a prologue and epilogue 'to be spoken by Fate or Destiny'.[46] We may note in passing that this last, is also a feature of *Tristan and Isolt*, but of greater interest are the details of the basic 'experiment'. 'The Hour Strikes', one of the 'Scenes' in *Minnie Maylow's Story*, is clearly the result of such an 'experiment'. In it, 'great figures' of Katharine of Aragon, Wolsey, Anne Bullen, and Henry VIII speak in turn. But they do so as the result of the inquiry of 'The Seeker', who climbs a hill on Midsummer Night, to find them. Whether 'Midsummer Night' is also the fruit of such 'experiments', or, alternatively, an inspiration of the method, the similarities are striking. Drafts of its opening come at the end of the second notebook, while drafts of possible speeches by various persons survive on eleven loose sheets. Though begun before Masefield had decided on his new tale of 'The Breaking of the Links', 'Midsummer Night' is not simply a part of the cycle in the same way as even the dramatic monologues of Gwenivach and Gwenivere are. It clearly proved an economical means of organizing the parts that are included in *Midsummer Night* – that, together with 'Dust to Dust' and 'On the Coming of Arthur', it also does much more than this, will be suggested below.

We may here note four other works and their possible

connexions with Masefield's retelling. The first two of these are 'The Love Gift' and 'Tristan's Singing', which come together in that order in *Minnie Maylow's Story*, each written in a different stanza varied from rime royal. 'The Love Gift' would seem to be strictly compatible with *Tristan and Isolt*, but also seems very much a companion-piece of 'Tristan's Singing', which is simply incompatible with the play. 'Tristan's Singing', at least, must either displace the play from the retelling, or represent the luxuriant strand of Masefield's imagination in approaching the Arthurian material, content to multiply versions of a tale.

Masefield's other Arthurian drama, *When Good King Arthur*, is itself concerned with a verse-speaking contest – one held at Tintagel, to which 'Each kingdom in the country sends one poet / To speak his poetry against the rest' – and a preliminary contest at Arthur's court to determine which of two poets to send. The world of the play seems very much that of the retelling.[47] For example, in an early version, Geraint, to discredit his rival, quotes from a supposed letter from his 'friend, the king of Vectis', which says of Owain:

> He came here in a ship from Brittany, [. . .]
> His stay in Vectis ended suddenly.
> He disappeared on board a pirate cruiser,
> Whose men landed and sacked the temples here.
> Undoubtedly he acted as their guide.

But this play and the final form of the retelling do not seem compatible in all details: here, during Marc's lifetime, Arthur is very much a local king, rather than *dux bellorum*, and is married. The character of Arthur seems to represent another incompatibility. In an early version, a stern and furious Arthur is about to pronounce sentence on his daughter Helen upon ancient, potent relics which include 'A finger-nail of Lear, who cursed his daughter'. Whether he would have sentenced her to marry Geraint against her will, or to immediate confinement in a nunnery, we do not know, for here the Soothsayer

20

intervenes. This Arthur, who is a kind of tragicomic analogue of Lear, effectively disappears in revision. But the Arthur of the later version presented here, after the princess Helen has become his ward rather than his daughter, still lacks the sharp intelligence of the Arthur of the retelling. The plot gives another example of Masefield's transposing a non-Arthurian story to an Arthurian setting for its reworking: in this case, the story of the poet Arion (Herodotus I, 23–24).

When Good King Arthur remains fraught with practical mysteries. It was clearly intended for performance, and was cast, and presumably rehearsed – some of the manuscripts bear marginal timing notes. But whether it was performed, and when, and in how many versions, we cannot say. For parts of the play, a good number of different stages of composition are discernable (often with more than one earlier stage in typescript), but whether these – and the two cast lists – testify to one continuous process of revision, or whether the play was in fact produced in different versions at different times, is unclear. It is usually possible to tell which are Masefield's latest drafts of a given part: that these also represent his final intentions is not so easy to say, for nothing like a fair copy of a final version survives among the manuscripts. It has therefore been necessary to reconstruct a conjectural final version from the materials which do survive.

We do not yet know when this considerably revised play was written. Of the possible clues discovered so far, none is decisive. Thus, it could be anything from Masefield's first major Arthurian work to be completed, to the last one of this intensely Arthurian period. All we can say certainly, is that it must have been written between 1919 and 1932, when Masefield was living on Boars Hill and active in amateur drama – and almost surely after 1922, when he became so interested in the speaking of poetry.[48]

About the poem, 'All Hallow Night', which occurs among the manuscripts of *When Good King Arthur*, nothing more certain can be said than about the play. It has the feel of a self-contained tale – presumably an independent variant –

though it could be a draft of a poem intended, at some stage (probably early) to be a part of Masefield's retelling.[49]

When Masefield first encountered the Arthurian stories, he 'supposed that these old romances were all retellings of British history or traditions, and that all of them had been founded on fact.'[50] His interest in archaeology and the historical geography of Britain always included the Arthurian.[51] And his retelling is among the early examples in this century of something which has since become quite characteristic – the Roman British Arthur. In this context, we may note that, however different Masefield, Charles Williams, and David Jones are their Arthurian poetry, they have three notable things in common: they make particular use of Welsh sources, and, by no means excluding the matter of mediaeval romance, they yet give special prominence to the relation of Britain to the Roman Empire and civilization.[52]

As *Notes 1* show, in the Welsh sources, the historical triumph of the Saxons has various contributory causes of Arthurian provenance. In *Notes 2*, the *Prospectus* and *Sketch*, and throughout the stages of the retelling, we can see Masefield working to achieve a satisfactory imaginative reconstruction and integration of the Welsh materials with essential 'tragic' elements of Malory – Arthur's incestuous begetting of Modred and the adulterous love of Gwenivere and Lancelot – to provide an account of the failure of the last great hope for Roman Britain.

Masefield's Arthur comes at the culmination of a long process: in 'The Birth of Arthur' the Kings and Queens who have built up Britain say to him 'What we made you will keep.' The virtuous begetting in pure love which Masefield provides for Arthur is the last contribution to this. But from the responses of Merchyon and Breuse – and then of the kings of Uther's league – come potentialities of future disaster.

Through the confessions and claims of responsibility in 'Midsummer Night', Masefield shows what a complex business the actualization of such potentialities is. He is attentive both to the reality of human freedom, and to its effective conditioning.

In this context, he neither simply celebrates, nor simply con-demns, nor only makes pragmatic allowance for, the passionate loves of Tristan and Isolt and Gwenivere and Lancelot. In *Tristan and Isolt*, for example, we see Isolt to some extent truly – and properly – freed by Marc's generous action from a love she then sees as 'blindness and greed': yet again, we see both that she is not in fact thoroughly freed, and that the love is not wholly or essentially something evil.

We may now consider the midsummer symbolism which not only runs through the retelling, but is a feature of 'The Love Gift' and 'Tristan's Singing' as well.[53] Midsummer, 'the summit of the year', can mark a return to the beginning, presenting new opportunities. It is apparently at midsummer that Ygerna takes the baby Arthur to Pendragon Ledge that the Powers and Helpers may come to him. It is, indeed, summer, and perhaps near midsummer, when Arthur is conceived, and summer and June imagery are associated with him. That triumph of Badon would seem to follow not long after such a solstitial new begin-ning. On the other hand, Morgause is taken in June, Modred is also conceived 'one summer night', perhaps around midsum-mer, and Camlan certainly takes place as the 'season neared midsummer'. What follows midsummer midnight is 'the first hour of the year's decay'. It is perfectly fitting that the testing involving the Fruit of Immortal Life in 'The Love Gift' should begin on Midsummer Eve and that the poem should end with 'deeper sorrows' laid bare, than Marc's over his betrayal – with a confrontation with the mystery of death in the context of

> The inmost ache within the mortal breast,
> The pitiful child's crying of the race
> For comfort of a soul no longer there.[54]

No one has so partaken of Immortality as to escape dying. Together with the fact of new opportunities, the midsummer symbolism presents the fact that the best that can be achieved within the world is radically impermanent.

It is this, with its temptations to surrender and despair,

which Arthur must finally face in 'The Sailing of Hell Race'. By then, he has already confronted other dangers – and temptations – of misrule and disordered societies, which illustrate the importance of striving for the fragile best which may be achieved. Even so, it is only through the intervention of his Helper, and through his response to her, that Arthur is delivered from the despair and paralysis that attend this final confrontation.

This Helper is part of a careful structuring of the *Midsummer Night* cycle. In 'The Birth of Arthur' she says that at three crises 'My beauty as Helper / Shall not let you fail', and that 'at passing' she will bring him 'Where nothing grows old' – to 'Avalon', in fact. The first of the three occasions we have just noted; the third comes in 'Arthur in the Ruins'. Before we attend to the second, we must consider the matter of 'Avalon'.

In 'The Fight on the Beach or The Passing', Arthur's Helper and seven queens 'bear him to the isle of Avalon, / Where everlasting summer has abode.' Gwenivere seems immediately to contradict this, saying 'That ship reached Avalon with Arthur dead; / I, Gwenivere, helped cere him, within lead.'

Here, we may at last attend to the three poems which go beyond a simple retelling of Arthurian events – and are essential to Masefield's purpose. 'Dust to Dust' makes it clear that this latter 'Avalon' is Glastonbury. Both that poem and 'Gwenivere Tells' present the fact of Arthur dead, though with significant differences. In 'Dust to Dust', Masefield imagines the excavation of Arthur's grave as taking place during the lifetime not only of Henry II, but of Rosamund, and in their presence. Here is a later word than those of the still-living Gwenivere in the two-part monologue 'Gwenivere Tells' – 'The Death of Lancelot'. Here are Gwenivere and Arthur apparently reconciled, 'dead ones' together 'Untouched by any semblance of decay, / Liker to things immortal than things dead' like the bodies of some saints – though at the touch of a rose petal 'Those bodies ceast, as though they had not been'.[55] This 'Avalon' is a place of wonders, but need not be the only

'Avalon'. Nor does the fact of Arthur's body, wonderful yet 'ceasing' to powder, necessitate the reduction of 'Arthur' to his corpse.

Gwenivere had said, 'Men watch for him on each Midsummer Eve. / They watch in vain'. But the speaker of 'Midsummer Night', going within a hill 'to Arthur's bower', seems to hear not only Arthur, but Gwenivere, and others of the court (though before midnight he 'could not know / If they were dead, or carved, or living all', and after one o'clock chimes 'those figures lapsed again to stone'). The 'Arthur' here says they will rise and return, and the speaker of 'On the Coming of Arthur' echoes him, and invokes: 'O Arthur, come.'

Two other works present returns of Arthur and his companions. One is 'Simkin, Tomkin and Jack' (which immediately follows 'Tristan's Singing' in *Minnie Maylow's Story*). The other is *The Midnight Folk*.

'Midsummer Night' suggests that Gwenivere's defiant assertion in 'The Death of Lancelot' – 'What though I broke both nun's and marriage-vows, / April will out [. . .] / And though my spirit be a lost thing blown, / It, in its waste [. . .] / Will glimmer still from Love, that will atone' – is not, in any such defiant sense, the last word on the subject. There she seems no 'lost thing blown', but one gathered to table with a company which includes not only Arthur but Modred, too, where each, 'Smiling a little, turned towards the King'. This circumstance, and the fact that Arthur says 'We' collectively – 'We will take horse and come / To purge the blot' – must be given their due weight, though it is clear from what the 'figures' actually say that they are not – or not yet – equally 'lamenting of the ancient woe'.

In the final sonnet of *Animula*, the speaker says of wife, lover, and fierce husband, after all are dead, that 'now, perhaps, the memory of their hate / Has passed from them, and they are friends again' and that they may go in the wind

> Exulting now, and helping sorrowing men
> To do some little good before they die.

25

For from these ploughed-up souls the spirit brings
Harvest at last, and sweet from bitter things.

Some such idea, though in far more complex circumstances, is implicit in 'Midsummer Night'. In order to 'come / To purge the blot', Arthur, Lancelot, Gwenivere, Gwenivach, and Modred must themselves be purged, reconciled, purified. Here, the 'midsummer' opportunity for a return to beginnings allows a search for the causes of destruction, that they may be lamented, and turned from. 'Above those forms the Helper stood alone, / Shining with hope.' The idea is essential to *The Midnight Folk*, and there it is clear that actively helping people is part of the purgatorial process: as Lancelot tells one of those who are helped, the young protagonist, Kay Harker, 'Now we are re-making what we undid.'[56]

The subject of 'helpers' is one to which Masefield frequently returned. In the first notebook occurs a group of non-Arthurian drafts which include 'I know that some, whom we think dead, have come / To visit us, whom we account alive, / With help or comfort, or with pure delight' and 'I cannot reach the country where they dwell, / Only am certain that they live and see / The sorrow and injustice among men, / And from eternity / Come down'. Earlier in the group is this stanza about soul and church:

There was a time when that old house of pray'r
Would shelter her and comfort and console;
For angels used to dwell
About that doorway of escape from hell
Angels who gave men strength against despair
And strewed God's beauty into dusty soul.

Those of whom it is said 'I know they visit thus, for I have felt / The mercy of their presence and their touch / Those whom an unknown grave has buried deep' are clearly very like the 'angels' of 'that old certainty' – and, one might add, also like the saints. These drafts follow that of 'Arthur and His Ring'. We are now in a position to consider that poem, with its second intervention of Arthur's Helper.

26

Venus's words in the penultimate stanza make quite clear her identity with Arthur's 'Helper from Heaven'. Masefield presumable knew the story of 'The Ring Given to Venus' from William Morris's poem of that title in The Earthly Paradise, though his use of the place of 'three meeting roads' suggests that poem was not his only source. Masefield's reworking is very different in many essentials from the story as told by Morris or by Vincent of Beauvais in his Speculum Historiale.[57] One of the most important of these differences, is the character of the pagan gods (so to call them), and particularly Venus. In Masefield's Arthurian novel, Badon Parchments (1947), there is a very clear opposition between Roman British Christians, supported by Byzantine Christian aid, and the 'Heathen' Germanic invaders. In the earlier verse retelling, the situation lacks such clarity. Thus, for example, Uther and Ygern are married by the hermit 'Bran the Blest' in his chapel, but 'Arthur and His Ring' seems to assume a vital and unquestioned pagan Roman religious practice – and to present its end. None of the obviously demonic terms in Vincent and Morris are here used of the 'gods' involved, however. 'Strong' and 'fair' they are, as the itinerant teacher says, who also says 'My Master is the Master of their chief', but more than 'erring thoughts and empty air' is the Venus who remains Arthur's Helper and comes with her Queens to bring him to 'Avalon' – and may well be the Helper brooding over all in 'Arthur's bower'. Perhaps such Helpers, whether non-human or divinized human, are also undergoing purification. Whatever they are, they seem neither final nor evil. In any case, Masefield's Venus effectively – and, it seems, deliberately – tests Arthur so as to confirm him in his intentions, by his proper preference of 'pain / On earth' while trying to fulfil his kingly calling, to any attempt at immediate escape 'to bliss such as immortals take'.[58] Surely this Arthur knows, and serves, the spiritual ends of earthly government, and already submits to his purification. Uther's mercy to, and alliance with, Lot, and Arthur's willingness to work with the usurper Kolbein, and even his last appeal to Modred in 'The Fight on the

Beach', may testify to such an awareness and intent, rather than to either foolish idealism or cynical 'realism'. And 'Midsummer Night' reveals the depth of Arthur's words to Marc and Isolt, and suggests that they have an application beyond death: 'Life will have to be lived when this is settled. / Do not make life more hard by bitterness now.'

Whatever Masefield may have thought about the afterlife, or for that matter, preëxistence and reincarnation,[59] in his retelling he presents a myth of judgement, and of the need and hope of repentence, purgation, and forgiveness, which speaks now to those who can hear. Here is his theme of slavery and the release from slavery in its fullness.

'Simkin, Tomkin and Jack' recapitulates it. Simkin puts aside his aspiration to produce a slave-class with 'synthetic Man's Flesh' and Tomkin his, of artificially enhancing intelligence through 'an Essence of the Soul of Man', to collaborate on a kind of technological resurrection of one of Arthur's comrades whose bones they have found in a barrow. Their declared aim is to gain data about 'the past'. But the 'warrior's figure', rather than submitting to the interrogation of the historicizing brothers to provide such external information as they seek, addresses the 'Sun that I have worshippt' and whose fires 'confess / A power supreme above their mightiness / Who captains Heaven and many millions such', and invokes Arthur and his comrades to come – and 'They came to carry light to human souls.' The figure is then freed from technological bondage, and the brothers hear 'a cry begin / "Open your doors and let the new life in." ' Arthur returns, mythically, to purify by speaking, and inviting to, a proper spiritual orientation. Masefield wrote, of the 'greater life' which he began to experience as a boy,

> I believe that life to be the source of all that is of glory or goodness in this world; and that modern man, not knowing that life, is dwelling in death.[60]

Masefield's last published Arthurian poem, the sonnet about

Gwenivere, 'Caer Ocvran', speaks of her heart as 'pardoned now, where beauty still avails', and ends 'The heart that beat to beauty is forgiven.' The foregoing suggests, at least, that such pardon and forgiveness, and the atoning which Gwenivere looked for from Love in 'The Death of Lancelot', do not exist apart from the purification of the soul.[61]

Charles Williams's comment about the conclusion of Masefield's play *Good Friday* – 'It ought, one feels, to be more effective than it is' – will not lack for applications in Masefield's Arthurian poetry.[62] One strand of Williams's critique is that, in various ways, Masefield often tries to bring together what cannot – or cannot easily – be brought together, and fails in the attempt. This, too, could well be elaborated and applied with reference to the Arthurian poetry. For whatever reason, Masefield was more regularly and thoroughly successful in this respect in his Arthurian fiction – in *Badon Parchments* with its combination of a satirical reflection of Parliamentary debate on the eve of the Second World War,[63] and a more 'realistic' attempt at the imaginative reconstruction of late Roman Britain, including a compelling exercise in fictional military history – and far more so in *The Midnight Folk* (which, according to his daughter Judith, Masefield himself liked the best of any of his books[64]), with its wonderfully adept interweaving of styles, genres, and matters. Nonetheless, the Arthurian poetry is full of interest and enjoyment – whether one thinks of examples of grim humour, vivid description, polished storytelling, lyric beauty, or narrative invention – and it embodies an experience and faith which can seem not undeserving of the name Platonic.

BIBLIOGRAPHICAL NOTE

Fraser Drew, *John Masefield's England* (1973) includes the only recent bibliography of works about Masefield of which I am aware. I have made no attempt to discover if Masefield's Arthurian poetry is treated in the general works listed there, and have been unable to consult J. Dwyer, *John Masefield* (Boston: G.K. Hall [Twayne], 1987). In drawing attention to Vida D. Scudder, 'Masefield's Arthurian Poems', *The Yale Review*, 18 (Spring 1929), 592–94, I note that no attempt has been made, either by Professor Drew or myself, to register all reviews of Masefield's Arthurian publications. I am aware of four works directly concerned with Masefield's Arthurian writings which were not included in Professor Drew's select bibliography:

Garnette Shelley Hogan, 'A Comparative Study of the Treatment of Lancelot in Tennyson, Morris, and Masefield', unpublished M.A. dissertation, University of Souty Carolina, 1930.

Katherine Jones, 'King Mark Disguised as Himself', *American Imago* XVI (1959), 115–25.

Estelle Morgan, 'Some Modern English Versions of the Legend of Tristan and Isolde', *Die Neueren Sprachen* X (1952), 374–83, 418–24.

Gertraud Wurnig, *Arthur und sein Kreis in der englischen Literatur von Spenser bis Masefield*, dissertation, Innsbruck, 1952.

Perhaps the essay by Dr Peter S. Noble on *Badon Parchments* in *Quondam et Futurus: A Journal of Arthurian Interpretations* (1994) will herald (together with the present volume) further attention to Masefield as an Arthurian writer.

Bibliographies of Masefield's own works include: Charles H. Simmons, *A Bibliography of John Masefield* (NY: Columbia UP, 1930); Fraser Drew, *Some Contributions to the Bibliography of*

John Masefield (NY: Papers of the Bibliographical Society of America, June and October, 1959); Geoffrey Handley-Taylor, *John Masefield, O.M., The Queen's Poet Laureate: A Bibliography and Eighty-First Birthday Tribute* (London: Cranbrook Tower Press, 1960); Crocker Wight, *John Masefield: A Bibliographical Description of His First, Limited, Signed and Special Editions* (Boston: The Library of the Boston Athenaeum, ed. 2, 1992). For some information about Masefield's papers, see Constance Babington Smith, *John Masefield: A Life*.

Those wishing to read (or reread) Masefield's significantly Arthurian fantasy, *The Midnight Folk* (1927), and its dream-sequel, *The Box of Delights* (1935), should note that in recent years abridgements of these have sometimes been issued which are not as enjoyable as the original, complete novels.

Part I

PUBLISHED POEMS AND PLAY

The Ballad of Sir Bors

Would I could win some quiet and rest, and a little ease,
In the cool grey hush of the dusk, in the dim green place of the trees,
Where the birds are singing, singing, singing, crying aloud
The song of the red, red rose that blossoms beyond the seas.

Would I could see it, the rose, when the light begins to fail,
And a lone white star in the West is glimmering on the mail;
The red, red passionate rose of the sacred blood of the Christ,
In the shining chalice of God, the cup of the Holy Grail.

The dusk comes gathering grey, and the darkness dims the West,
The oxen low to the byre, and all bells ring to rest;
But I ride over the moors, for the dusk still bides and waits,
That brims my soul with the glow of the rose that ends the Quest.

My horse is spavined and ribbed, and his bones come through his
    hide,
My sword is rotten with rust, but I shake the reins and ride,
For the bright white birds of God that nest in the rose have called,
And never a township now is a town where I can bide.

It will happen at last, at dusk, as my horse limps down the fell,
A star will glow like a note God strikes on a silver bell,
And the bright white birds of God will carry my soul to Christ,
And the sight of the Rose, the Rose, will pay for the years of hell.

The Begetting of Arthur

Uther, the Prince, succeeding to the post
Of Red Pendragon, or Anointed Chief
Of all the Kings in Britain, saw with grief
How jealousy and spite
King against King, let in the heathen host,
Who, coming in their hundreds, found a land
Of warring Kingdoms owning no command,
And therefore sackt, uncheckt, from Tyne to Wight.

So when he took the purple he began,
Among his friends, to build a league of Kings:
Iddoc of Kent, among the Easterlings;
The Orkney pirate, Lot;
Then, from the North, the golden hero, Ban;
And having these, he greatly longed to win
Old Merchyon, King of Cornwall rich in tin,
Whose strength would bind the leaguers like a knot.

None loved King Merchyon: Prince Uther knew
That he was aged, savage, mean and grim;
That baron Breuse, the Heartless, lived with him,
Of all bad men the worst;
That in Tintagel, nest-rock of the mew,
His daughters lived with him, the dark Ygraine,
That moon of women; then the bright Elaine,
And little Morgause, whom a witch had curst.

So, knowing that the urger of a cause
Must urge the cause in person, Uther rode
With Kol and Guy, to Merchyon's abode,
And in Tintagel tower
Pled eloquently to him without pause,
With all a young man's beauty, flusht and true;
And as he pled, Ygerna watcht, and knew
That of all knights Prince Uther was the flower.

36

Then Merchyon answered, 'I have heard your plea.
I will not mingle in remote affairs,
I can mind mine, let others manage theirs:
What can the East, or Wales,
Or all of northern Britain, mean to me?
No Cornish men shall bleed in the employ
Of you, or others like you, Roman boy.
Your schemes are childish and your fears are tales.

Or if not so, perhaps the Romans plan
To recommence their empire, for in truth
Taxes and tribute and conscripted youth
Are playthings dear to Rome.
But you, my Roman, come to the wrong man.'
So raging, wrapping close his scarlet cloak,
He left the hall: Breuse, as he followed, spoke.
'That was your answer, Uther; make for home.'

Breuse and his sworders followed Merchyon out,
Uther had neither welcome nor farewell,
Comfort, nor rest, nor water from the well,
Nor food for man or horse.
He stood a moment, betwixt rage and doubt.
'Sir,' said Ygerna, coming from her place,
'Father is old: forgive his want of grace.
To-morrow he'll be broken with remorse.'

Then Uther for the first time saw Ygern;
And at her voice and at her wistful glance,
Love stabbed his spirit with her beauty's lance;
While she, made faint with love,
Felt the hot blush upon her temples burn.
Love to both startled mortals made it known
That each was other's to the inward bone
Through some old passion in the stars above.

As in October when the Channel mist
With silent swathes of greyness hides the sea
Until none knows where land or waters be,
And suddenly a blast

37

Scatters and shreds the vapours into twist
And all is glorious sunlight, wind and foam,
Through which a towering ship comes striding home,
Spray to the rail, with colours at her mast;

Or as, in mild Novembers, when the pack
Whimpers in covert and the hunters wait,
Under slow-dropping oak-leaves falling late,
Making no sound at all,
And suddenly the fox with hollow back
Breaks, with a crying leader at his brush,
And all those riders gathered for the rush
Surge for the fence, not heeding any call,

So, to those two, the greyness and delay
Of all their lives' endeavour and employ,
The hollowness which they had counted joy,
The hopes which had been dear
Until that instant, all were swept away;
They were alone upon an ocean shore
Where nothing meant nor mattered any more
Save their two souls and being without fear.

'O Princess,' he began, 'O dark-haired Queen,
O moon of women, we have met again,
We who are one yet have been cut atwain
To seek ourselves till now.
Whatever griefs are coming or have been,
Love in his glory grants us to make whole
Our bleeding portions of divided soul
That our last dying sundered with the plough.'

And she replied, 'Even as a winter bird,
Robin or chaffinch, in the iron day
Mopes, with pufft feathers, on the snowy spray,
Too pincht with cold to fly,
Too starved with bitter need to sing a word,
Till, from the farm, maid Gillian scatters crumbs,
And the bird, gladdened, knows that April comes
And carols his thanksgiving, so am I.'

Then, being in the certainty of love,
That cannot doubt, however it be blind,
Those two young lovers plighted mind to mind,
And straightway told the King;
Who cried, 'A pretty plot, by Heaven above.
Since I, as King, refused to be allied,
You think to win my power through a bride
Whose loving father grants her everything.

Not so, my Roman, for I see your plot.
Keep to your own princesses; she shall wed
My Breuse, who has no Latin in his head,
And you shall go out shamed. . . .
You sworders, make this loving swain less hot . . .
Set him ahorseback with his head for home.
And keep from Cornwall henceforth, man of Rome,
Or Cornish hands will swiftly have you tamed.'

Then instantly, before Ygraine could plead,
Or Uther answer, he was hustled forth
(He and his Knights) and headed for the north,
With orders not to turn.
Since three alone were helpless, they agreed
To the tide's setting, but they rode in rage,
Vowing to set King Merchyon in a cage
Next Sarum Fair, to suffer and to learn.

Yet, after noon, as Uther stayed to look
West, from the moorland, at Ygerna's home,
There, on the moor, he saw a horseman come
Black against burning sky,
Galloping tow'rds him, by the way he took.
And being near, behold, it was Elaine,
Flusht, tousled, riding on a tautened rein,
Calling, 'O Uther, help, or she will die . . .

Help us to-night, because my Father swears
That Breuse shall wed Ygerna before Prime . . .
Friend, can you help her in so little time? . . .
Not let her go to Breuse . . .'

'Men have plucked women out of dragons' lairs,'
King Uther said, 'And I will pluck Ygraine.
O Rose in briars difficult to gain,
Lighten my mind with strategems to use.'

Then, having thought, he said, 'This seems a chance.
Your porter's old: suppose I climb the rock,
Dresst like the King your father, and then knock
At midnight on the door.
He, being old and drowsy, may but glance,
Think me your father, bow, and open gates,
Then, when I bring Ygern from where she waits,
He may unfasten for me as before.

It is worth trying, for, if it succeed,
Ygern and I will be beyond the wall;
And I can see no other chance at all
Of saving her to-night . . .
And if I save her, sister, as God speed,
I swear to take her to the hermit's cell
And marry her before we cross the fell,
Making her Queen from Isis to the Wight.

You, Kol and Guy, arrange for horse-relays,
From here to where King Merchyon's country ends;
Swift horses, mind. About it: gallop, friends:
And if the luck be fair,
We'll meet again in Sarum in three days.
Sister, be ready when the moon goes west.
The hermit knows me, he is Bran the Blest,
He will assist us: have the horses there.'

*   *   *

Who longs for time to pass? The child at school,
Sick for his home where understandings dwell;
He who counts tiles within a prison-cell;
The broken, with her wrongs;
Eagles in cages stared at by the fool;
To all these dreary longers, at the last,

Some bell of blessing tells *the hour is past*:
But none longs for it as the lover longs.

Still, at the last, to Uther, the sun dimmed;
Men drew old sails across the half-built ricks;
The quarrymen trudged home with shouldered picks;
Slow-footed cows turned home;
After the chapel-bell ceast, voices hymned;
Evening came quiet: all the world had turned
To rest and supper where the rushlights burned:
Tintagel blackened like a dragon's comb.

By moonlight Uther came to Bran the Blest
Whose shed now held the horses of Elaine,
Bold-eyed, high-mettled, leaners on the rein,
Waiting their King and Queen.
At moonset, helped by Bran, Prince Uther dresst
With crown and scarlet and a sheep's-wool beard
Like Merchyon's self; then down he went, and neared
The rock-cut stairway slimy with sea-green.

He clambered up, while far above his head,
Black on the sky, the battlements were grim;
The sentries paced above, not seeing him,
Nor hearing how he climbed.
Beneath, within the bay, the ripples spread
One after other slowly to the shore,
Where, gleaming but unbroken, they gave o'er
Like breathing from a sleeper, husht and timed.

Upon the topmost stair he stood intent
Outside the gate, to listen, while the feet
Of drowsy sentries passed upon their beat.
He heard, beyond the door,
The porter, breathing deeply where he leant
Sprawled over table near the charcoal pan.
'Come, courage,' thought Prince Uther, 'play the man.'
He knocked King Merchyon's knocking and gave o'er.

As he had hoped, he heard the porter rouse,
Garble some words, unhook the lantern-ring,

Kick back the bench, and mutter, 'It's the King!'
Then fumble on the bar,
Pulling it weakly, gulping down his drowse.
The oaken barbolt loitered slowly back,
The latchet clicked, light yellowed at the crack,
An old man louted with the door ajar.

And as he louted low, Prince Uther passt . . .
There was Elaine, to take him to Ygern,
Telling the porter to expect return
Within few moments more.
All ways are long to lovers, but at last
He found Ygerna waiting in the dim,
Her great eyes bright, her white arms stretcht to him;
He drew her back along the corridor.

They trod the dark stone passage between rooms
Where people slept beneath the sentry's tread;
Tintagel seemed a castle of the dead.
A horse-hoof scraped the stone
Where the King's stallion waked among the grooms.
The porter, with his old eyes full of sleep,
Opened the gate to let them from the keep;
Its clang behind them thrilled them to the bone.

They crept like spies adown the cragside stair,
Into the gully's blackness between crags;
They heard the spear-butts clang upon the flags
At changing of the guard.
No challenge came: the world was unaware
How lovers fled: they reached the castle brook
Where ever-changing gleaming ever shook
An image of the zenith many-starred.

No sentry saw them; no one challenged; no,
Not when they moved across the moorland crest
Leaving the castle black against the west,
Grim guardian of the sea.
Their footsteps made a drowsy cock to crow,
A dog barked at their passing by the farm,

But no one stirred nor answered the alarm:
They reached the hermit's chapel: they were free.

There in the little chapel of the well,
By taper-light, the hermit made them one.
'Now cross the moor,' he said, 'before the sun
God be your guard and speed.'
They turned the chafing horses to the fell,
That King and bride upon their marriage day;
The nightingale still sang upon the spray,
The glow-worm's lamp still burned among the weed.

All day and night they hurried from pursuit;
Next morning found them out of Merchyon's land
Beside a brook with wood on either hand,
Deep in a dell of green:
Cool water wrinkled at the flag-flower-root,
The meadowsweet her heavy fragrance shed:
'Here,' the pair thought, 'shall be our marriage bed,
Here, in this orchard of the fairy queen.'

So there they halted in the summer flowers,
The speedwell blue, the stitchwort starry bright,
The dog-rose not yet opened, pink or white,
But sweet as very love.
Blackbirds and thrushes sang the lovers' hours,
And when the young moon brightened golden-pale
In the blue heaven, lo, a nightingale
Singing her heart out on the spray above.

There the two loved. Alas! ere morning came,
There Breuse and Merchyon, finding them asleep,
Stabbed Uther dead, and took Ygern to weep
In grim Tintagel tower.
There she sat weeping at the weaving-frame,
Waiting to bear her son before she died;
And as she wept, poor woman, hollow-eyed,
She wove the story of her happy hour:–

The creeping from the castle in the dark,
The blinking porter drowsed in lantern light,

The hermit and the chapel and the rite,
The horses tried and true;
Dawn on the moorland with the singing lark,
The ride for safety ever glancing round;
Then the sweet loving place, where they were found
At dawn among the speedwell in the dew.

And sometimes Merchyon, mindful of his girl,
In mercy of her health, would have her ta'en
To rest beside the Alan with Elaine,
Guarded by Breuse's band.
There as she watcht the water-eddies whirl,
Often a dark-eyed deer with fawn at heel,
Would shyly nuzzle her to share her meal,
And robin redbreasts percht upon her hand.

The Birth of Arthur

When the wind from East changes
Through South into West,
And the hard-frozen brooklets
Thaw out from their rest,

And come shining and leaping
Past the snowdrop's drooped head
Through the green-pushing pastures
Where moles burrow red;

Then the rooks call from elm-tops,
And lambs from the fold;
And the larks joy in heaven
For death of the cold;

And the blackbird calls clearest
Of sweet birds that sing,
And the dear becomes dearest
Because it is Spring;

And a joy of rejoicing
Springs green in the corn;
Such a joy was Ygerna's
When Arthur was born.

When the midsummer dog-rose
Was sweet in each hedge,
She took little Arthur
To Pendragon Ledge,

And at moonrise she laid him
On the Dragon's stone chair
Looking out over ocean,
Grey rock in keen air.

For the wise ones had told her
That to children so laid
Come the Powers who fill them,
And the Helpers who aid.

*   *   *

She laid the child sleeping
When all things were still
Save the sea-water creeping
And wind on the hill,

And the full moon came climbing
Till Time made the hour
For the foot of the Helper
And the wing of the Power.

Then at midnight Ygerna
Bent low at a cry,
For a night-laughing curlew
Laughed loud in the sky;

Such a night-laughing curlew
As never was heard:
It laughed in grey heaven,
But was not a bird.

Then again there was silence;
Then, whirling on wings,
Came the long-ago heroes,
The Queens and the Kings,

All the beast-quelling heroes
Who ruled and made tame,
All the women of glory,
All the spirits of flame

Who had wrought in this island
To make her more fair,

And exist now forever
In the beauty they bare.

There they gazed upon Arthur
With their light-giving eyes,
All the lovely true-hearted,
True-sighted and wise.

Then a King said: 'Our harvest . . .
This corn coming green.'
And a Queen said: 'This captain
Will be loved by a Queen.'

Then they laughed all together,
And the babe laughed in sleep,
And they said: 'Little Arthur,
What we made you will keep.'

Then, as seabirds at sunrise
Fly seawards from ken
To a rock of fair fishing
Untrodden by men,

Flying after their leader,
White wings on red sky,
So those heroes flew seawards
And a wonder drew nigh.

For from out of the water
A mailed man arose,
Fierce-eyed as the eagle,
But bearing a rose.

And as manes stream from racers
In wind on the down,
So flames streamed behind him
From under his crown.

He said: 'Thoughts are many
But wisdom is one.

Your way, being wisdom,
Will shine like the sun.

You will shine on this island
Till green corn be gold,
And the tale of your harvest
Will never be told.

All the Power within me
Shall stablish your peace;
But at evening comes darkness
When sunlight must cease.'

He ceased into darkness
As meteors that die;
A night-laughing curlew
Laughed loud in the sky:

The night-laughing curlew
Cried loud in the air,
A wonder stole forward
And stood by the chair.

He was dim as an evening
Whose moon sets apace,
Green light as of glow-worms
Was pale on his face.

He said 'Little Arthur,
Our passings will meet:
My moon will be sickle
To garner thy wheat.

Thyself shall create me
To ruin thy joy,
Yet though I shall break thee,
I cannot destroy.'

He ceased into darkness
As sea-mist that dies;

The night-laughing curlew
Made mirth in the skies.

Then a wonder most lovely
Swept in from the west,
As a sea-bird white-pinioned
Who glides to her rest;

Her face had the quiet
Of night at an end,
Her gift was the glory
Of beauty for friend;

In the gold of her crownal
White flowers were fair;
She stood like the morning
With stars in her hair.

And as Arthur woke laughing
And stretcht out his hands,
She said: 'The deep currents
Stir even the sands;

As high as the planets
And deep as the sea
Are the currents of living
That bind you to me.

To each spirit fashioned,
To each creature born,
Is a Helper from Heaven,
A Rose to the Thorn.

Myself am your Helper;
My beauty will stir
As a dream in your spirit,
As the prick of a spur:

Though others' the Power
And yours be the seed,

My beauty as Helper
Will bring it to deed.

You are frail now as snowdrops
That come before Spring;
My beauty as Helper
Shall crown you the King.

And thrice in your kingship
Your manhood shall quail;
My beauty as Helper
Shall not let you fail.

And at passing, my Arthur,
I'll bring you to fold
In the violet meadows
Where nothing grows old.'

She ceased into twilight;
A lark carolled sweet,
The blue-blossomed speedwell
Were bright at her feet.

As Ygrain took her baby
The seabirds flew low,
Singing: 'Whither man wanders
No mortal can know.

But rise, little Arthur,
Like the green corn in pride,
And a Power shall fill you
And a Helper shall guide.'

The Taking of Morgause

Morgause the Merry played beside the burn:
The otter said 'Go home: return, return.'

But no; she wandered down to the seaside;
'Go home, O little friend,' the gannets cried.

But no; she strayed to Erbin heaping wrack:
'Morgause,' he said, 'Beware, my dear; turn back.'

But no; she laughed, and ran along the beach:
Blind Erbin cried: 'Come back, dear, I beseech.'

She ran with naked feet in the bright foam:
The shepherd on the cliff-top called 'Go home.'

But no, she did not hear, or could not care.
The little vixen stopped her with 'Beware . . .

Beyond this jutting headland, drawn to land,
A pirate's Drake-Ship lies upon the sand.

There, filling water, is the pirate's crew . . .
Beware, lest, with the water, they take you.'

But no, she heard the sweet-voiced pirates sing,
Filling their earthen breakers at the spring.

Above the cuckoos and the bees of June,
She heard the voices at the ancient tune:–

    'My spear will feed me with another's bread,
    House me, where once another laid his head,
    And bride me with the girl another wed.

    'Farewell, you women all, that once were dear;

Lovely is love, but warring makes more near
The man beside me with a fellow spear.'

Then little Morgause longed to see and know
These dreaded pirates who were singing so.

She thought: 'One little peep among the fern
To say I've seen them, then I will return.'

But as she went, the black-backed adder cried:
'You tread the road to trouble; turn aside.'

The blunt-tailed field-mouse called with shrilly shrieks:
'Beware of iron claws and horny beaks.'

Then the red robin, hopping, twittered: 'Flee . . .
These men are wicked, they flung stones at me.'

*   *   *

Now, as she crouched among the grasses' stalks,
She saw the Drake-Ship on the roller-balks.

She was red-painted with a sweeping run,
Rowlocked for twelve, with shields for everyone.

A gilded Dragon eyed the way she went,
Aft, were Thor's Hammer and a scarlet tent.

Below the cataract that leapt the rock
The gold-ringed pirates filled their water-stock.

They filled red earthern jars: their King stood near
Whetting the deadly edges of a spear.

He was a young man, smiling, with black eyes;
In all a pirate's wisdom he was wise.

He wore a scarlet cloak above a mail
Of shining silver wrought like salmon-scale.

52

He eyed the grass where little Morgause lay,
But did not seem to see: he looked away.

He ceased the whetting of his weapon: then
He watched the work and chatted with his men.

At flood, he bade them run the Dragon down
To sea, across the beach-wrack tumbled brown.

They ran her seaward, crying 'Heave' and 'Hale';
'Now,' (little Morgause thought) 'I'll see her sail.'

*　　*　　*

They hoised her red sail, singing to the pull
A song which Morgause thought most beautiful.

The red sail filled and jangled; the calm sea
Lifted and lapsed the vessel not yet free.

The wading pirates loaded her with stores,
Unlasht the steering, shipped the rowing oars.

'There,' (Morgause thought) 'they are about to go,
And I, alone, of all the castle, know . . .

I shall return and tell them: 'Look at me . . .
I saw the pirates whom you did not see.

They could not see me hidden in the flowers,
But there I snuggled, watching them for hours.

I was as near as you are to the King,
I heard him tell his boatswain what to sing.

He never saw me, but he came so near,
I could have touched him with a hunting-spear.

Now, after this, I'll wander where I choose,
And when I wish to, nor shall you refuse.'

*　　*　　*

So Morgause thought, but now the Dragon's sheets
Were homed; the after rowers took their seats;

The moorings slackt; the silver-harnesst lord
Spoke to two seamen as he climbed aboard.

The two men trotted inland: a call blew
Shrill, as the captain passed among his crew.

The oars were tosst together and let fall
Into the rowlocks at the 'Ready all.'

*   *   *

'Now,' (Morgause thought) 'they go away, away
Oar-blades green-swirling, Dragon spouting spray;

Would I could go with them, to see and know
Where all the setting suns and planets go;

To hear the Mermaids singing, and to see
The spicy Phœnix in her burning tree;

And all the golden Apples that the Snake
Guards, lest the neighing Centaurs come to take;

And that dim Valley of the silver corn
Browsed in the moonlight by the Unicorn;

O would I could . . .' And suddenly she felt
Two pirates grip her grimly as she knelt.

*   *   *

King Lot, the silver-scaled, said 'By-and-by,
When you are wiser, you will make a spy . . .

Meanwhile, my Morgause, you shall come with me
Over the thoughtless, ship-destroying sea,

54

North, to my Orkney kingdom's granite tower;
In that grim garden you shall be the flower.'

*   *   *

Thither she went: within that stony place
She grew to loveliness of form and face.

And when the seasons made her seventeen,
King Lot of Orkney took her as his Queen.

The Begetting of Modred

When berries were scarlet
In the holly's dark green,
To the court at Caerleon
Came Morgause the Queen,

Being charged by her husband
To spy and report
On the troops under Arthur
From Caerleon court.

There she lived as a lady
From autumn to spring,
But she learned little tidings
To send to her King;

Save that soldiers were mustered
From Uskmouth to Wye,
But for all of her serpent
She could not learn why.

Then she tempted Prince Arthur,
The youth in command,
Till she saw his eyes brighten
At the touch of her hand.

There she baited her beauty
With the lures women use,
But for all of her serpent
She gathered no news.

When the daffodils flowered
In the fields of red clay
And the apple trees blossomed
And the birds sang all day,

When the swallows were building
And the cuckoo had come,
All the camps of Caerleon
Were loud with the drum.

All the troops in Caerleon
Were packing their gear;
All the whets in Caerleon
Whipped sword-edge or spear.

Queen Morgause of Orkney
Knew wars did prepare,
But for all of her serpent
She could not tell where.

In her room hung with purple
She baited her hooks
With her sweet-smelling body,
Sweet words and sweet looks.

There she tempted Prince Arthur
With beauty's delight,
So that love was between them
For one summer night.

Then when first the red cock crew
The trumpet blew shrill,
And the Caerleon legion
Came down from the hill.

And Prince Arthur rode with them
And left her in doubt,
For, for all of her serpent,
She had not found out.

But in Orkney in winter,
When waiting was done,
She bare the boy Modred
From the evil begun,
And the father, the uncle,
Had a nephew for son.

57

Badon Hill

Loki the Dragon Killer mustered men
To harry through the western isles agen.

Five thousand raiders in a hundred ships
Sailed with him to put Britain in eclipse.

For many days they loitered to the south,
Pausing to raid at every river-mouth.

Always they met good fortune and good reive.
Kol, with his pirates, joined them in the Sleeve.

They sacked the Roman seaport: they laid bare
Down to its plinth, the marble-covered phare.

Then, growing bold, they sacked Augusta town.
Temples of many gods came crashing down.

Then Loki said, 'My grand-dad, in his prime,
Burned a great city into building lime.

Upstream it was and many miles from here.
No man has harried there this many a year.

Then, as his gang dissolved, he went alone
Upstream from there, exploring the unknown,

And reached a reed-mere, whence a trackway led
Up to an ancient fort called Badon Head.

And looking thence (he said) beheld what we
Dream of perhaps but very seldom see:–

Sway-footed cows in thousands, deep in grass,
Unraided reiving such as never was,

And distant downland stretching, green with keep,
White as its chalk with moving flocks of sheep.

He swore to raid there with a gang, but Fate
That loves but ruins boldness, shut the gate . . .

Ambrose the Briton maimed him with a spear
So that he lingered helpless many a year

And never came to keep his oath, nor saw
That land again, that pasture without flaw;

Nor did his son, my father: no one has;
Unraided lie those pastures of deep grass.

Now I will raid them: you and I, my spears,
Will make the greatest raid of fifty years.

We will go up the river, we will take
That land and sack it for my grand-dad's sake.'

'Right,' Wolf the Red Fang said; 'But people tell
Those Westers' leader is a cub of hell.

Arthur, they call him: people get their fill
Coming for cattle against Arthur's will.'

'Arthur to Hell,' said Loki; 'I shall go.'
'Right,' Red Fang answered; 'I have warned you though.'

Upstream they rowed their Dragons: on the banks
The horsemen scouted, keeping clear their flanks.

O'er many a mudbank jammed with rotting drift
The harnessed horses gave the ships a lift.

After some days, King Loki trod the wracked
Shell of the city that his grand-dad sacked;

Then on he passed, now poling, now with oars,
Now dragged by horse-teams straining on the shores,

Now sailing, till he sailed into the green
Reed-shadowed mere his ancestor had seen.

There was the trackway, there the Badon Hill
Notched on the skyline by its rampart still.

'This is the place,' said Loki. 'Here we'll drive
Those sway-foot cattle to the ships alive.'

He moored his ships and marched his men ashore.
He eyed those pastures of his ancestor.

No herd, no head, was in those miles of grass.
The fields were empty as the downland was.

No smoke from any house, no noise of men,
Empty the cottage as the cattle-pen.

King Loki pitched his awnings in the camp,
And bade his men new-palisade the ramp.

He said to Wolf the Red Fang, 'Mount and scout
West, with the horse, to seek the cattle out.'

'Right,' Wolf the Red Fang said: 'But Arthur calls
All cattle in, and shuts it within walls,

Soon as he hears of wolf-packs near the house.
Mounting and scouting will not bring you cows.'

'Mount,' Loki said. 'I do not ask advice.'
'Right,' the Wolf answered. 'Now I've warned you twice.'

Wolf Red Fang took the horse into the west,
Over green pastures better than the best.

Green though the pastures were, that summer land
Was bare of people as a desert sand.

No scout of all his raiding horsemen heard
Voice of aught living save the summer bird.

Nothing was heard by them, and nothing seen
Save summer blue above the summer green.

Nothing but summer greenness stretching on
Marked by the tracks by which the herds had gone.

'Where have they gone?' they murmured. 'We have come.
Heel-scenting, sure, or we'd have met with some.'

And others said. 'We must be under curse.
Let's back to camp before we meet with worse.'

But Wolf replied, 'A man who won't believe
Has got to learn: come, ride ahead and reive.'

The sun declined, the misty west grew red,
But still no cattle, not a single head.

The dusk grew dim: they trembled as they rode,
For no dog barked at all, and no light showed.

At star-time they unsaddled for the night
Beside a chalk-brook, water-crowfoot-white.

They did not help again in Loki's plan,
Arthur at dawn destroyed them to a man.

Arthur pushed onward: before dawn next day
He eyed the reed-mere where the longships lay;

Those servants of the water-spooning oar
Lay flank to flank, their noses from the shore.

Their pine-plank, painted red, the hot July
had burned to be like bonework, blister dry.

Up in the pirate's camp no watch was kept,
Drunk Kol was dicing, drunken Loki slept.

Arthur and Lancelot the son of Ban
Took burning touchwood in an iron pan;

They slid into the water among reed,
No pirate saw their coming, none gave heed.

They pushed their gear before them on a raft,
The ripples spread in little gleams that laught.

The weather Dragon-ship rose overhead
Like a house-pale, sun-blistered, painted red.

Arthur and Lancelot together smeard
Tar to the leadings whence her hawsers veered,

Then heaping twigs and pine-cones, they gave touch,
And blew, until the little flames took clutch.

No watcher heard or saw them, no one came.
The little flame became a bigger flame.

It spread along the seams and thrust its tongues
Out, till the straikings looked like ladder-rungs.

First, the wind bowed it down, then, at a gust
The flame, that had been greedy, became lust;

And like a wave that lifts against a rock
Up, into shattering shining at the shock,

So it upshattered into spangs of flame
That writhelled red, and settled, and laid claim

And tore the Dragon's planking from her bones
Roaring: the Dragon sighed with little moans.

Now swearing pirates ran to fight the flame
And Arthur's archers shot them as they came.

And Loki, rising from his drunken sweven,
Saw all his longships blazing red to heaven

And Arthur's army coming with a will
Straight from the fire up the Badon Hill.

All Britons know the stories that are told
Of Arthur's battle for that pirates' hold:–

How first he tried the flank, and failed, and then
Tried at the gate and was repulsed agen;

How at the broken stakes where flints were flying,
He burst a way among the dead and dying,

And held the gap, the while his meyny all
Shovelled and picked, to totter down the wall;

How Loki charged and beat him headlong thence
With pirates in a spear-gang matted dense;

How Lancelot and Hector and Gawaine
Routed the spears and bore him back again;

And how they beat a little breach and stood
Crouched under lifted shields to make it good;

While from the upper wall about their ears
Came flying flints and fire, darts and spears.

And how that lower ditch was filled with dead
Men taking death there like their daily bread.

How Loki, growing anxious, strove to cut
His passage out but had his pathway shut;

How thrice he tried, with three defeats, and each
Time found him fewer, with a bigger breach.

Then how, like wolves entrapped, those pirates raged,
Horseless, without a navy, foodless, caged.

With Loki sorely wounded and Kol killed.
Men also tell how Arthur's fifers thrilled

Along his front, in that late afternoon,
While all his army, in a demi-lune,

Trod to that fifing up the slope and stayed;
And how the trumpets all together brayed

Along the front, and all the army swarmed
Upward together, till the wall was stormed;

Till, on the crest, beyond the tumbled pales,
They saw all-glorious Fortune turn her scales;

And how the horse came thrusting to the wrench,
Trampling the rampart fallen in the trench;

And how the trumpets all together blew,
And Arthur's army charged and overthrew.

Under the grasses where the cattle browse,
King Loki's army keep eternal house

In Badon earth, for none escaped alive.
Thereafter Arthur's realm was free to thrive.

For many years, no pirates had the will
To band against him, after Badon Hill.

The Sailing of Hell Race

When Arthur came from warring, having won
A name in Britain and a peace secure,
He felt the red horizon cast her lure
To set him hunting of the setting sun,
To take a ship and sail
West, through the grassless pastures of the whale,
West, to the wilderness of nothing sure
But tests for manhood in the deeds undone.

So, in his ship, the *Britain*, with her crew,
He sailed at all adventure for the west:
The Severn glittered at the *Britain*'s breast
As first her set sail wrinkled and then drew;
She dropped down with the tide,
Then, ere the changing, leaned upon her side
And smote the spindrift from the billow-crest
And strode from raddled waters into blue.

Westward she sailed, beyond familiar seas,
Beyond the landmarks and the ships of home,
To seas where never ship had broken foam,
Past all encounter with man's argosies.
The skies shone blue; the sun
Burned hotter at each marking of the run;
Out of the sea the summer islands clomb;
For many happy days they passt by these.

And there, between the surf-break and the snow
Bright on the pinnacles of crags, the land
Grew fruits of blessing ready to man's hand,
In deathless green an ever-golden glow:
And brown-skinned Indians came
Bringing them wreaths of flowers red as flame,
And plaques of gold-leaf beaten from the sand,
And begged them stay and wept to see them go.

But on they stood, until the sea-most peak
Was sunken as Polaris; till the day
No longer burned with summer but was gray
With iron snow-clouds over waters bleak.
A granite coast appeared,
Beaten by breakers; thither Arthur steered
Into the desolation of a bay
Where the scared seahawks made the echoes shriek.

All still it was, save for the seabird's cry
And for the thunder when the glacier broke
Her seaward iceberg in a spray like smoke.
All iron-gray the land was, like the sky;
But on the beach were heapt
The harvest wreckage which the sea had reapt,
Mastings of pine, fir plankings, ribs of oak;
The bones of ships, suckt bloodless, flung up dry.

There lay the helm, the yard, the figurehead;
Nay, even a ship that had been painted green;
Nay, all the wreckings that had ever been
Seemed to have stored that dockyard of the dead.
And there a cairn of stones
Rose as a tomb above the broken bones,
And on the cairn a wooden box was seen
Which held a script in heart's blood. Thus it read:

'Beyond this harbour are the granite rocks
Which are the gates of Hell, where courage dies.
Brother, I call upon you to be wise;
Return, before the Key turns in the locks.
Return, and do not dare
Death beyond death, the Cities of Despair.
Return, to where the lark sings in the skies
And on the Down the shepherd keeps his flocks.'

Then Arthur said: 'We have adventured far,
And tread upon the bones of what has failed;
The door of hell is dark until assailed,
But every night of blackness hides a star.

66

Come: even if we end,
Courage will bring immortals to befriend,
By whom the precipices shall be scaled
And bolted doors forever flung ajar.'

Then: 'On,' they cried, 'good captain, let us go.'
Onward they sailed, till sunset, when they neared
Two forms (or were they goddesses?) upreared
On crags with wrack above and foam below,
And from their granite lips
A laughter cackled like the death of ships.
Into the race between them Arthur steered,
Dreading lest they should murder him. But no . . .

Under those awful figures and between
He passed into a race of toppling seas
That broke and back-lasht at the granite knees
And scurft with salt the figures of each queen.
Those Furies' shadows fell
Dark on that channel of the way to Hell;
But Arthur's ship was built of sacred trees,
She stood, although the billows swept her clean.

On, through the turmoil of Hell Race, she swept,
The darkness, with her rooky wings of fear,
Covered the starless sunset's crimson smear;
Into the midnight of the sky there crept
Ahead, a glare, as though
The world were all afire smouldering slow.
Black towers on the glaring stood up sheer,
Lit windows in them sleepless vigil kept.

'Friends,' Arthur called, 'we have adventured well:
Ahead is all the glittering and pride
Of power of the devils satisfied,
The triple City where destructions dwell.
We will adventure on
And face their death together.' Then anon
Furling their sail, they made the *Britain* glide
Safe to a pier below the citadel.

67

Hell Race, the channel of the ocean, thrust
Tongue-like throughout the City: her two banks
Glittered and glowed with lamplight, ranks on ranks,
Higher than March's madness flings the dust;
Within some topmost towers
Flames out of cressets tosst like scarlet flowers
Where some exultant devil uttered thanks
For will indulged in executed lust.

Where Arthur lay, the City's dreadful joy
Came to him from the streets, for devils dirled
Pan upon iron pan, for glee; or hurled
Crockery crash, to shatter and destroy;
With shrieking horns they sped;
Explosions burst; the fire rusht up red;
Devils of discord, dancing, shriekt and skirled,
Beating at doors their brothers to annoy.

The naked women devils lured their prey
To dens or corners where, alert, in wait,
Murder stood tiptoe by the side of Hate;
Vice stole in flusht, and, glutted, slunk out gray.
And all life went at speed,
Each for himself and let the other heed.
Life was a fury roaring like a spate,
To fall, and to keep falling, or to slay.

And, drunk with vanity, their poets barkt
The glory of great Hell, the joy, the pride,
Of being devil-born in Hell to bide,
As devil-spawn by other devils sharkt.
The shrieks of women sped:
'Bring us your brother's blood if you would wed;
Blood, that our day-old mantles may be dyed,
That Mammon may be snared and we be markt.'

Within his vast and dirty temple sat
Mammon, the god and monarch of that Hell,
With sharp suspicion blinking through his fell,
Toad-throated, hooft, yet pinioned like a bat.

Athwart the temple's span,
Across the walls, a fire-writing ran,
Blazing the prices of the souls to sell
For all to read, the devils yelled thereat.

Multitudes trampled in the temple nave,
Fighting like wolves in quarrel for a bone;
The brazen forehead with the heart of stone,
Rat with hyena, murderer with knave;
Then from a gallery's height
The tiger devils cast into the fight
Spirits of men like dirty papers blown
That raved in dropping down as madmen rave.

And at the dropping down, the mob beneath
Leapt, like starved dogs at feeding time, to snatch
Each one a dropping from the tempter's catch;
With filthy claws they clutcht, or filthy teeth;
They tattered into rags
Those faded floatings that had once been flags;
Roaring they fought for them with kick and scratch:
They trod the quivering anguish underneath.

Yet more than Mammon, Lady Self was lord
Within that city of the lust for gold,
The jewelled thing, bespiced, bepainted, cold,
Whom Mammon purchased for his bed and board.
A varnisht shell was she,
Exquisite emptiness of vanity,
Unbodied and unminded and unsouled,
The mirror Self, whom all who saw adored.

She, and her mighty husband, and the game,
The roar, the glitter, and the zest of sin,
The prices offered by the Mammon Kin,
The gold all chinking when the moment came,
All these temptations drew
Some of the seamen of King Arthur's crew;
They stole ashore to Mammon, there to win
The worm's eternity in lasting flame.

So ere they all should leave him, and because
The Mammon people, hating foreign breeds,
Denounced him as perverter of their creeds,
One fit for burning by their holy laws,
King Arthur cut his ropes
And thrust to seaward, leaving to their hopes
His nine deserters, there to reap their seeds.
He sailed, with bubbling water at his hawse.

Soon in Hell Race a City loomed ahead,
Unlit, unlovely, under a dark star,
Girded by forts, each scaled with many a scar,
And toppped by cloud where fire glittered red.
A roaring filled the air
With thunder and destruction and despair,
As engines flung the fireballs afar
And fireballs Hell's dissolution shed.

And here the Searcher-Devils, grim with steel,
Boarded them out at sea and led them in
Within defences jaw-tootht like a gin
That kept without the port the foeman's keel.
'We are at war,' they said,
'The justest war that devils ever made,
Waged as a vengeance on our neighbours' sin,
To blast them into carrion till they kneel.

Why are we fighting? That's forgotten now;
No matter why; we are, let that suffice . . .
Yes, and those cannibals shall pay the price
Before we end, nor shall we scruple how.
And you . . . remember here . . .
We end all question-askers with the spear.
Wisdom is treason not committed twice;
We make it Death with branding on the brow.'

Then did those devils prison ship and crew
Under grim guard, where, natheless, they could tell
The progress of that war of Nether Hell:
No peace nor any joy that City knew.

The trumpet called the hours,
Trampling of troops had trodden out the flowers,
The trees were rampikes blasted by the shell;
Babes starved and women maddened, and men slew.

Bright-eyed with sharp starvation and with hate,
Twitching their bitter mouths from nerves gone mad,
With homes long since destroyed, in rags half clad,
(No craft save war being practist in the state)
They lusted, like the stoat,
To meet their teeth within a foeman's throat,
Or, like the wolf, to see the corpses shrad
With even thirsty Earth blood-satiate.

All day, all night, the shrieking and the crash
Of battle shook the town, as hate grew worse.
The elements were peopled with the fierce;
Insanity was captain of the rash.
Then cries arose 'Kill, kill! . . .
Those foreigners are workers of our ill,
Spies to a man and bringers of the curse;
Brothers, come slay and burn them to an ash.'

Then some of Arthur's crew were killed; and all
Would have been killed, had not the stunt and wizen
Starved doers of the slaughtering arisen
Against their Emperor and General,
And forkt to hideous ends
Those profiters by battle and their friends.
They hurried Arthur and his crew from prison,
Then made their town a pyre of funeral.

As Arthur sailed, he saw a lightning run
Along that City's ramparts with the thirst
Of fire licking up those bricks accurst;
Then thunder blasted from it and did stun;
Then its immense strength shot
Skywards in sooty fire withering hot,
Where trembling planks and figures were immerst
In glare that slowly darkened into dun.

Then as that fiery cloud came scattering down,
Blackness oppresst that City from the sight;
The foeman's fireballs came flaming bright
Into the crater that had been a town;
The devil's laughter cackled,
As fever laughs, like fetters being shackled.
King Arthur's ship drove on into the night;
A darkness toppt the battle like a crown.

Throughout the night they sailed, till morning showed
Mudbanks and salted marshes with sparse hair
Or stubble-stalks, of herbage blasted bare.
Then, the wind failing, up the creek they rowed:
Grey wisps of vapour curled
Above that marish of the underworld;
A droning and a whining filled the air
As though small devils in the mist abode.

Then, as the sullen sun rose, they beheld
Smoke rising up from pyres of the dead;
A granite statue sat there without head;
Beyond, arose a City gray with eld,
Nay, green with dropping mould;
That which had ruined her had made her old;
Cricketless were her ovens without bread;
A wind-stirred jangle from her ruins knelled.

There the pale fevers issued from the fen
To yellow human cheeks and cloud the mind;
There tetters dwelt, that writhel skin to rind,
Or rash the forehead with a savage pen;
Palsies, that twitch the lips
Or hamstring men with anguish in the hips;
These, too, were there, and sloughings that make blind,
And all the madnesses that unmake men.

They forct those Britons to that City's Queen,
A winged and browless fierceness on the throne,
Vert-adamantine in her hall of bone,
Fang'd, sting'd and mail'd in metal gleaming green:

72

No thought was in her eyes;
In where her victims' blood ran she was wise;
Her death-horns filled the palace with their drone,
Her dart of death out-quivered and was keen.

'Arthur,' she said, 'you stand in Nether Hell
Upon the sediments of greed and pride,
The rotted dust of nations that have died,
Amidst the foulness where destructions dwell.
Here the strong hand grows faint;
Here poison saps the manhood of the saint;
Here beauty sickens, joy goes hollow-eyed;
What else of glory is, my minions quell.

I slay the nations, one by one, that stood
Fierce-eyed in rapine and the fire of sacks,
Bright-eyed in ringing breaches in attacks,
Glad-eyed in glory from the beauty good.
I am the final Death,
Unseen and unsuspected as the breath,
Yet fatal as the crashing of the axe.
I am the ender of all hardihood.

You, too, with your adventurers, are sealed
As mine already: see, your cheeks are pale,
Your scarlet currents in their courses fail;
However lusty, they will swiftly yield,
And you will dwindle down
To beg among the ruins of the town.'
Then Arthur felt a weariness assail,
Nor could he struggle, nor oppose a shield.

And there with yellowing skins his seamen drooped,
Their arms too sick to pull upon the oar,
Forgetting how the sail rose to the roar
Of singing, as the gleaming clipper swooped.
'We've done enough,' they cried,
'Leave us alone.' There seven of them died:
Their burials were the vulture and the boar,
Whose scavengings the shallow graveyards scooped.

73

There Arthur saw the chickweed green the deck,
The halliard rot, the anchor-cable rust;
Gone was all order, gone were hope and lust,
The sick mind stared contended with the wreck.
Then in a midnight drear,
As Arthur tossed, a brightness hurried near,
A sudden glory on his senses thrust,
A terror prickt the hair upon his neck.

There, in her blue robe, the immortal queen
His Helper, stood, the calm one, the benign,
Crowned with forget-me-not and columbine,
And speedwells blue and never-withering green;
No darkness nor disgrace
Could bide the beauty of that steadfast face.
'Arthur,' she said, 'from birth devoted mine,
Now flung as straw for devils' hands to glean,

Take power from my touch; arise, arise,
Cast loose these prison-tacklings and begone
Forth from these dens where sunlight never shone,
Nor flower throve, nor spirit saw the skies.
My power gives you strength.'
Then spirit kindled Arthur, and at length
It stirred his seamen from the malison
Of that third monarchy of the unwise.

So, with that Helper at the helm, they stood
Clear from that City's mudbanks, and away,
To seas where flying fishes skimmed the spray
And every blowing air gave hardihood.
Homeward the *Britain* cleft,
Of all her company but seven left.
Soon the blue water dimmed into the gray
And bright Polaris rose as they pursued.

Till, as they sailed, they saw the seaweed float
And felt a changing tide. When darkness came
They watched for sight of land or beacon-flame,
Or any friendly sail or fisher's boat.

The steering lantern purred;
Then through the haze before the dawn they heard
Triumphantly a red cock call his dame,
Making a stallion challenge with full throat.

Then as the haze blew seaward, they beheld
The hills of home, the country green with corn,
Blossom upon the blackness of the thorn,
The hedgerows with the pretty primrose stelled;
They heard the blackbird sing,
They heard the chiff-chaff and the birds of spring,
The early cuckoo wandering forlorn
In woods whose millioned green was still unshelled.

Till noon they coasted, reach by lovely reach,
Beyond King Dyved's, past King Ryence' lands,
Past mountains casting shadows on the sands
And river water shining over beach.
Then lo, a brazen-poled
Bright chariot driving, all aflame with gold,
A chariot driven by princesses' hands:—
A princess drove to welcome them with speech.

Two stallions dragged that chariot like a spate,
White stallions lovely as the leaping pard,
Pickt stallions of King Ocvran's bodyguard,
Urged by a green-clad woman, who, elate,
With streaming red-gold hair
And eyes like stars illumined and aware,
Croucht watchful, to the grippt reins straining hard,
As one who lifts a winner up the Straight.

There did the giant Ocvran leave the car
And welcome Arthur to the shining shore;
There Arthur furled the sail and tosst the oar
And dragged the ship where billows could not mar.
The red-gold lady dear
Was Ocvran's daughter, princess Gwenivere,
Whom Arthur worshippt then and evermore,
As in the night the traveller the star.

Arthur and his Ring

Beauty's Delight, the Princes Gwenivere,
The day she promist marriage to the King
Drew from her hand the gem she held most dear,
Kisst it, to Arthur gave,
Saying, 'O love, I plight me with this ring,
This sapphire, my most precious marvellous thing.'
Her hair was in it, red as corn in ear.
'This,' Arthur said, 'I'll carry to my grave.'

And being filled with joy, he went to thank
The goddess Venus who had blest his love.
Her image stood before a marble tank
In which, in glittering falls,
A fountain sprinkled water-rings that clove
The shadows of the temple myrtle-grove;
There her bright-breasted pigeons preened and drank,
Sidling and ruckling ever with douce calls.

In marble was the goddess, fashioned well,
Yearning a little forward as she stared;
Men thought her holy bosom rose and fell;
Her robe drooped to her hip,
Fallen in folds, while all above was bared . . .
The myrtle shadows and the water fared
Into the pool before her, there to dwell
With the statue's shadow for companionship.

And Arthur, passing, saw his shadow pass
Along that water on the imaged sky
Wherein the evenings planet's glitter was.
He reacht the shape of stone,
Love's very Queen who gives the victory;
He saw her sweet, proud face, her steadfast eye,
Her crown that gleamed, like glow-worms among grass,
Her left hand stretcht, her right hand at her zone.

76

'O lovely Queen,' he cried, 'to whom all hearts
That ever suffered Love's intensest ache,
Turn with most passionate crying from all parts,
Take now my thanks, most sweet;
All my heart's deepest thankfulnesses take,
Because, to-day, thy Loveliness didst make
Me, thy poor servant, healed from many smarts
By granted love;' he bent and kisst her feet.

And as he kisst, he felt the marble thrill
As though alive; he felt her garment stir;
Her awful beauty made his heart stand still;
His spirit understood
The cryings of the birds attending her;
Light beat upon him, and the smell of myrrh;
Ecstasy rapt him to a greater will;
A peace that burnt like fire, a pain most good.

'O goddess, risen from the sea,' he cried,
'Grant that this ring which my beloved gave
May touch your finger and be sanctified;
And make my love endure
Like to the mountain, not the breaking wave;
Make it my star to shine beyond the grave.
O rose, whom men adore in every bride,
Grant me this boon, most beautiful, most pure.

Behold the ring.' At this, he tendered it
To Venus' self, and with his gentlest touch
Upon her outstretcht finger made it fit . . .
But to his utmost awe,
The finger bent to take the ring in clutch;
Then, instantly, his ecstasy was such
That the green leaf was speaking to his wit
And the gold glow-worm telling him his law.

He felt the goddess' hand caress his head;
He hard the music that the planets sing;
Strange flowers fell upon him, scarlet-red,
And glow-worms gleaming green . . .

Yet in the midmost of his joy, the King
Still strove amidst it all to take the ring,
But, lo, it clippt the hand that never bled,
Merged to the finger of the marble Queen.

And as his fingers pluckt, the glory went;
The twilight's wind was in the myrtle grove,
Rattling the leaves and killing all the scent;
The goddess was but stone,
A marble thing to which his jewel clove;
He wrested at it, but it would not move,
It could not move, the finger being bent,
The goddess meant to keep it for her own.

Even with unguents, even when he smeared
Finger and ring with oil, the gem remained
Fast on the stone; until King Arthur feared
That it was lost indeed.
'And yet,' he murmured, 'if the stone were planed,
By some good craftsman when to-night has waned,
Then, without any doubt it could be cleared.'
He went to bed, praying that dawn might speed.

But being abed, the midnight glowed with fire.
There, standing radiant in her crescent moon,
Was Venus' self, the Granter of Desire,
The Hope forever green.
Her quire of lovebirds carolled all in tune,
Her laughing eyes were glowing like the noon,
Joy was her gift and beauty her attire.
'Arthur,' she said, 'will you not take your Queen?

For I am yours, you wedded me this night;
Take me, beloved: I was never won
Before by mortal man beneath the light,
But I am won by you.'
Then Arthur cried, 'O creature of the sun,
Have pity on me, O immortal one,
Give back the jewel that my lover plight,
It is Queen Gwenivere's and I am true.'

'Behold it, set upon my hand,' she said;
'You placed it there with many words of love;
Though I am deathless, do not be afraid,
I am your wedded wife.'
'O lady, no,' he cried. 'By heaven above,
By you, the Blesser and by judging Jove,
My love is Gwenivere, the royal maid,
I neither wooed nor wed you, on my life.'

Her crescent moon dimmed down, her eyes seemed stone,
Her scarlet lovebirds dimmed and ceast to sing;
He heard the bloodhounds in the courtyard moan.
'So, Arthur, you deny
Me, the immortal, you an earthly King.
God has your words recorded, I your ring,'
The goddess said: 'But she whom you disown
Will come again.' She dimmed into the sky.

All day he urged his craftsmen, one by one,
To break away the ring; but all from fear
Of goddess or of priest, refused, and none
Would lift a tool or hand.
Then as he sorrowed in the midnight drear,
His bloodhounds whimpered like a stricken steer,
Venus again came shining like the sun,
With eyes not glad, but gleaming like a brand.

'Arthur,' she said 'Behold your Queen again . . .
I come out of the brightness of the sky
To seek my husband; must it be in vain?'
Then he, in sore distress,
Said: 'Queen, return the jewel. I deny
I ever gave, or thought of giving. I . . .
Goddess, take pity on a mortal's pain.'
'So,' she said, 'twice you spurn my happiness.

Be wise in time, my Arthur, and beware
A third denial.' Then, with dimming light,
She faded from the room and left him there
Shaken at loss and threat.

Unhappy dreams tormented him all night,
Hell-hounds, with yellow eyes and fang-teeth white,
Trotted about his bed with the night-mare.
He rose like one well taken in a net.

And looking at the quay below his tower,
He saw a stranger landing from a ship;
A dark, fierce man, with bright eyes full of power
Blazing beneath a hood . . .
One swift and telling as a cutting whip,
Keen, with a King's decision on his lip.
He smiled on Arthur; Arthur toiled an hour,
Then sought the garden where the statue stood.

And lo, a curse had fallen: fungus grew
Over the goddess in a lace of green;
No sparrows chirruped nor did pigeons coo,
And mat-weed chokt the tank.
The smell of dying made the place unclean,
All withered were the myrtles of the Queen.
'This cannot be the garden that I knew,'
King Arthur thought, and yet his spirit sank.

'Alas,' he muttered, 'I have brought a curse
Through scorning of the goddess in the night.'
Yet in Apollo's House the wreck was worse;
Jove's House was in decay,
The altars bloodless without gift or rite:
No sweet blue incense-smoke, no votive light,
The golden serpents broken from the thyrse,
And no one there to sacrifice or pray.

No pine torch streamed to Mars in tongues of flame,
The Sanctuary of the Sun was shut,
And in the Moon's House kittens were at game:
To Mercury no oil
Poured, and to Saturn was no offering put,
Vine-prunings, milk, or cornshoots newly-cut;
No woman called aloud on Juno's name,
Nor brought her wool, or balm, or household spoil.

And no man was at work at field or craft,
Nor loitering in the market or the lanes,
No hawkers cried, no children screamed or laught,
No women tended stall:
The world seemed weary of its fight for gains,
Its daily battle with its daily pains,
Its daily acquiescence in the daft;
A strange awakening had come to all.

But turning tow'rds a lifted voice he heard,
He found them in the circus at the gates,
Intently listening to a teacher's word.
That same fierce foreign man,
Whom he had seen on quayside midst the freights,
Was speaking to them about life and fates.
His spirit quelled them like the eagle-bird,
The hearers trembled as his message ran.

And when he ceast, those tremblers rose as one,
Eyeing each other for a man to lead;
Then, at a word, they all began to run
Towards the city gate,
Crying, 'Destroy the idols, the whole breed . . .
Destroy these statues of the devil's seed!'
Then household idols from their niches spun
Crashing: the stranger bade King Arthur wait.

'Arthur,' he said, 'I see you have a grief
Tormenting to your spirit: lay it bare.'
Then, having heard, he said: 'I bring relief;
Their strength begins to fail.
They are but erring thoughts and empty air,
Though some of them are strong and other fair.
My Master is the Master of their chief;
Trust to my Master, for his words avail.

But, hark. To-night, at midnight, you must go
Out of the city to that open space
Where the three highways all together flow
Before the bridge-gate fort.

You know the spot, it is an evil place:
Blood-sodden spirits haunt there without grace.
Natheless, go boldly, for ere cocks shall crow,
Their King will travel thither with his court.

Go to that Sovereign and demand your ring
Before he pass the gateway with his crew;
Many and deadly evils do they bring. . .
My Master be your guide.
Ask for that stolen sapphire as your due
And do not blench nor quaver: if you do,
Then truly it will be an evil thing;
But to the valiant nothing is denied.'

*   *   *

At midnight Arthur crept outside the gate
Over the causeway to the river bank,
There where the bridge-head tower rose up great
Above three meeting roads.
A fire-basket swung there from a crank,
Lighting the river-ripples rank on rank;
Nothing was there but darkness full of fate
And spirits without pardon or abodes.

And Arthur, standing at the meeting ways,
Lit by the fire swinging from the tower,
Heard voices crying in a meteor-blaze
That streamed across the air.
One voice was calling: 'They have had their hour!'
Then one: 'All changes, even Beauty and Power.'
Then one:'Eternity has many days . . .
The things that will be are the things that were.'

Then from the city, horses' clattering feet,
Trotting upon the causeway, swiftly neared . . .
There came an old King, in a winding sheet,
Whose gemless crown was lead.
Long-boned he was, sunk-eyed, with scanty beard,
Old beyond human telling, bowed and sered,

Tapping the ass he rode with ancient wheat
That, like a sceptre, dreary lustre shed.

And after him, on horseback, came a crew
Of figures, wrapped in cloaks inscribed with signs,
Each tended by the symbol creature due,
The eagle and the pard,
The wolf, the peacock and the stag with tines,
The ox, the goat, the hedgehog with his spines:
The last was one whose looking almost slew,
Who bore no symbol but a broken shard.

Then Arthur, catching at the donkey's rein,
Challenged the Sovereign as the priest had told,
Saying, 'O Saturn, give my ring again!'
Then Saturn slowly spake.
'I, ageless, am most aged: I was old
Ere first a lichen sprouted upon mould,
And now I meet a man who prefers pain
On earth to bliss such as immortals take.

Accept your lesser fortune: take your gem.'
Then, with a sudden waft of holy scent,
That loveliest flower of the immortal stem,
Venus herself, the Queen,
To Arthur from her golden saddle leant.
'Take back the troth-plight that you never meant,'
She said, and gave it. 'Think not I condemn.
In exile I shall keep your memory green.

We pass to exile, you to reap your sowing,
We to the violet fields, you to your end,
We into peace and you to ebb and flowing;
But when the Fate cuts short,
When life has no more penny left to spend,
When Will no longer makes your elbow bend,
Then, from my sea, O Love, I will come rowing,
My Queens and I, to bring you into port.

And now, farewell.' And, as she spoke, a cock
Crowed from the gateway tower; the brazen gate

Jarred, rolling open at King Saturn's knock;
And all the glimmering crowd
Rode slowly through, those forces of no date:
Last went the Death that held the broken fate.
Then Arthur, stunned, recovering from his shock,
Kissed his belovèd's ring and sang aloud.

Midsummer Night

Midsummer night had fallen at full moon,
So, being weary of my ancient tale,
I turned into the night,
Up the old trackway leading from the vale.
The downland dimmed before me, dune on dune,
Pale dogrose buds about me shed their scent;
The startled peewits glimmered as they went,
The moonlight made the earth and heaven white;
The heaven and earth together uttered June.

So perfect was the beauty, that the air
Was like immortal presence thrilling all
The downland with deep life;
Presences communed in the white owl's call;
The rampart of the hill-top stood up bare,
High on the windy hill a brightness shone –
I wondered whose, since shepherd-men had gone
Homeward a long time since to food and wife;
Yet brightness shone, as from a lantern there.

Then, as the valley belfries chimed the hour,
I thought: 'On summer nights King Arthur's door,
By yonder sarsens shut,
Is said to open to a corridor
Hewn far within the hill to Arthur's bower,
Where he and Gwenivere, with all the tale
Of captains toughened by the weight of mail,
Bide in a hall within the limestone cut:
That is the doorway, this is Arthur's hour.'

So, pressing near, behold, a door was wide
Flung open on the steepness of the hill,
Showing a lighted shaft.
A footlift fox was paused upon the sill;
Eyes gleaming green, he fled. I stepped inside.

85

The passage led within all brightly lit,
Deft limestone hewers' hands had fashioned it.
Behind me (as I thought) the white owl laught.
The lighted way before me was my guide.

Till deep within the hill, I reacht a hall
Lit, but so vast that all aloft was dim.
The chivalry below
Sat at their table stirring not a limb.
Even as frost arrests the waterfall,
So had a power frozen that array,
There at the banquet of the holy day,
Into such stillness that I could not know
If they were dead, or carved, or living all.

Then, entering in, accustomed to the light,
I marked them well: King Arthur, black and keen,
Pale, eager, wise, intense;
Lime-blossom Gwenivere, the red-gold queen;
Ban's son, the kingly, Lancelot the bright;
Gawaine, Bors, Hector; all whom trumpets drew
Up Badon at the falling of the dew:
And over them there brooded the immense
Helper or Spirit with immortal sight.

All was most silent in that cavern nave
Save a far water dripping, drop by drop,
In some dark way of time.
Power had brought that Knighthood to a stop,
Not even their ragged banners seemed to wave,
No whisper stirred the muscle of a cheek,
Yet all seemed waiting for the King to speak.
Far, far below I heard the midnight chime,
The valley bells that buried silence clave.

Then, at that distant music Arthur stirred;
His scarlet mantle quivered like a wing.
Each, in his golden stall,
Smiling a little, turned towards the King,
Who from his throne of glory spoke this word:–

'Midsummer Night permits us to declare
How Nature's sickle cut us from the air
And made the splendour of our summer fall.'
Then one by one they answered as I heard.

KING ARTHUR:

I was the cause of the disastrous end. . .
I in my early manhood sowed the seed
That made the Kingdom rend.
I begot Modred in my young man's greed.
When the hot blood betrays us, who gives heed?
Morgause and I were lovers for a night,
Not knowing how the fates had made us kin.
So came the sword to smite,
So was the weapon whetted that made bleed:
That young man's loving let the ruin in.

GWENIVERE:

I, Gwenivere the Queen, destroyed the realm;
I, by my love of Lancelot the Bright;
Destiny being strong and mortals weak,
And women loving as the summer night.
When I was seized by Kolgrim Dragon Helm,
Lancelot saved me from the Dragon-beak,
Love for my saviour came to overwhelm.

Too well I loved him, for my only son,
Lacheu, was his, not Arthur's as men thought.
I longed to see my lover's son the King;
But Lacheu, riding into Wales, was caught
By pirates near St. David's and undone . . .
They killed my Lacheu there.
The primroses of spring,
Red with his blood, were scattered in his hair:
Thereafter nothing mattered to me aught . . .

Save Lancelot perhaps at bitter whiles,
When the long pain was more than I could stand;
He being Arthur's cousin, was his heir
Till base-born Modred reacht us from the isles.

87

Thereafter was no comfort anywhere,
But Modred's plottings and my sister's wiles,
And love that lit me ruining the land.

LANCELOT:

I, who am Lancelot, the son of Ban,
King Arthur's cousin, dealt the land the blow
From which the griefs began.
I, who loved Gwenivere, as all men know,
Was primal cause that brought the kingdom low,
For all was peace until that quarrel fell;
Thereafter red destruction followed fast.
The gates of hell
Hedge every daily track by which men go;
My loving flung them open as I passt.

GWENIVACH:

I, who am Princess Gwenivach the Fair,
Compasst the kingdom's ruin by my hate,
The poisonous hate I bare
For Gwenivere, my sister, Arthur's mate.
My mind was as a murderer in wait
Behind a door, on tiptoe, with a knife,
Ready to stab her at the slightest chance,
Stab to the life.
I stabbed her to the heart in her estate;
Disaster was my blow's inheritance.

MODRED:

Not you, with your begettings, father mine;
Not you, my red-gold Queen, adultress proud;
Not you, Sir Lancelot, whom none could beat;
Not you, my princess sweet;
Not one of all you waters was worth wine.
Mine was the hand that smote this royal seat,
Mine was the moving darkness that made cloud;
You were but nerves; I, Modred, was the spine.

You were poor puppets in a master's game;
I Modred, was the cause of what befell.

I, Modred, Arthur's bastard, schemed and planned;
I, with my single hand,
Gave but a touch, and, lo, the troubles came;
And royalty was ended in the land.
When shut from Heaven, devils create hell:
Those who ignore this shall repent the same.

You were at peace, King Arthur (cuckold's peace);
Your queen had both her lover and her son;
And I, your bastard by your aunt, was far,
Where Orkney tide-rips jar.
Your Kingdom was all golden with increase.
Then your son's killing happened: Modred's star
Rose; I was heir, my bastardy was done;
Or (with more truth) I swore to make it cease.

But coming to your court with double claim
(As son and nephew) to the British crown,
You and the Queen named Lancelot the heir:
A brave man and a rare;
Your cousin King, the cuckoo to your dame,
Whom nobody opposed till I was there.
But I opposed, until I tumbled down
The realm to ruin and the Queen to shame.

GWENIVACH TO GWENIVERE.

And I, your younger sister, whom you slighted,
Loved Modred from the first and took his part.
That made the milk of your sweet fortune sour.
I told you in the tower,
The green-hung tower, by the sunset lighted,
Sunset and moonrise falling the same hour;
Then I declared how Modred had my heart,
That we were lovers, that our troths were plighted.

You could have won our love, had you been wise;
Then, when, as lovers, we confesst and pled
Together with you for a lasting truce.
No blood would have been shed,
April and June had had their natural use,

89

And autumn come with brimming granaries.
But no; you gave refusal and abuse;
Therefore I smote your lips so harlot-red . . .
The joy of that one buffet never dies.

I see you at this moment, standing still,
White, by the window in that green-hung tower,
Just as I struck you, while your great eyes gleamed.
Till then, I had but seemed . . .
My striking showed you how I longed to kill.
O through what years of insult had I dreamed
For that one stroke in the avenging hour!
The devil of my hatred had her will:
God pity me, fate fell not as I deemed.'

So, with lamenting of the ancient woe
They told their playings in the tragic plot,
Until their eyes were bright:
The red-gold beauty wept for Lancelot.
Then the church belfries in the vale below
Chimed the first hour of the year's decay,
And Arthur spoke: 'Our hour glides away;
Gone is the dim perfection of the night,
Not yet does any trumpet bid us go.

But when the trumpet summons, we will rise,
We, who are fibres of the country's soul,
We will take horse and come
To purge the blot and make the broken whole;
And make a green abundance seem more wise,
And build the lasting beauty left unbuilt
Because of all the follies of our guilt.
But now the belfry chimes us to be dumb,
Colour is coming in the eastern skies.'

Then as those figures lapsed again to stone,
The horses stamped, the cock his challenge flung,
The gold-wrought banners stirred,
The air was trembling from the belfry's tongue.
Above those forms the Helper stood alone,

90

Shining with hope. But now the dew was falling,
In unseen downland roosts the cocks were calling,
And dogrose petals shaken by a bird
Dropped from the blossomed briar and were strown.

The Fight on the Wall

Modred was in the Water Tower
At Caerleon-on-Usk,
He saw Queen Gwenivere the flower
Go by at dusk.

She was disguised, but Modred knew her,
No cloak could veil such grace:
She was Queen Gwenivere: What drew her
To such a place?

She past beneath the phare new-lighted,
He spied a red-gold tress
And gems upon a hand that righted
The wind-blown dress.

'Aha,' he said, 'My golden plover . . .
What go you out to do?
Queen, you are going to your lover;
I will go, too.'

He dogged her through the unbuilt quarter,
Past heaps of brick and slate,
Scantlings and smoking lime and mortar,
To the East Gate.

Behind the East Gate turret-curtain
A rushlight flickered dim.
'Lancelot's room,' he said; 'It's certain
She goes to him.'

He crouched behind her as she listened
And watched, to know all clear.
He thought: 'You think it safe. It isn't . . .
Go on, my dear.'

Then with a little clink, her sandal
Trod on the East Gate stair . . .
At turret-door one held a candle,
Her Knight was there.

'Lancelot,' Modred said. 'We take him;
His golden Queen and he;
Arthur will burn the slut and break him.
What joy for me.'

Back to the palace Modred fareth
And there he finds Gawaine,
With's brothers Gaheris and Gareth
And Agravaine.

When Agravaine had learned the matter,
He said: 'Knights, hearken here:
You thought my charges wicked chatter
Of Gwenivere.

Now she is trulling with her master,
That Lancelot of fame,
This spotless Queen of Alabaster . . .
It is a shame . . .

It is a shame to them who do it
And worse to us who see.
I say, tell Arthur: let them rue it.
Do you agree?'

Then Gawaine said: 'Be silent, brother,
And move no more in this:
Leave evil-speaking to another,
Leave it as 'tis.'

Gareth and Gaheris replying
Said: 'We will take no part
In dirty treacheries and spying
Foul as your heart.'

'But I,' Sir Modred answered sour,
'I will make one with you.
Arthur shall know within the hour
About these two.

You dainty Knights of spotless honour
May watch your Queen's disgrace,
But we will bring a judgment on her
And brand her face.

And Lancelot, that peer of traitors,
Shall be a public show.'
Gawaine said: 'You accursèd haters
About it: go.

But know, that what you do will issue
In every grief made worse.
The present world of men will hiss you,
The future curse.'

Gawaine and's brothers left in anger:
King Arthur entered in.
Modred said: 'Take your Queen and hang her,
She lives in sin.

She trulls with Lancelot the splendid
Atop the East Gate stair;
Attack them now and they'll be ended,
Caught unaware.'

'If it be so,' said Arthur, 'surely
The pair of them shall die.
Take men and bind the two securely.'
Modred said 'Ay.'

Modred took Kolgrevance and's brothers
Kurslin and Petipase,
Galleron, Joure and seven others,
They went their ways . . .

They crosst the city's narrow alleys,
Now dark, the shops being shut;
They heard the night-wind in the salleys,
The fox in rut:

They heard the screech-owl at his calling
That charms the wood-mouse' ears,
And the tinkle of the water falling
At the bridge piers.

Soon they were near the East Gate tower;
A small light showed aloft.
'See,' Modred said, 'they're in our power:
Now creep in soft.

There's where the deer lies in her cover,
The red stag keeping guard:
Now we shall take her with her lover.
Bind them both hard.'

They tiptoed up the winding stairway,
But Modred tiptoed last.
The jackdaw in the archer's airway
Blinkt as they passt.

They crept out on the paven landing
Atop the city wall.
It had a parapet and banding
Lest men should fall.

Between these ridges ran the footing
To where the tower rose;
The East Gate flanking-tower for shooting,
Loopholed for bows.

Thither they crept and stood there, straining
Their ears at the barred door:
The wind-cock up above complaining,
Creaked and gave o'er.

A silence was within the tower,
Naught touched on wood or stone;
Joure whispered: 'This may be the bower,
The birds are flown.'

They listened: then, within the hiding,
Gwenivere's voice said: 'No . . .
It was the wind-cock spindle griding
As the flaws blow . . .'

Lancelot answered: 'Not the spindle . . .
No; but another sound.'
The listeners felt their spirits kindle,
The game was found.

Then beating on the door in fury,
They cried: 'You traitor Knight!
You are taken now. We're judge and jury,
Come out and fight.

Come out!' and at the panels rashing
They strove to beat a way,
As through the scrum a pack goes crashing
In football play.

The door held to its bolts, being oaken.
'Come out,' the dozen cried.
They rashed again: no bolts were broken,
No hinges wried.

Gwenivere whispered to her lover:
'Alas, we both are lost.'
Lancelot had no arms nor cover,
A cloak at most.

'Alas, my Queen,' Lancelot muttered,
'That I should die thus tamed;
Snuffed, like a candle that has guttered,
Leaving you shamed.'

The arm-chest in the chamber angle
Was bare of points and blades,
He had two hands with which to strangle:
No other aids.

'Come out,' the dozen cried: 'No quarter
If we are forced to storm.'
'Go, Joure,' said Modred, 'to the dorter . . .
Bring up a form . . .

We're bringing up a form to batter
The door about your ears . . .
We'll have your head upon a platter,
My prince, sans peers.

And you, my red-haired queen, your trollop,
Let you make no mistake,
Shall go in smock like a cook's collop
To burn at stake.'

Lancelot said: 'This filthy crying
Is more than I can stand:
Better than hearing this were dying
Death out of hand

O Queen,' he said, 'the times are over
That you and I have known.
Belovéd Queen, I am your lover,
Body and bone,

Spirit and all of me, past knowing,
Most beautiful, though sin.
Now the old lovely days are going
And bad begin.

I shall die here, but whatsoever
May come of me, my friends
Will stand to succour you forever
Until life ends.

Farewell, beloved beauty peerless,
My star since I began;
You were my light when life was cheerless,
You made me man.

In many a foray, many a stour,
In many a deathy place,
Your thought has blesst me like a flower
And given me grace.

Now would that I had arms upon me
Until my powers fail,
What I would do before they won me
Would make a tale.'

At this, the running twelve came battering
Their form against the door,
A panel yielded to the shattering,
They staved two more . . .

They cried: 'Three more, and we shall take him,
This captain of the King;
Let this one hit the bolt and break him
Together . . . Ding.'

Lancelot said: 'Give over knocking,
I will unbar: let be . . .
I will undo . . . I am not mocking . . .
Come capture me.'

He drew the bolt and opened to them
And stared into the dark,
By the thin taper's light he knew them
All he could mark.

Even as wolf-hounds snarl and cower
About the wolf at bay,
Those shrank till Kolgrevance of Gower
Leapt at his prey.

Kolgrevance shouted: 'Now I have him,'
And slashed, but the cut misst.
Then Lancelot a buffet gave him
With the clencht fist:

A brain-pan blow that laid him sprawling
Dead on the turret floor;
Lancelot, while the corpse was falling
Bolted the door.

Bolted it just before the others
Charged with their blows, too late.
Lancelot said: 'You misst me, brothers,
Now you must wait.'

Then as they beat the panels, railing
Like dogs the stag has gored,
Lancelot donned the corpse's mailing
And took his sword.

Modred and Agravaine together
Cried: 'Out, you traitor, out.'
Lancelot answered: 'Cease your blether;
You need not shout.

Go from the door: I promise truly
That if you go from here,
Naming your place and hour, duly
I will appear

Before the Court in judgment sitting
Against what charge you bring
I'll answer all, to my acquitting
From him the King.'

'Arthur has damned you both already,
To death,' Modred replied,
'To death by us, and we are ready,
So come outside.'

'If that be so,' he answered, 'surely
My portion is but hard.
I warn you, keep yourselves securely' . . .
Then he unbarred.

Then storming armoured from his prison
He strode out to the wall.
Since the man's death the moon had risen:
He saw them all.

There was no room in that grim alley
For more than two abreast.
The meyny charged him at his sally,
They smote his crest.

But ducking from their swords uplifted,
He grappled those who led –
Agravaine, Lot's son, called The Gifted,
Lovel the Red.

Agravaine cried to those behind him:
'Stand back, friends; give us room.'
He felt a sudden lightning blind him,
He felt Death's doom;

Knew not how Lancelot had stricken,
But felt the blow destroy
The gifts that made his hearers quicken
From calm to joy.

Stumbling, he saw bright waters gleaming
With star-gleams spark on spark,
Then he struck stone, then all was seeming,
Then all was dark.

Before he clanged upon the paving,
Lovel the Red was in,
Crying: 'Come, friends; he's ours past saving . . .
Die in your sin . . .

Die,' and he struck, struck twice, but tamely,
Being too near his mark.
Lancelot, closing, gripped him gamely
And struck him stark,

And swung him as a shield before him
As guard to Kurslin's axe,
Which struck Sir Lovel fair and tore him
As cards tear flax.

Lovel fell back upon his slayer
But Kurslin thrust him clear:
He cried, 'Where is this Queen's betrayer?
I'll kill him here.'

But Lovel's body made him stumble,
And Lancelot cried: 'Not so . . .
I betray no one, friend, be humble,
Get out, man . . . go.'

And Lancelot struck him surely straightway
Over the gangway wall,
Down to the entrance of the gateway;
Men heard the fall.

And at the crash the party wavered
And fell back to the stair;
Having four champions dead, they quavered;
He watched them there.

Then Mador, of the White Rock Leaguer
That guards the Wye Mouth Ford,
Lured by the smile of death was eager
And tosst his sword,

And cried: 'Now, Lancelot, my brother,
Have at you, with good heart,
One of us two will kill the other
Before we part.

101

Remember now our ancient quarrel
About that pasture-right.
Now one of us shall earn a laurel:
Have at you . . . fight.'

Then rushing as the wild boar rushes
In some oak glade of Dean,
He scored his gashes with his tushes
So bitter keen.

Two slashes right and left made fire
On Lancelot's armour bright:
Lancelot's sword fell like a geier
From heaven's height,

A geier, that aloft in heaven
Stares at the sun unblind . . .
Then plunges headlong like the leven
Upon the hind:

So swept the broadsword from its eyry
Shrieking to seek its own,
Beating its port and clanging fiery
Through steel, through bone,

Through marrow to the life, so sweeping
Lancelot's smiting scored . . .
And Mador's soul had done with keeping
The swift Wye ford.

And Mador drooped and toppled over,
That loud-voiced ward of Wye,
To feed no more on the green clover
The white-faced kye,

To hear no more sand-raddled Severn
Pass out to sea in song,
But fill a grass-plot at St. Keverne
Not six feet long.

And seeing Mador dead, the seven
Cried: 'All together . . . now,
Down with the traitor: help us heaven,
Pull stroke, pull bow.'

Petipase led their meyny shouting
The cries of the sea host,
He being a sailor tanned from scouting
The Saxon coast.

He had a short axe poised for striking
Lancelot's skull apart,
Lancelot sent his sword-point spiking
Athwart his heart.

And leaping, Petipase remembered
The red sails of his ships,
Then he collapsed like one dismembered
And in eclipse.

But knew among the gleams and crying
Through which his soul was wrencht,
That other men than he were dying
And that they blencht.

For Lancelot, his point withdrawing,
Struck Florens with the edge
Over the brow, that he fell clawing
Against the ledge.

Then as Joure sprang, the great Knight quickly
So smote him with his shield,
That Joure's manhood was made sickly,
He drooped, he reeled.

And straight, before he fell, the ravage
Of the sharp sword-edge came
Swift as the coming of the savage
Who goes in flame.

And Joure fell and clanged in falling,
But heard before he died
The ring of the triumphant calling
Lancelot cried:

For as the shaken four were backing,
Lancelot cried his cry
That led like trumpets in attacking
To victory,

And charging as he cried, he drove them
Back to the winding stair,
Where two men making stand, he clove them,
Maelgon and Gare.

Then leaping down the steps pursuing,
He cut down Galleron:
But he who set the trouble brewing,
Modred, was gone . . .

Gone screaming in his dread to cover
Across the sleeping town.
Lancelot turned him to his lover
And sat him down.

Then after all that crash of warring
Came silence, without thrill:
Kolgrevance quiet on the flooring,
The lovers still.

Outside, the city slept; the water
Moaned at the bridge's piers,
The moonlight blancht that place of slaughter,
The dew dripped tears.

The white mist, from the river wreathing,
Shrouded the river ground:
But for the dew and the two breathing,
There was no sound.

Gwenivere spoke at last: 'O glory
Of all Knights among men,
This of to-night will be a story
Not matched agen.'

A silence followed in the tower
Save for the Knight's deep breath.
Horror had followed on the power
Of dealing death.

By the dim flicker of the taper
Sir Lancelot discerned
How in her face as white as paper
The Queen's eyes burned.

Deep in the panels of the walling
He heard the death-tick knock,
The dewdrops from the aspens falling
Ticked like a clock.

Then in the convent tower a tolling
Called nuns into the tower.
Lancelot said: 'Past man's controlling
Are place and hour.

I had no quarrel with the meyny
Nor did I know them all,
But life is not at peace with any
And her blows fall.

Now all our hours of joy together
Are past, our share henceforth
Will be but bitterness, with weather
Out of the north.

This day, beginning in the quire
Where now the ladies sing,
Will make our glory of desire
Another thing.

For I foresee the Kingdom breaking
Asunder from all this:
Out of the welter of man's making
What must be is.

Here is the prelude to the story
That leads us to the grave.
So be it: we have had a glory
Not many have.

Though what to-morrow may discover
Be harsh to what has been,
No matter, I am still your lover
And you my queen.'

The Breaking of the Links

They told King Arthur how the Knights were killed,
He saw the bodies carried by on biers
By torchlight, among faces, under spears,
He knew what misery had been begun;
The doors and shutters banged: the city thrilled.
'The mob will murder Gwenivere,' he thought.
The Queen sat haggard like a soul distraught.
'Courage,' he whispered; 'Much may yet be done.'
He led her quaywards as the forum filled.

And while the rabble gathered in the square,
He set her in his galley and bade sail.
He watched the galley whitening a trail
Down eddied Usk for towered Camelot.
'But Lancelot,' he thought, 'they will not spare,
These widows and these takers of the feud.
He must begone at once before pursued.'
Therefore he sent Sir Bors to Lancelot,
Who drew him north, the townsfolk unaware.

Soon, when the colour-giving dawn had come,
The kinsfolk of the dead came, crying all
For vengeance on the killer, to the hall.
'Bring out this royal harlot and her man.
These ruiners of all shall pay for some.
Where are they, Arthur? Bring them out,' they cried.
'Where are this strumpet and her homicide?
Burn them, the traitor and his harridan;
Punish their murderings by martyrdom.'

Then Arthur said, 'Keep silence here; the Queen
Is gone from here: so Lancelot has gone.
As to the killings, we shall think thereon
At ripest leisure.' Modred answered 'No.
No royalty or loyalty can screen

Treason like theirs; their hot adulteries,
Their plots that sought the Kingdom for a prize,
Their slaughterings, that laid our kinsmen low.'
'No,' the crowd yelled, 'they shall not get off clean.'

'No,' Modred said. 'For, King, you cannot know
The truth of this. Last night at your behest
I went, with friends, with warrant, to arrest
This Lancelot for treasons to the crown.
We summoned him to court: he would not go.
We strove to take him, he resisted: then,
Doing their duty, all those dozen men,
Man after man, were harshly beaten down.
Not by the killer's greater manhood; no . . .

No, but because within that narrow hold
Only one man could reach him at a time;
Nor was the Queen inactive in the crime . . .
Those dozen sworders held her in regard;
Her presence helped the one a hundredfold;
She helped to arm him; being armed, she stood
So that we dared not tackle nor make good
Our comrades' efforts; our approach was barred,
We must have wounded her had we been bold.

True, harsher captains might indeed have laid
Hands on the Queen and dragged her headlong thence;
But with what scandal and with what offence?
Mad as we were, we would not shame her thus.
Besides, the only purpose of the raid
Was to take Lancelot; we held no brief
To touch the partner, but arrest the chief . . .
So, holding back, destruction fell on us.
They have escaped, but God will see us paid.'

Then Gawaine said: 'What need was there to send
Armed men upon the Queen and Lancelot,
The King's wife and King's cousin, as all wot?
The two are daily in the palace here;
At one word spoken, either would attend.

But I perceive that jealousy begins
To conquer wisdom by imputing sins . . .
With Lancelot away and Modred near,
A royal bastard's fortune might amend. . . .

I will not silence, I will speak my word
To you, my cousin Arthur, and to one
At once my mother's and my cousin's son,
Who, with twelve captains, made a night surprise;
Against one lion, thirteen in a herd,
(Or fourteen was it?) By the starry skies
God made His vision of the matter plain.
Yet here this mongrel Modred dares complain . . .
I say he should be branded and unspurred.'

Then Arthur said, 'But I support him, I.
Against your cavils in the present cause;
He served against a breaker of the laws
At his life's peril, among comrades killed.
And proven treasons, not a jealousy,
Make the foundations upon which we build.
Treasons that amply justified arrest.
As Fate has fallen, I have judged it best
To wait a certain season ere we try . . .

Therefore the two accused are banisht hence,
Awaiting trial. Meanwhile Modred did,
Or strove to do, exactly as I bid.'
'Ay,' the crowd shouted, 'everybody knows
Gawaine can argue in a trot's defence.
He takes their part.' Gawaine said, 'I suppose
My cousin-brother now will govern us.
Now I remember what the ship-rat does . . .
When the ships begin to leak, he scuttles thence.

Therefore, my cousin Arthur, chief and King,
I say good-bye: I say you are misled
By plottings from this misbegotten head.
Not lightly will this cloud of evil pass.
I, like the swallow, joined you in your spring,

When first the daisies whitened all the grass;
Now autumn spiders come and leaves are blowing,
The summer being gone, I must be going.'
Then Bors and Hector strode into the ring.

Bors said, 'I brought Sir Lancelot away
For Gloucester and the north, as I was told.
The time has come for speakers to be bold.
Why was our captain banisht without trial?
Who sent the gang, commanding them to slay?
Since when were Tablers subject to espial?
I say, as Gawaine says, you take advice
From one whose plottings shall not use me twice.
Since Modred governs, I shall not obey.'

Sir Hector said, 'I do not ask the cause . . .
For men who fling the best and keep the worst
Are men whose fortunes are about to burst,
As yours are, Arthur, acting as you do.
A golden eagle cannot sort with daws,
Nor will this mongrel Modred sort with you;
Nor we with him, by heaven, so farewell.
We choose the Queen and Lancelot and hell,
And leave you folly, Modred and the laws.'

Then out the three defiant captains strode.
Their friends and kin, the party of the Queen,
Followed them out: all silent was the scene;
All present knew what breaking of the links
That bound the provinces together bode:
Nothing was heard except the little clinks
Of spurs on flagstones: then the horses sparred,
Sidling from men who mounted in the yard;
Then the slow horse-hoofs died along the road.

And while their going sounded, men were still.
Then Agravaine's gaunt widow, white with hate,
Cried, 'Shall our murdered darlings' spirits wait
Thus long for simple justice for their death?'
Then horse-hoofs clattered to the portal-sill,

110

A rider tottered to them spent for breath;
He cried, 'I've galloped from the Kentish prince,
I have not drunk these thirty hours since.
Get ready for a second Badon Hill.'

Then he sank, panting, till they gave him wine
And splashed his face with water; then he said;
'King Iddoc says this is no common raid,
No, but an over-swarming, such as comes
Only when blazing comets give the sign
And banded nations seek elysiums . . .
Three hundred ships were counted at the first,
More follow fast, we haven't toucht the worst.
They made our army snap like broken twine.

Who are they? Why, the manhood of a race
Or races, banded by an oath to seize
A Kingdom for themselves beyond the seas:
The summer pirates join with them besides.
Our ships attacked them at the landing-place,
Their ships destroyed them; now their navy rides
Holding the ocean to Augusta tower.
King Iddoc fought them in an evil hour.
They thrashed us out of knowledge and gave chase.

Briefly, the width of Kent is overrun;
They hold the Channel; beyond any doubt
They will advance before the moon is out
And toss your men-at-arms like meadow-hay;
They are fell fighters, every mother's son.
But will you muster with what men you may
And join King Iddoc? If the truth be told,
Whatever line we take we cannot hold;
They are our masters, Arthur, we are done.'

Then Arthur said, 'Whatever fair success
These pirates have, I never knew it last.
For when they seem the worst the worst is past;
They conquer first, then suffer for supply.
Therefore be comforted in your distress,

111

We suffer first and conquer by-and-by.
I start for Camelot at once from here;
By harvest we will have the Kingdom clear . . .
Whatever Iddoc's fears are, I say yes.

Come, Modred, we must sail for Camelot
Within the hour, or we lose the tide.
Dismiss, the court, the other things must bide.'
But as he passt, that wraith of Agravaine's
Cried, 'You have trickt us, Modred misbegot,
You killed our loves and leave us to our pains.
You shall not go until our cause is heard.'
Here the guards seized her, but her witch's gird
Rang through the hall and was forgotten not.

'Modred betrayed us, it is all laid bare.
He used our husbands only to disgrace
The Queen and Lancelot and take their place.
And all our lovely lovers are laid dead,
While he removes to Camelot to share
King Arthur's favour; curses on his head.
But you shall perish by the plots begun,
Son by the sire, sire by the son,
Before one swallow seeks the southern air.'

But now King Arthur was aboard his ship,
Rushing from Usk athwart the Severn stream:
War lay ahead, the rest was but a dream:
Modred beside him shared his busy brain.
His galley took a white bone in her grip,
The running bubbles made a noise like rain;
And though he missed two comrades from of old,
His son was by him and his heart was bold
To break the raid by this new comradeship.

Gwenivach Tells

I, Gwenivach, King Modred's queen, declare
What happened next: I, Gwenivach, accurst,
Being born very little but most fair.
King Arthur marched his army into Kent
And suffered loss at first:
I said to Modred, 'See, the gods prepare
Your fortunes for you; take the chances sent.'

Small need had he for prompting; he arose,
He and myself and all our chosen band;
He seized the crown and governed as he chose.
The gutters reddened from our glutted hate.
Had we but laid a hand
On Gwenivere, she should have died, God knows;
But she escaped us for a bitterer fate.

Throughout we triumphed: Modred was the King,
I was the Queen, from Gelliwic to Wales.
Sir Kolgrim joined us from his pirating,
Bringing, to swell our army, all the crews
That manned his hundred sails.
Well to our side did Fortune's balance swing:
Then Fortune changed; a rider came with news.

These were the news: that, Arthur had destroyed
The heathen fleet and army and had turned
To make our treasoned usurpation void,
Marching like fire on a windy day;
That, when our subjects learned
His coming, they renounced us overjoyed.
So our red morning had an evening gray.

We saw their malice snicker in the street
In Camelot: would God we had had time
To blast their pleasure in my love's defeat;

Some of those sneerers should have had white lips,
And eyeballs seared with lime.
But Modred gave the order to retreat;
We marched to Cornwall to Sir Kolgrim's ships.

And there we waited Fate and Fortune's chance,
Camped above harbour on the windy down.
Spies brought us word of Arthur's swift advance,
Then that he halted like a man in doubt
In that burnt Roman town.
Then lurching at us like a launching lance,
He camped in hail and hung his colours out.

Arthur in the Ruins

King Arthur watched within the ruined town,
Debating what to do and what avoid;
No sleep was there for his tormented brain.
War lay behind; before, were war and pain,
The column of the Kingdom fallen down,
With all that he had struggled for destroyed.
For if he fought his son,
The heathen would re-win what he had won;
And if he did not . . . there it was again.

So, being heart-sick, saying 'I must rest,'
He turned him to his blanket on the stones
Grass-sprouted, of a roofless temple's floor.
The sky above her bright-eyed watchers bore
Now that the youngling moon had wilted west.
Miswandered beetles fumbled out with drones.
And there a woman stood
Star-semée, with a planet in her hood,
Live with such beauty as the morning owns.

'Arthur,' she said, 'these many weary days
You have desired help where none has been.
To captain souls, in their intensest grief,
No comrade understanding gives relief,
Or brings that balm of the discouraged, praise:
Sweet friendship cannot come to King and Queen;
But we immortals come,
Sometimes, to help them in their martyrdom,
As sunlight comes upon the summer leaf.

You know that what I counsel will be true,
True as your inmost self at whitest heat
That touches All-Truth, and, as such, endures.
All courses that perplex men with their lures
Perplex you now with anguish, which to do.

115

So may the summer poppies hide the wheat.
This single thing must be:–
Battle with Modred by the western sea;
Of all man's destined courses, this is yours.

This will but seem a vision of the night
Rede-ing you falsely: let me prove it true:–
In the gray morning, as you march the Heath,
Left of the road a woman with a wreath,
Broad-browed, like me, in raiment crosst with white,
Yearning towards you there, will welcome you.
"King," she will say, "Go on.
Eternal glory waits in Avalon,
In Avalon the sword will find its sheath." '

At dawn King Arthur bade the trumpets call
'Strike camp and march;' and as King Arthur rode,
Lo, by the crossways in the heathy place,
A broad-browed woman with a noble face,
Wreathed with the little toadflax from the wall,
With white-crosst garments, from the heather strode
Towards him, and declared
Those self-same words: then on King Arthur fared
West, from the downlands to the Cornish chase.

The Fight at Camlan

Soon the two armies were in touch, and soon
Camped, face to face, upon the windy, high,
Thyme-scented barren where the wild bees croon.
Southward and westward was the wrinkled sea
Where Kolgrim's ships lay black.
Now must they treat or battle, since to fly
No longer was a solace that might be.
The season neared midsummer and full moon;
His impulse urged King Arthur to attack.

Then thought, and pity of his son, and hate
Of shedding subjects' blood, made him resolve
To make an offer ere he shut the gate
On every end save battle to the death.
He sent Sir Bedwyr forth
To Modred, to discover what might solve
Their quarrel without quell of living breath.
Modred replied, 'Let Arthur abdicate
This southern half the realm, and keep the north.

If he contemn this, say I shall not treat
Or commune, save as King with equal King.
Here is my army, yonder is my fleet;
Cornwall is mine, I can maintain it mine;
I am prepared to fight.
But if my modest terms can end the thing,
And all this southern realm be paid as fine,
We'll choose ambassadors and let them meet
There on that barrow, in the armies' sight.'

So, to be brief, both men empowered peers
To make discussion of the terms of peace.
The barrow, of the King of ancient years,
Topped by a thorn tree, was the meeting-place.
There six from either side

117

Went, while the heralds bade all warfare cease,
No sword to leave its sheath, no bow its case,
The horsemen to dismount and pile their spears
And all keep camp till all were ratified.

The twelve Knights went unarmed up to the howe
Between the armies, to debate together;
They hung a white flag on the hawthorn bough
And started talking, while the troops in camp
Disarmed, and cleaned their gear,
Or stretcht to sleep upon the matted heather;
Or with their comrades sat upon the ramp,
Sure that the quarrel would be settled now;
Each hailed the other side with mock or cheer.

To eastwards of the campments was a mound
Or rise of earth from some old fallen fence
Of ancient village, camp, or cattle-pound;
Three rebels flung themselves upon its top
With Kolgrim, Modred's friend,
Who mocked and said 'These talkers have no sense.'
Then, hours later, 'Let this folly stop . . .
There goes King Arthur; let us shoot the hound,
Crown Modred King and bring it to an end.'

Prone in the heath the four uncased their bows,
They strung them, on each other's bodies stayed;
Then from their quivers each an arrow chose.
Arthur was sitting with Sir Kai in talk,
Making an easy mark.
Back to the ears the arrow-feathers laid,
Then, as the hornet leaves his hollow balk
Humming with evil, so the arrows rose,
Shot from the string to strike the victim stark.

Sweeping the space those shafted barbings sped,
Like golden birds athwart the light they thrilled:
One pierced Kai's bitter heart and struck him dead,
Another cut King Arthur's purple cloak;
Another, by his hand

Stuck quivering in the table till it stilled;
The last struck sideways on a shield and broke
Below the barbs, its venomed fang unfed.
'Quick, mates, again,' said Kolgrim to his band.

But as they drew, King Arthur's herald cried:
'Treason! The men are shooting! Quick. Beware.'
Then, leaping up, he thrust the King aside
And shouted 'Treason! Fall in, Arthur's men.'
And as he snatcht a shield
The second flighting shafted through the air
That struck him through and put him out of ken
Of wife and home by pleasant Severnside.
Then trumpets blew and tumult filled the field.

The counsellors upon the barrow fled,
Each to his camp, not knowing what betid;
King Arthur's men into their cohorts sped,
Swearing, 'We'll pay those breakers of the truce,
Oath-breaking, treacherous swine.'
The black-backt adder to her cavern glid;
Now Modred's archers let their arrows loose,
And many a grey goose-feather was made red,
Ere either army formed a battle-line.

Now the armies stood as walls of spears
Beneath the ever-passing shriek and strike
Of arrows wavering in their careers.
Modred came swooping as a falcon swoops,
On horseback down his ranks,
Crying: 'Behold your sparrows: play the shrike.'
The trumpets blared among the rebel troops,
King Arthur galloped to his front with cheers;
He cried: 'If fronts are stubborn, try the flanks.'

Then as in thunderstorms the wind-vanes shift
On towers, against blackness, with a gleam,
So did his riders' spearheads glitter swift
Above the blowing pennons as they drooped
As one, down to the charge.

119

Then did the stallions bare their gums and scream,
The bright bits tightened as the riders stooped;
Then like a lightning from a thunder rift
The squadrons clashed together, lance on targe.

For hours they fought: then Arthur, beaten back
From camp and downland to the planted fields,
Steadied his line against the spent attack;
The armies stopped the battle to re-form.
Thirst-broken soldiers quencht
Their thirsts, and dropped their lances and their shields.
There fell the central quiet of the storm,
And spearmen strayed, to rob the haversack
Of friend or rebel prone with muscles clencht.

And while the battle stayed, Sir Modred found
No plenishment of spears and arrows spent
Save what the fight had scattered on the ground;
But Arthur formed upon his waggon-train
That brought him up new gear.
Archers and lancers took fresh armament
And faced to front, resolved to fight again.
Then Arthur heard a distant trumpet sound,
And, looking, saw strange horsemen in his rear.

And as he moved some lancers as a guard,
Thinking that Modred threatened his retreat,
He saw the banner of the golden pard;
Sir Lancelot was riding in to aid
With squadrons of picked horse.
Lancelot said, 'Though banisht, let us meet
To put an ending to this renegade:
See, his line wavers: let us push him hard;
He'll break as sure as prickles grow on gorse.'

It was now drawing to the summer dusk,
The sun, low fallen, reddened on the sea,
Dog-rose and honeysuckle shed their musk,
Lancelot's troops moved up upon the left,
King Arthur took the right.

It was the hour of the homing bee.
Then up the bright blades glittered on the heft,
The dragon of red battle bared her tusk,
King Arthur's tattering trumpets sounded Fight.

At a slow trot they started, keeping touch,
Elbow to elbow, upon rested horses
That strove to get the bits within their clutch,
Troop after troop the hoof-beat thunder grew;
Slowly the trot increast
As Lammas torrents grow in watercourses;
Then, utterly triumphant trumpets blew
And as a mounting wave, already much
Mounts mighty ere it smashes into yeast,

So mounted there that billow ere it broke;
Then, at its breaking, Modred, branch and root,
Horseman and footman, scattered like blown smoke
From burning leaves on an October blast.
Then mile on moorland mile,
King Arthur's army had them in pursuit;
Arthur with six Knights followed Modred fast,
Till on a beach he turned to strike a stroke.
Ten, against Arthur's seven, seemed worth while.

The Fight on the Beach or The Passing

These were the nine with Modred:– Kolgrim, Gor,
Bein Bloodsark, Stagfoot, Odwin, Addersfang,
Math, Erbin, Breuse, nine scoundrels in a gang,
Three pirates and three outlaws and three knaves.
They turned upon the shore,
And Kolgrim said, 'The battle has been lost,
But some beside the beaten shall have graves:
Some of these conquerors shall pay the cost.'
These were the six with Arthur:– Owain Mor,

(Gwenivere's brother), from the March of Wales,
Bedwyr, the Cornish Knight, whom Tristan fooled;
Lucan, the Golden, whom King Ban had schooled;
Prince Ryence, Girl-Face, beautiful as spring;
Ambrose of whom the tales
Still linger by the hearthstones of the west;
And Maximin, the son of Ban the King,
Of all deer-footed runners he was best:
These six now cast their lives into the scales.

And first the giant Owain, called the Red,
Riding in front, put spurs, and with his axe
Killed Math and Sigurd Stagfoot with two hacks;
The Stagfoot, falling, wrenched the haft away.
Here Owain's horse was sped.
He snatched Breuse' javelin as the stallion fell,
He speared Breuse through beneath the shoulder stay,
Addersfang cracked his helmet like a shell;
He grappled Addersfang as Breuse fell dead.

Bein Bloodsark struck him in the back, but he
Brought Addersfang from saddle; then he reeled,
Clutching that panting body as a shield.
Addersfang's horse upset him, Erbin struck,
He could no longer see:

But with his knife he thrust at Addersfang
Under the buckles, twice, and had good luck,
Leaving the hangman but a corpse to hang;
Dying, he muttered, 'Four, or was it three?'

King Kolgrim rode at Ryence with a thrust
That speared him through and flung him to the sand;
The lance-head broke, but with the stump in hand
Kolgrim struck Ambrose overthwart the face;
Ambrose reeled back, but just
Just as King Kolgrim had his axe to strike,
Miximin knocked him over with a mace;
Kolgrim rose dizzy, grinning like a pike,
Ambrose's javelin struck him to the dust.

Bein Bloodsark strode across him and cleared ground.
Men were dismounted now, their horses loose.
Kolgrim rose dying with, 'I broke the truce . . .
One other thing I'll break before I die.'
His sinews were unbound,
He lapsed face forward slowly and forgot.
Then each man shouted out his battle-cry,
The two sides clashed together in a clot,
Iron with iron meeting, wolf with hound.

Modred killed Ambrose dead, that Knight of Dean;
Erbin sore-wounded Bedwyr; Lucan dropped,
Stunned by a mace-blow which his helmet stopped,
(Odwin the Smiter dealt it as he rushed);
Odwin struck Maximin,
Breaking his guard; he swung and struck again;
The golden leopard of the crest was crushed,
Swift darkness crashed upon the young man's brain,
Dead fell that youngling of the golden queen.

Then for an instant Arthur fought with five.
He slipped from Modred's blow and swept at Gor
A slash athwart the neck that made them four;
Bein stabbed him at the sword-belt as he smote.
Arthur saw Odwin drive

123

Towards him, with his mallet swung aloft;
Short'ning his point, he took him in the throat;
Odwins mace toppled from his grip, he coughed
And fell upon the sand no more alive.

Erbin struck Arthur on the shoulder: Bein
Stabbed him again, a short-arm body-stab:
Then Modred gripped his ankles like a crab,
Meaning to trip, but Arthur shook him clear,
Then slipped in the bright brine,
For now the tide was coming. As he slipped
His left hand clutcht the butt of Erbin's spear;
He wrencht the shaft from Erbin as he dipped
And stabbed him through the heartspoon with the tine.

Modred and Bein came at him as he rose
Among the ripples of the gleaming sea.
He swerved aside and stumbled on his knee:
Bein fell across him, blocking Modred's way.
With moonlight-glinting blows
They struck each other, and the splashings shone,
Like salmon-leapings, as they tried to slay:
Then, at a lunge from Arthur, Bein was gone,
Heart-stricken, with his vague hands clutching oaze.

Modred drew backward, seeing Bloodsark killed.
'Modred,' King Arthur said, 'surrender here.
Your treacheries have cost this Kingdom dear.
They cannot prosper, Modred: let them end.'
The brimming ripples spilled
Their brightness on the bodies of the dead.
'I am your father, Modred, and your friend,'
King Arthur pleaded, 'and your shot has sped.
I would have granted much of what you willed

Had you but told me: it is not too late
To come to some agreement, you and I.
Come up, above the tides, and let us try.'
He stood near Modred on the moonlit sand.
Modred was still as hate;

124

He made no answer, but he breathed deep breath.
Sore-wounded Bedwyr, propping with his hand,
Cried, 'Arthur, bind me: I shall bleed to death.'
'I'll bind you, Lucan answered, 'only wait . . .

One moment, till this dizziness is past.'
The ripples swayed the bodies up the beach.
Then Modred said, 'A sweet forgiving speech,
More than a bastard rebel can deserve.
I shook the dice and cast
A great throw to be quit of men's contempt.
"Bastard," they called me; but the bastard's nerve
Came nearer Kingdom's conquest than they dreamt.
I fail; my one endeavour is my last.

I spit upon your fatherhood and you.
You be my friend, who made me suffer scorn
From every living soul since I was born?
My friend, you think? You sorry cuckold; no.
But an account is due
And shall be paid, O luster that begat.
Down to the hell of all my hating, go.'
Then, leaping forward like an angry cat,
He struck his father on the headpiece, through.

Three blows he struck, not heeding Arthur's thrust;
Then, shaking clear, his features wrenched aside,
Marshlighted deathward, he collapsed and died:
'Thirty years' anguish,' were his latest words,
'Made by your idle lust.'
Arthur, with both hands groping outward, swayed;
The tide-brink touched his ankles with its curds:
Sick Bedwyr was beginning to upbraid:–
'O come to stop this bleeding! O you must.'

Then Arthur reeled towards him, saying 'Where?
Where are you wounded, Bedwyr?' Then he knelt,
Tented the wound and bound it with his belt,
And raised Sir Bedwyr's head; his own bled fast.
Then Lucan, crawling, bare

125

Drink from the brook for Bedwyr, but it spilled.
Then Arthur said, 'This hour is my last.
Modred is dead, I killed him; I am killed.
Call, Lucan, if our friends are anywhere.'

So Lucan called, a hurt man's feeble cry.
No answer followed save a stir of wings,
That and the creeping water's whisperings
Ant-like about the bodies of the dead.
Then Arthur said, 'Good-bye,
O you two faithful who have followed me
With loving service ever since I led.
I give as bitter payment as the sea,
Hard days when living, hard death when you die.'

Then, moving from them for a little space,
His spirit felt the promptings of the blood,
That now the brimming tides were at the flood,
And that the ebb would carry him afar.
West from the rocks a race
Streamed seawards, speckt with bubble-broken white.
Lamplike before him was the evening star.
He said, 'My comrades perish, touch and sight . . .
The feast is finished: let me utter grace.'

He faced the western star with lifted hand,
While muddled thoughts and clear thoughts clanged and
          passt,
Of splendid things, if life could only last,
And long-dead friends, and kindnesses undone
And good things hoped or planned
That life would none of: then he took his sword,
Red once at Badon, red, now, from his son.
He bound about its hilt the priested cord;
He said, 'The tide is setting from the land,

And I, too, set; but yet, before I go,
This that King Uther, yes, and Ambrose bare
In battle with the pirates everywhere,
Our House's Luck, this Britain's Bright Defence,

126

My Fortune in the Flow,
Must take the Ebb, if I have strength to fling.'
He tottered to the water and stood tense;
The moon and the moon's image watched the King,
The weltering water ceased her to-and-fro.

He gathered up his dying strength, he swung
The weapon thrice and hurled it in the stream;
It whirled like a white gannet with a gleam,
Turning blade up in moonlight as it fell;
Bright-flying foam-drops stung
The steel, the spray leapt as it disappeared.
'No other man shall have you: all is well,'
King Arthur said; and now his moment neared;
The tide was ebbing and his heart was wrung.

A curlew called: he fell upon his knees,
And lo, his failing eyes beheld a ship
Burning a path athwart the water-rip;
The water gleamed about her like soft flame,
Her gear creaked in the breeze;
Towards him, nosing through the soaken sand,
To rest her at his side, the vessel came.
His Helper held the tiller in her hand;
His Friend was come, to comfort his disease.

Then seven queens upraised the dying king
And laid him quiet in a bed aboard,
And balmed the gashes smitten with the sword;
Immortal life upon their faces glowed.
Then they began to sing:–
  'We bear him to the isle of Avalon,
  Where everlasting summer has abode.'
An unheard summons bade the ship begone,
She headed seawards with a stooping wing.

Lucan and Bedwyr, propping as they might,
Watched as she passed: they heard the singing range
Through secrets of things hidden and things strange,
And things of beauty not yet found in thought.

The ship seemed made of light,
She travelled by the thrilling of the hymn;
The race a moment with her passing fought,
Then she was on into the distance dim,
And on beyond, and on, and out of sight.

Gwenivere Tells

So Arthur passed, but country-folk believe
He will return, to triumph and achieve;
Men watch for him on each Midsummer Eve.

They watch in vain, for ere that night was sped,
That ship reached Avalon with Arthur dead;
I, Gwenivere, helped cere him, within lead.

I, Gwenivere, helped bury him in crypt,
Under cold flagstones that the ringbolts shipped;
The hangings waved, the yellow candles dripped.

Anon I made profession, and took vows
As nun encloistered: I became Christ's spouse,
At Amesbury, as Abbess to the house.

I changed my ermines for a goat-hair stole,
I broke my beauty there, with dule and dole,
But love remained a flame within my soul.

What though I watched and fasted and did good
Like any saint among my sisterhood,
God could not be deceived, God understood

How night and day my love was as a cry
Calling my lover out of earth and sky
The while I shut the bars against reply.

Years thence a message came: I stood to deal
The lepers' portions through the bars of steel;
A pilgrim thrust me something shut with seal.

I could not know him in his hoodings hid;
Besides, he fled: his package I undid;
Lancelot's leopard-crest was on the lid.

129

Within, on scarlet ivory, there lay
A withered branchlet, having leaves of gray.
A writing said: 'This is an olive spray

Picked for your blessing from a deathless tree
That shades the garden of Gethsemane;
May it give peace, as it has given me.'

Did it give peace? Alas, a woman knows
The rind without may deaden under blows;
But who has peace when all within's a rose?

The Death of Lancelot as told by Gwenivere

Then, after many years, a rider came,
An old lame man upon a horse as lame,
Hailing me 'Queen' and calling me by name.

I knew him; he was Bors of Gannis, he.
He said that in his chapel by the sea
My lover on his death-bed longed for me.

No vows could check me at that dying cry,
I cast my abbess-ship and nunhood by . . .
I prayed, 'God, let me see him ere he die.'

We passt the walls of Camelot: we passt
Sand-raddled Severn shadowing many a mast,
And bright Caerleon where I saw him last.

Westward we went, till, in an evening, lo,
A bay of bareness with the tide at flow,
And one green headland in the sunset's glow.

There was the chapel, at a brooklet's side.
I galloped downhill to it with my guide.
I was too late, for Lancelot had died.

I had last seen him as a flag in air,
A battle banner bidding men out-dare.
Now he lay dead; old, old, with silver hair.

I had not ever thought of him as old . . .
This hurt me most: his sword-hand could not hold
Even the cross upon the sacking-fold.

They had a garden-close outside the church
With Hector's grave, where robins came to perch.
When I could see again, I went to search

For flowers for him dead, my king of men.
I wandered up the brooklet, up the glen:
A robin watched me and a water-hen.

There I picked honeysuckles, many a bine
Of golden trumpets budding red as wine,
With dark green leaves, each with a yellow spine.

We buried him by Hector, covered close
With these, and elder-flower, and wild rose.
His friends are gone thence now: no other goes.

He once so ringing glad among the spears,
Lies where the rabbit browses with droppt ears
And shy-foot stags come when the moon appears.

Myself shall follow, when it be God's will;
But whatso'er my death be, good or ill,
Surely my love will burn within me still.

Death cannot make so great a fire drowse;
What though I broke both nun's and marriage-vows,
April will out, however hard the boughs:

And though my spirit be a lost thing blown,
It, in its waste, and, in the grave, my bone,
Will glimmer still from Love, that will atone.

Dust to Dust

Henry Plantagenet, the English King,
Came with Fair Rosamond, for monkish picks
Had lifted flaggings set in Roman bricks
And cleared a Latin-carven slab which told
That Arthur and his Queen were buried there . . .

They watched: the diggers raised the covering . . .
There lay those great ones placid under pyx;
Arthur enswathed as by a burning wing
Or wave of Gwenivere's undying hair,
Which lit the vaulty darkness with its gold.

Seeing such peace the living lovers knelt
And sought each other's hands: those dead ones lay
Untouched by any semblance of decay,
Liker to things immortal than things dead,
Manhood's undying glory, beauty's queen.

The crimson rose in Rosamunda's belt
Dropped, on the dead, one petal, soft as may.
Like ice that unseen April makes to melt,
Those bodies ceast, as though they had not been;
The petal lay on powder within lead.

On the Coming of Arthur

By ways unknown, unseen,
The summer makes things green,
The pastures and the boughs
Wherein birds house.

Summer will come again,
For sick things become sane,
And dead things fat the root
That brings forth fruit.

Arthur, like summer, waits,
For Wit and Will are gates,
Like those the summers pass
To green earth's grass.

Arthur will come like June,
Full meadow and full moon,
With roses up above
As red as love,

And may-bloom down below,
As white as fallen snow,
And no least linnet dumb;
O Arthur, come.

The Old Tale of the Begetting

The men of old, who made the tale for us,
Declare that Uther begat Arthur thus:–

Queen Ygrain sat in her bower
Looking from Tintagel tower.

Uther saw Ygrain the Bright,
His heart went pit-pat at the sight.

He said to Merlin, 'Make her mine,
Or you'll be hog's meat for my swine.'

Merlin wrought all day with pray'r,
With water, earth and fire and air.

He made a mask that had the look,
Colour and speech of Ygrain's Duke.

Uther wore it and came late
And knocked upon Tintagel gate.

He cried, with the mask's voice, 'Fair Ygrain,
Open, it is your lord again.'

The dogs howled and the owls cried,
But Uther came to the Queen's side.

As he climbed to the Queen's bed,
Ygrain's Duke on the moors fell dead.

*   *   *

Uther drinks and boasts at his board,
Ygrain sings for her dead lord:
'Would I were pierced through with a sword!'

135

The Old Tale of the Breaking of the Links

French poets write:– That, Lancelot the brave
Fought and defeated Arthur's Knights, to save
Queen Gwenivere, then sentenced to the fire:–

That, he and she then lived in heart's desire
At Joyous Gard, for certain months or years.

This is Queen Isolt's tale, not Gwenivere's,
Tristan's, not Lancelot's: but since men know
This version best, I tell it also so.

———

Soon as the colour-giving dawn was seen,
Arthur bade call
His Court, to judge the sinning of his Queen
There in the hall.
Himself, in scarlet, sat upon his throne
To hear her plead;
She, with her beauty only, stood alone;
Alone indeed.

For round her stood the widows and the young
Of all the Knights
Whose limbs and lives her lover had unstrung
On the wall's heights;
And with them were the rabble of the Court
And Modred's friends,
Thinking the baiting of the Queen a sport
That made amends.

And in the shrilling of the threats and cries
That nothing stilled,
Sir Modred told of Lancelot's emprise
And how he killed
The meyny sent against him to discover
The wicked thing.

'He killed them,' Modred cried, 'this woman's lover.
Be just, O King.'

Then Arthur spoke: 'You bid me to be just . . .
Justice decrees
Death for the petty treason of a lust
And brooks no pleas;
"Death for the wife by burning at the stake,"
The law is clear;
No shadow of exception will I make,
It is death here

Unless the one accused can bring defence
Of such a kind
That we be certain of her innocence . . .
Now let us find
What answer the accused, Queen Gwenivere,
Makes to the tale
Of petty treason brought against her here.
Let truth prevail.'

The red-gold Queen replied: 'O tender lord
To grant this grace,
To let me answer as you sit at board
To try the case.
A few short hours ago you ordered men
To take and kill
My friend and me. Since murder throve not then,
Now justice will.'

'No,' Arthur said, 'they were not sent to slay,
But to arrest
And bring to me: they charged you to obey
The Kings behest.
Resistance to my order was the cause
Of twelve men's death;
For that there shall be answer to the laws
As the law saith.

But the main question now is treason, Queen.
This Knight and you

137

Met to be lovers as you long have been.
Is that not true?
You went disguised, in darkness and alone,
To this man's lair,
Because you are his woman to the bone
And loved him there.

If not to love this captain, tell us then
Why did you go
To meet him, hidden from the eyes of men
In darkness so?
Answer us that . . . remember that you stand
On a pit's brink.
Speak truth as one in judgment on God's hand,
But ere speech . . . think.'

The colour came to Gwenivere's pale cheek,
Her great eyes shone:
Why should I think,' she asked, 'before I speak?
All thought is gone
From you and all the rabble kennelled here
To hear me cast . . .
You mean to burn me living on a bier
By sentence past.

I say you lie. Your killers never spoke
Of the King's will,
But beat the turret door until it broke,
Meaning to kill.
Then Lancelot to save me (me, the Queen)
From the King's friends,
Made such a story as will last, I ween,
Till the world ends.

There were thirteen against a man and me;
These two remain:
Modred and Mullet in their infamy,
The things unslain . . .
They disobeyed your orders without cause,
They mocked your will:

138

No matter: they may much assist your laws
To kill me still.'

'Queen,' Arthur answered, 'if they disobeyed,
That cannot clear
You, the accused one, of the charges made
Against you here.
The chief of which is, that unlawful love
Sways you from me,
And has done long, as many people prove
To certainty.

What the Court asks from you is a defence.
That you must make,
Or our unchanging law will send you hence
To burn at stake.
Why did you go by night to Lancelot
If not for sin?
Let royal indignation be forgot,
Let truth begin.'

Then the proud red-gold lady, beauty's peer,
Answered: 'Proceed . . .
Burn me, to soothe this kennel barking here,
Your friends in need,
Your haters and your killers and your two
Flee-ers, who ran.
Know, there is warrantise for all you do:
I loved this man.'

Then Arthur said: 'No need to question more . . .
Since you are his,
Doubly a traitor to the oaths you swore,
Your sentence is
That you be burned within the public ring
Outside the wall,
Before this noon: thus sentences the King . . .
Bear witness all.'

Then Gawaine said: 'King Arthur, you are mad,
And act from spite . . .

139

This is no trial that the Queen has had . . .
You have no right
To sentence on confession, without proof,
As the world knows.'
Then Arthur said: 'Peace, Gawaine, stand aloof.
To stake she goes.'

Then Gawaine said: 'You turn all upside down
For one hour's rage . . .
She is the chiefest sapphire in your crown,
Star of her age:
And you, because your bastard Modred wills,
Cast her to die.
It is not justice, no, but he that kills . . .
That infamy.'

Then Arthur said: 'You, for this insolence
To me, the King,
Shall call the bodyguard and take her hence
Out to the Ring,
And there see sentence done as I command.'
Gawaine said: 'No.
Let Modred be your foul act's dirty hand,
I will not go.

No; let your bastard do your hangman's task;
I, a King's son,
Refuse it, whether you command or ask.'
Then everyone
Cried: 'Down with Gawaine!' But Sir Gawaine turned
Scorning them all;
He shouldered through the mob that milled and churned
And left the hall.

Then Arthur cried to Gareth, Gawaine's brother,
Still but a boy:
'You, Gareth, shall not question, like the other,
Your King's employ.
You, on your knightly service, take the Queen,
This proven trash,

140

And burn her as a felon on the green
To bitter ash.

About it: go: fall in the bodyguard.'
At this he rose
And left the Queen sans counsel or regard
Alone with foes.
The widows and the children of those killed,
And all the mean
With nails that clutcht and savagery that shrilled,
Assailed the Queen,

So that the spearmen had ado to check
The rush that came
With sharp claws stretching for the victim's neck
And shrieks of shame.
But Gareth with a spear-butt beat them back
And kept space free,
Then said to her: 'O lovely Queen, alack
That this should be . . .

Now I am shamed whatever thing I do:
Letting you live,
I break my oath; and if I murder you,
None will forgive
And nought atone, forever, till I die . . .
These curs at least
Shall all behave or show a reason why.'
Then like a beast,

A bull that sees his foe, or wolves made one,
Seeing their prey,
That crowd of haters brought with malison
The Queen to bay . . .
They beat the spearmen back, they spat, they struck,
They overwhelmed . . .
Gareth was gallant but had little luck,
That lad unhelmed;

So, in an instant, Queen and guard were reeds
Tosst in a flood

Of devils utterly possesst by greeds
For human blood . . .
They screamed: 'You golden harlot, once so proud,
Shall now be tame;
Come to the fire, malkin, in your shroud,
And feed the flame.'

Then suddenly, while all the building rang
From those who curst,
The bronze doors were forct open with a clang,
And in there burst
Lancelot and his meyny, with Sir Bors,
Ector and Urre,
Cutting a pathway to her from the doors
To rescue her.

In that fierce mellay of the charge none knew
What foe he hit;
Each in his headlong fury struck and slew,
Steel on steel bit.
Lancelot cleared the crowd, his meyny broke
The King's array;
There Lancelot killed Gareth with a stroke,
And Ector, Kai.

And Bors killed Gauter, and Sir Safer clave
Driant the Bright;
There Bel the Proud was toppled to his grave,
And Tor the Knight.
Lancelot at the Queen's side cleared a ring
And shouted: 'Swine . . .
I take this royal lady from the King,
She is now mine.

Tell Arthur therefore that I take her hence . . .
If he demur,
Let him give battle; I will make defence
For love of her.'
Then, with his arm about her, forth he stalkt
Out, through the crowd,

Who shrank away from him like jackals baulkt,
Snarling but cowed.

Then at the gateway taking horse, he passt
Usk bridge at trot,
And on the green beyond it trotted fast
From archer's shot.
Th' alarm bull in the tower boomed like surf,
But fear was gone
From all those comrades trotting on the turf
While the sun shone.

Till noon they trotted, then, near Braddock reach,
They turned aside
From raddled Severn babbling in soft speech,
To a green ride;
Through ancient oakwoods where the ravens built,
All day they went,
Till sunset found them on the western tilt
Of the bare bent.

There, looking back across the misty woods
Topped by red sky,
They saw white Venus star the solitudes
Above the Wye;
They saw the Severn sandy to the mouth,
Arthur's domain,
The forest and the mountains to the south,
Chain in blue chain.

Then Lancelot and Gwenivere were sure
That they were done
With all their past, however long might dure
Their share of sun.
That they were finisht with that realm of gold
As Knight and Queen;
The glory of their living was grown old,
Their joy had been.

Above the rock, above the well, above
The grove of thorn,

That couple stood, those burners in great love,
On the forlorn
Lean neck of hill surmounted by the caer,
The glow of light
Shone in the Captain's eyes and the Queen's hair
Before the night.

They set their tired horses to the east
Over the crest.
Beyond, the colours had already ceast,
Birds were at rest.
The mist was creeping on the Seven Springs
Where no light glowed,
A darkness was upon the face of things:
To that they rode.

South and East

When good King Arthur ruled these western hursts,
That farmhouse held a farmer with three sons,
Gai, Kai and Kradoc, so the story runs.
All of the hollow where the water bursts
They reckoned holy land,
For there, they said, the gods came, hand in hand,
At midnight, in full moon, to quench their thirsts.

So by the hollow's western edge they fenc't
With unhewn stone and hawthorn and wild rose,
A little meadow as a holy close
Not to be trodden in by foot uncleanst . . .
And from the harvests rare
Which filled their granaries, they were aware
That the great gods this service recompenst.

Gai was a hunter through the country-side;
Kai was a braggart little prone to truth;
Kradoc was reckoned but a simple youth,
Though kind and good and all his mother's pride.
He loved his mother well;
He loved his mare and dog; but it befell
That sorrow smote him young, for all three died.

Now it befell in grass-time, late in May,
That Gai, the hunter, going out at dawn,
Found the grass trampled in that sacred lawn,
All trodden as by feet the flowers lay.
He thought, 'Some godless men
Have done this evil; lest they come agen
I'll watch to-night beside the holy hay.'

Yet in his watch he slept, and when the east
Grew bright with primrose-coloured morning, lo,
The grass again was laid past power to mow;

145

By godless men, it seemed, not any beast.
So, when the next night fell,
Kai came to watch, but slept, not waking well;
At dawn the trodden portion had increast.

Then, on the third night, Kradoc said, 'Let me
Be guard to-night'; so, when the dusk was dim,
He took his hunting-spear and stationed him
Beside the close beneath a hawthorn-tree.
The thin moon westered out,
The midnight covered all things with her doubt,
The summer made the world one mystery.

Then, when the hunting owls had ceast to cry,
There came a sound like birds upon the wing,
And shapes within the close were glimmering,
Hushing, and putting glittering raiment by . . .
Then the shapes moved: they seemed
Three women, dancing, but their moving gleamed:
Or were they birds? because they seemed to fly.

'They are the goddesses,' he thought, 'at game . . .
Soon they will blast me;' but he watcht intent . . .
Starlight and dawn a little colour lent;
They were three women, each like moving flame
In some old dance of glee,
All lovely, but the leader of the three
Beauty so great as hers can have no name.

For hours he stared, not moving, while they danced;
Then in the brightening dusk a blackbird cried;
The dancing stopped, the women slipped aside,
There to the grey wall where their plumage glanced,
They donned it and were gone
Up, upon wings; across the sky they shone,
Gleams on the darkness where the dawn advanced.

And being vanisht, all his heart was sore
With love of that fair Queen. 'Alas, I kept
Ill watch,' he said, 'and all the grass is stepped

As though it had been danct on o'er and o'er.
To-night I'll try again,
A second night I will not watch in vain.'
All day at work love searcht him to the core.

At night, his father and his brothers both
Came with him to the holy close to guard;
But long before the midnight many-starred,
His comrades slept, forgetting boast and oath.
The hours went by: he heard
The darkness laughing with the marvellous bird
Who husht the woodland with her plighting troth.

Then, suddenly, with linnet cryings sweet,
The shapes were near him, putting off their wings;
Then all the close was swift with glimmerings
Of silvery figures upon flying feet
White as the thorn that blows,
Skimming the daisies as the swallow goes
Or as the sunlight ripples upon wheat.

Then, as he stared and prayed, the thought came bold.
'There are their wings upon the wall, put by . . .
If I should take them, then they could not fly . . .
But these are gods, immortal from of old,
And they would blast me dead
If I should touch their plumage silver-spread,
Let alone gather it and try to hold.'

But as the moth about the candle tries
To know the beauty of the inmost fire,
And feels no burning but his heart's desire,
And even by scorching cannot be made wise,
He took the wings: a lark
Twittered, and colour stood out from the dark;
Those figures sought their wings with passionate cries.

'They are not goddesses,' he thought; and then
Seeing who held their wings, those lovely birds
Were pleading with him with caressing words:

147

'Friend, we shall die if we are seen by men.
Give us our wings, oh, give;
We may not look upon the sun and live:
Sweet mortal, let us have our plumes agen.'

Then, to the first, he gave the plumes, from fear;
Then, to the second, gave them out of grace;
Then she, the Queen, was with him, face to face,
Within the touch of hand, she was so near
The two spread wings and sailed
Up to the summer heaven primrose-paled.
'O lovely Queen,' he cried, 'for pity, hear.

These two nights now I have beheld your dance,
And nothing matters now, but only you;
You are so beautiful, it shakes me through,
The thought of you is my inheritance.
I am unfit to speak
To such as you, but, lovely Queen, I seek
Only to love you, leaving life to chance.

I am unfit to touch your wings; but quake
At thought of losing you; for pity, tell
How I may reach the Kingdom where you dwell,
There to be slave or servant for your sake;
O bird of beauty bright,
Teach me the way, or come again to-night
And have some pity or my heart will break.'

Then looking on the lovely lad's distress,
She loved his love for her and pitied him;
But now the morning made the stars all dim;
She took the wings from his unhappiness.
She said, 'We have been seen,
We cannot dance again upon this green,
And where I dwell is past the wilderness.'

'O tell me where,' he cried, 'for I shall find
The way there.' 'Ah,' she answered, 'Way is none.
We dwell South of the Earth, East of the Sun,

Beyond the savage rocks and seas unkind;
You have no wings for flight,
No earthly mortal knows the course aright,
Unless the Three Queens have it still in mind.'

'And where are they' he asked. 'Far, far,' she said,
'Somewhere beyond the sunset in the West;
In seeking me you choose a weary quest.
Now, friend, farewell.' 'One minute more,' he prayed:
'Beloved, I shall try . . .
For I shall love you only till I die . . .
And seeking you, I shall not be afraid.'

Her glowing face was noble with sweet thought.
'O friend,' she said, 'the love of me will bring
Loneliness, toil and many a bitter thing;
Nor can the friend you strive to help in aught.
But I will wait you there . . .
Come, even with palsied limbs and snowy hair,
All things are truly found if truly sought.'

Then, leaning suddenly, she kisst his lips,
And pressed one glittering feather in his hand,
And swept away above the wakening land
As the white owl at dusk from cover slips . . .
Up the dark wood her gleam
Shone, as adown a basalt shines a stream;
Then she was gone and joy was in eclipse.

At first, he hoped that she would come again:
He watched the next night through: no dancers shone;
Then the next night, until the stars were gone;
Then the third night, but vigil was in vain.
'She cannot come,' he cried,
'I will go seek her Kingdom far and wide;
Better to die in search than live in pain.'

So at the downland market he enquired
Of all the tinkers, if they knew the way
South of the Earth? 'There's no such land,' said they;

'We have gone roving Earth till we are tired
And never heard the name.'
The wandering merchants told the lad the same:
They knew all lands, but not the one desired.

And in the inn, a travelling minstel told
Of lands beyond the sea, both East and West,
Lands where the phoenix has her burning nest,
And trees have emerald leaves and fruits of gold,
But no land East the Sun . . .
'Boy, I have been,' he said, 'There is not one.'
'None,' Kradoc thought, 'There must be, to the bold.'

He bade farewell to father, brothers, home,
Friends, and the grasses that her feet had prest;
He sailed to find the Three Queens in the West,
O'er many a billow with a toppling comb,
Till, 'neath the western star,
He trod the forest where the were-wolves are
And spied a hut, as of some witch or gnome.

There sat an old crone wrinkled nose to chin.
'Lady,' hs said, 'Since I have gone astray,
Seeking the queens to tell me of my way,
Have you some shed that I can rest me in?
In recompense, I'll cut
Your winter's firing and repair your hut.'
'O wonderful,' she said, 'New times begin.

I have reigned here for twenty oak-tree lives,
Yet never once has stranger spoken thus,
Bowing, uncovered, thoughtful, courteous:
What marvellous young noble here arrives?
One who goes South the Earth?
I govern all four-footed beasts from birth,
To-morrow I will ask them and their wives,

If any know the way to that far land.
Rest here to-night.' And when the morrow came
All the four-footed creatures, wild and tame,

Ran thither at the lifting of her hand:
Slink tigers yellow-eyed,
The horse, the stag, the rabbit and his bride,
Fur, antlers, horns, as many as the sand.

They listened while she questioned of the way:
'South of the Earth?' they answered, 'Madam, no . . .
It is no country where the winter go . . .
There is not such a land, the bisons say.
Ask of the birds who fly;
The eagle may have seen it from the sky,
If not the eagle, then the seagull may.'

'So,' the Queen said, 'My people cannot tell.
You must away to ask my Sister Queen
To ask her subject birds if they have seen
A country South the Earth where people dwell.
A year hence, travelling hard,
You may be with her, if no ills retard.
Good luck attend. Commend me to her well.'

*   *   *

After a twelvemonths' tramp he reacht a lake
Wide-shimmering, beyond a waste of reeds;
There by a hovel mouldered green with weeds,
An old hag mumbled, gap-tootht as a rake.
'Lady,' he pled, 'I pray
You grant me shelter, I have lost my way;
All such requital as I can I'll make.

I will re-thatch your house and cut your corn,
And gather in your apples from the tree.'
'O wonderful; new times begin,' said she.
'I have lived here since roses had a thorn,
Yet never once till now
Has courteous youth addressed me with a bow.
And you go East the Sun and are forlorn?

I govern all the birds that know the air;
Rest here to-night; to-morrow I will ask

151

If any of them all can help your task
Or know the ways by which men journey there.'
When morning came, she cried
'Come hither, birds,' and from the heavens wide
Came erne and geier, heron, finch and stare,

Jay, robin, blackbird, sparrow, croaking crow,
Hawks from the height their talons brown with blood,
Gannets that snatch the herring from the flood,
And fiery birds that glitter as they go.
'East of the Sun?' they said . . .
'We have flown windy space since wings were made . . .
There's no such land. Perhaps the fish may know.'

'So,' the Queen said, 'My subjects cannot guide.
You must go ask my Sister Queen, who rules
The dwellers in the rivers and the pools
And the green seas that waver yet abide.
A year's hard travelling hence
Should bring you there: her Kingdom is immense,
Her folk know every country washt by tide.'

      *   *   *

After another year he trod the beach
Beside an ocean breaking wave by wave.
There an old hag peered from a dripping cave,
'O ocean Queen,' he cried, 'grant, I beseech,
That I may rest till day.
To-morrow I will labour to repay
Your kindness to me as your wish shall teach.'

'O wonderful; new times begin,' she said.
'I have lived here since raindrops became sea;
Yet none till now has spoken thus to me,
Courteous and kind and modest as a maid.
South of the Earth you go?
Rest for to-night; to-morrow you shall know
If those I govern know it and can aid.'

When morning came, the Queen gave her command,
And straight the bay was white with many a streak
From the swift fins of those that cannot speak:
Whales, dolphins, salmon, hurrying to the land;
Herrings, the pickerels fierce,
Mackerel with blue flanks writ with magic verse,
And cuttles such as eye has never scanned.

The thought passed to and fro, without a word.
'Ah,' the Queen said, 'They cannot help you, friend.
Between the world's edge and the ocean's end
No fish, no four-foot beast, no flying bird
Has heard of any place
South of the Earth: you say the human race
Knows no such land. Your seeking is absurd.

Why not abandon what is surely vain?
Why not return to all you left at home,
To shear the shining furrow down the loam
Feeling the plough-team lean against the rein?
To marry; and be skilled
In all good crafts, and have your granaries filled
And live till Death comes gently without pain?

Were these not better than the life you choose,
Seeking the thing that is not?' 'No,' said he;
'This feather, that still shines, she gave to me;
I will go on, though every footstep bruise.'
Out in the bay a stir
Broke the land's quiet image into blur . . .
'Wait yet,' the Queen said, 'something comes with news.

Yes, news of South the Earth . . . the fish that flies,
The thing that beasts and birds and fish disown;
He has a rumour of it, he alone . . .
Go with him therefore, if you think it wise.
These silver wings and fins
Will help you thither; and Desire wins
Though the Desired, won, may prove no prize.'

*   *   *

153

Then with that silvery skimmer of the seas
He sped across the unquiet fatal field,
Now pastured on by haze, now ridged and steeled,
Now low, now loud, but never at its ease;
Till a last leaping flight
Bore him ashore through billows crashing white
Beneath a cliff of granite topped by trees.

And at the scree-top, lo, the crag was sheer,
Hard granite face, nine hundred feet and more,
Gleaming where drifts of cataracts came o'er
And trackless to the foot of mountaineer.
He traced along beneath,
Among the boulders and the stunted heath,
And ever and anon he seemed to hear

From somewhere up above, the cry and bay
Of dogs and hounds together giving tongue,
So that his spirit was with terror wrung
Lest these should be the hunting dogs who slay
Like wolves, what men they meet;
He was defenceless and without retreat,
But thought 'Since hounds are there, there is a way

Up to the summit; and perhaps the hounds
Have huntsmen with them who would succour me.'
So thrice he hailed, all unavailingly.
Then o'er the tumbled rocks with leaps and bounds
A dog came swiftly to him,
Barking and wagging tail as though he knew him.
It was his dog, long dead to smells and sounds,

Long buried in that distant Berkshire place,
Now here alive, and crying, 'Master, come,
This is our ever-living happy home . . .
Come with me up the track the rabbits trace;
This way, and have no fear.
Climb with me to the forest, Master dear.
We live there always in delightful chase.

All day we hunt whatever game we choose,
Then, in the dusk, we pull it down and eat;
But by the dawn it runs again on feet,
Alive and scattering scent across the dews . . .
Now, up the rock top; lo,
The forest, green as Berkshire long ago.
There run the hounds at game they cannot lose.'

And, as he spoke, the precipice was scaled.
There lay a marvellous land of oak-trees high,
With grass where hounds were running in full cry
After immortal game that never failed.
All dogs of every kind
Routed or hunted as they had the mind,
And all were glad, for all were waggy-tailed.

'Come with me, Master, through the forest green,'
The little dog said, 'as we went of old
Along the Icknield underneath the wold.
Here we forget, in time, what we have been;
But I remember well
The rabbits and the moles and the rich smell
Of those old warrens in that happy scene,

And mind your kindness to me.' Then they went
For three long days across the forest land,
Until they reacht a desert, white with sand.
'Stay here,' the dog said. Someone will be sent
To guide you further on.'
He licked his hand and bounded and was gone.
The desert stretcht its desolate extent.

Its saltness nourisht naught but poisonous things,
The moon in silence looked upon its waste,
Then, towards dawn, a something came in haste
Trotting the sand or skimming it on wings:
It was his long-dead mare,
Coming with whinnyings to greet him there,
Dreading no adder's bite nor scorpion stings.

155

'Master,' she said, 'I come out of my rest
To bear you hence upon my wings of flame,
For I can fly now, nothing makes me lame . . .
Mount me and lay both hands upon my crest.
O I remember well,
Deep in my spirit, all the Berkshire fell
And you and I at gallop, heading west.

Now for a time I rest me from the past,
But those old days recur; the huntsman's horn,
The opening of the bin-lid for the corn,
The sweet red apples tumbling to the blast.
You with the bit, which I
Dodged, till the oat-sieve shook too temptingly . . .
And all your kindness to me to the last.

Now mount and ride, together we will go
A swifter gallop than we ever knew.'
Then, when he mounted, instantly she flew
Over the desert white with salt like snow;
Skimming the sudden whip
Of the blunt adder with the swollen lip;
Making the sage flow back as waters flow.

Till after three long days she made a halt
Upon the beaches of a sea whose waves
Moaned like to cattle in the glittering caves
And fed the tremulous jellies with their salt.
'O Master mine, farewell,'
The mare said, 'Now I gallop back to dwell
In far green pastures without any fault.

For there we dwell together in the plain
Unbitted and unshod, in knee-deep grass,
Where never any gad nor botfly was,
But scarlet apples fall and golden grain.
And there we whinny and race
With streaming tails in the delight of pace,
And muse about old harness with disdain.'

So with a whinny as of old she sped,
Out of his sight across the desert sand,
Leaving him lonely on the ocean-strand
Where the spent tide its gathered seaweed spread:
Then, gliding over sea,
A woman came to him; no wings had she,
She moved by love, being his Mother dead.

'O lovely son,' she said, 'who have given all
For love, despite the hardness of the way,
I come to give such guidance as I may,
And be beside your going, lest you fall.
O often I have been
Close, as you travelled hither, though unseen,
And speaking, though you could not hear my call.

I live in the sweet world that love creates.
It is more beautiful than I can tell,
For we can go with water into hell,
With peace to pain, with gentleness to hates.
We have this joy, to strive
To help the grief of everything alive
And show where Heaven shines at open gates.

And some, if truly called by mortal need,
Can come, with light and courage and swift strength,
To vanquish the dull snake whose deadly length
Laps and would coil, round every human deed.
Give me your hand, my son,
The darkness shows that morning has begun,
And we have far to travel: let us speed.'

She took his hand, and, lo, they footed sure,
Unsunk upon the unsupporting sea;
They trod the air, unfallen, flying free,
High in the cloudless currents, mountain-pure,
Until a land arose,
Peak upon peak, with pinnacles of snows,
East of the Sun, where happy dreams endure.

His mother kissed his brow and then was gone;
He was alone upon the shore, his sight
Dazzled at first by plenitude of light,
For all things in that happy country shone.
A loitering cataract leapt . . .
A glittering people, crying 'Welcome,' swept
On wings above him, flying on and on.

'This is the land,' he cried. 'But where is she?
Where shall I find the wonder whom I love?'
Before him ran a brook out of a grove,
Bringing clear water to the clearer sea.
Within the green grove dim
Someone was singing at a morning hymn:
'O you,' he cried, 'Beloved, answer me.'

He thrust aside the myrtle and the rose:
There was his lover stitching, plume by plume,
Bright silver wings that glittered in the gloom,
And singing out her ballad to the close . . .
Seeing him there, she stood;
She shone as though the light were in her blood;
Gone was the waiting time with all its woes.

'I never ceased to trust,' she said, 'And lo,
The wings which I have wrought for you are made,
Save for one silver feather which I laid
Bright in your hand, beloved, long ago.
You have it still, I see.
We win the lovers' heaven, happy we,
The greatest happiness that heart can know.'

Then placing on his shoulders the bright pair
Of wings, she took her lover by the hand
And with him swept above that sunny land,
Thrusting aside, like swans, the rushing air,
To some green place of peace
Where love like theirs forever knows increase,
For nothing sad can ever trouble there.

But sometimes, ere the cuckoos lose their tune,
Ere pink has tinged the snowdrifts of the may
Or seething scythe has gleamed into the hay,
Or nightingales stopped singing to the moon
Whose whiteness climbs and rounds;
Then, in the peace which silences earth's sounds
Save the bird's triumph and the water's croon,

Then, sometimes, in the hush, a glimmering glows
Into a brightness in that Berkshire grass.
Those lovers come where their first meeting was
Beside the spring, within the holy close.
They dance there through the night,
Treading adown in patterns of delight
Moon-daisy, vetch, and fallen hawthorn blows.

The Love Gift

In King Marc's palace at the valley-head
All seem'd in happiness: Isolt the Queen
And Marc the King were lovers newly wed;
Brangwen, the maiden, watcht them with soft eyes;
Tristan would pluck his harp-strings till they pled
To all hearts there, and April flourisht green.
Men said, 'Our kingdom becomes Paradise.'

But Tristan and the Queen were lovers sworn
Both having drunk the love-drink meant for Marc.
Brangwen in bitter anguish went forlorn,
Loving the King: she, too, had drunk the dram,
Had played the Queen that marriage night till morn,
And lived upon her memory of the dark.
These souls, like petals in a mill-race swam.

It fell that Marc, upon Midsummer Eve,
Went to the holy hill above the wood
And saw the moon steal slowly up and cleave
The white, still clouds that glitterd as she came.
And lo, he saw the forest-goddess leave
The aged Oak of Watching that there stood;
She sped to him, and called him by his name.

She was a mighty lady crowned with oak
In its young green, with oak-apple; she held
In her left hand a spear clutcht to her cloak,
Her marvellous hair was gathered to her head.
Her sandals were bright fire without smoke.
Her robe was of fresh beechen leaves all stell'd
With hawthorn blossom that never would be dead.

Antlers she bore, and from her leafy dress
Peer'd squirrels' eyes intelligencing quick
All things that happen'd with all sudden-ness.

160

The swiftness of the forest life was hers
All, from the ousel running 'neath the cress
To soft-foot stags that never snap the stick;
Her voice was as the forest when it stirs.

'King Marc,' she said, 'Since you have honour'd me
At all times, having kept this holy copse
From hunting horn and hunting knives free,
Nor let the woodmen's axes lop and split
The branches of my oaken dwelling-tree,
Where falcons nest and the red squirrel hops,
Now you shall joy in my reward for it.

'I have three gifts to offer to your choice:
Wisdom and Power and Immortality,
Wisdom that makes the spinning stars rejoice;
Power that makes the singing stars to spin;
And last, that Death shall never still your voice,
Eternal Living, Marc, from Death set free.
Which shall I give you? you shall choose: begin.

'Each of the three gifts you may give away
But must not share: I cannot help you choose:–
Each is a glory wrested from the clay
By spirit striving against mortal odds
To hive a little sunlight from the day.
Each is a splendour for immortal use,
Each, being had, will make you like the gods.'

She waited, while Marc pondered which to take
Of those three glowing fruits the goddess had.
Rejecting any would be such mistake
But this he thought: 'Since any may be given,
Which were the loveliest gift for me to make
To my beloved Queen, to make her glad?
Which would my Isolt love, my bird of Heaven?'

And thought 'The gift of Immortality
Would be the loveliest gift, it would ensure
That Death would spare that living ecstasy,

161

That April, at whose passing the grass springs;
Death should be powerless on such as she;
That White Rose of Midsummer should endure,
Bringing forever the beauty that she brings. . .

'Therefore,' (he told the goddess) 'I will choose
Immortal Life of what you offer here
Healing to every cut, balm to each bruise,
Life, flowing in wherever fever is,
Life, the advancing knight who cannot lose,
Life, that is enemy to death and fear,
Life, that brings vision to the mind amiss.'

The goddess gave the central glowing fruit,
'This gives immortal life to whomso eats,'
She said, 'It grows upon a deathless root
Men see it glimmer if they give their lives.
Breath cannot falter nor the pulse be mute
Of whomso swallows its exciting sweets.
Eat and be quit of all that Death contrives:

Or give (you may not share) if give you must. . .
Only a god's gift should not lightly pass
At greedy bidding from a mortal lust.
God chooses the recipients of his gifts,
As earthly kings their messengers of trust,
The golden vessels not the things of brass,
Not clay that crumbles nor the sand that shifts.'

Then she was gone as stilly as the moon
Creeps into mist: not any hazel stirrd.
Marc lookt upon the goddess' glowing boon:–
A quince, like living ember to the sight;
Of intense tint, but ever changing soon,
As gorget jewels on the humming-bird;
Now drawing to itself, now giving, light.

Then hastening back to palace, Marc repair'd
Straight to the Queen and cry'd 'Isolt, my own,
I bring you here Life's very essence bared.

Accept the fruit of immortality;
The spirit powers forbid it to be shared;
Its excellence must be for you alone,
Life at its fullest, for eternity.

'The goddess gave this wonder even now
And said: 'The Eater cannot taste of Death,'
This apple grew on an immortal bough
Whose roots are thrusted in eternal things.
Beloved, with this gift I Thee endow,
Eat, my beloved, that your blood and breath
May be exempt from mortal sorrowings.

'And be, forever, beauty, as they are
Now, to myself, O treasure of the West.
My joy, my Morning and my Evening Star,
I have so long'd for such a gift to give. . .
The winds will blow my perisht dust afar
This dust that loves you and that you have blest.
What matters that, beloved: you will live.'

Then Isolt took the Fruit of Life and said
'Marc, you were ever generous, to the soul;
I take this precious gift that you have made.
But for the eating of this living fruit. . .
That is a question to be deeply weigh'd.
How beautiful it is . . . like glowing coal . . .
Ask me not what I purpose, but be mute

'About it: it were better if we both
Kept silence about this most marvellous gift.
My husband, ever since we plighted troth
You have been royal to me, gift and thought.
I who have profited have suffered sloth
To check the gratitude that should be swift
And generous as the gift, and as unsought.'

She bowed her lips upon the fruit and went.
That following afternoon at milking time
When all the palace hinds were up the bent

(Save the smiths shoeing and the men at mill)
She stole into the gallery and lent
Over the rail, and softly sang a rhyme,
And Tristan came at call to know her will.

'Tristan,' she said, 'My heart's beloved friend,
This fire-glowing fruit that has been given,
Gives to the Eater Life without an end.
I cannot share it; but I cannot eat
Taking a joy I cannot give nor lend
To you, beloved soul, my earthly Heaven.
Take it from me, and be immortal, sweet.

'For then I shall be happy, knowing this
'My Tristan is alive, through love of mine.'
Out of our loving and the joy it is
I give this golden apple of the sun;
Beloved, take it, though it once was his. . .
Marc's . . . it is yours, I kiss it for a sign,
Kiss it for my sake, my beloved one.'

So Tristan took the fruit, and as he took
An aged crone beside the fire awoke
In the dark settle in the chimney nook,
And whimper'd; 'Ai, my little grandchild's late,
And I'm forgotten being palsy-strook;
My breath is shocking and my heart is broke.'
Tristan slipt sidelong thence and out at gate.

But being by himself he thought, 'Alack,
I cannot take the gift that Marc has given
(Doubtless with passion), I must give it back.
How could I live forever without her?
We are two wild-duck in a single track
Bound to a mere whose reeds are tempest driven
But we are utterly one amid the stir.'

So, when he next met Isolt in the hall,
He said: 'I cannot keep your precious gift.
We are each other's, let us share in all,

Living or dying, O beloved heart.
Love is most royal, without self, or thrift,
Or wisdom, or concern for what may fall,
Beyond the longing for the counterpart.

'But Isolt, sweet, when first we plotted here
We trickt King Marc, that on his marriage night
He drank the philtre that makes people dear,
With Brangwen, not with you: and that offence
Leaves Brangwen sorrowing in love, and drear
With miseries of shame: it would be right
To give this fruit to her in recompense.

'But I refuse a life you cannot share:–
Therefore let Brangwen eat the fruit and live,'
Isolt agreed and calling Brangwen there
They gave the fruit to her, and Brangwen took.
Brangwen the sweet-faced woman with brown hair;
Eternal life, but peace they could not give
To her whom Love's devouring fever shook.

All day the gentle Brangwen ponder'd long
Trying to dare, but checkt by shame-facedness,
Then Love, which ever ventures and is strong
Drove her to presence of King Marc to speak.
'O King,' she said, 'Forgive me if I wrong
Custom or rule in daring to address
Your Majesty uncall'd: I do not seek

'Aught for myself, but humbly offer you
This fruit which makes immortal him who eats
Immortal, as the shining retinue
Of bringers of the Light of God to earth.
All sickness flesh of mortal ever knew
Fades from the eater of these living sweets.
It is for you: man cannot share its worth.'

Then Marc, in taking Brangwen's gift, was sure
That Isolt had betray'd him to the full,
Loving another someone beyond cure.

He said, 'I thank you, Brangwen, for this gift.
Life is a precious boon, if Love endure.
This way and that the angry passions pull;
Many are eager that the end be swift.

'I shall remember that you gave this thing,
And how you gave it, and be ever proud
That subject has so reckon'd of her King.'
Then carrying the gift he left the hall
And anguish from the poison of the sting
Wrought in him till he wept with forehead bow'd
Nor heeded whither he was bent at all.

But at the last, he sat beside a brook
And lo, beyond, a little seven year lad
Was weeping with such grief his body shook
Choking with sobs and moaning in between
That Marc, remembering childish sorrows, took
Pity, and askt, what misery he had?
What bitterness had happt to cut so keen?

Then the child answer'd 'Mother's going to die,
So Doctor says, of weakness; when she's dead
Bran says that she'll be somewhere in the sky
Where she can never talk to us, nor see.
And Father beats when Mother isn't by,
When drunk, he's beaten me until I've bled.
But Mother's kind: she makes him let us be.'

'But, Courage,' said King Marc, 'and lead me, straight,
To where your Mother lies;' then, being brought,
He paused beside the broken cottage-gate
And said, 'Go swiftly: make your Mother eat
This Fruit of Living ere it be too late.'
The lad ran to the cottage swift as thought.
And laughter follow'd after, that was sweet.

Then the King turned for home, no longer blest,
No longer home, but now the tragic place
Of passionate love's betrayal manifest.

166

But deeper sorrows than his own were bare,
The inmost ache within the mortal breast,
The pitiful child's crying of the race
For comfort of a soul no longer there.

Tristan's Singing

PART I

When Isolt quarrell'd with her Tristan there
In the green forest, and returnd to Marc,
Tristan was in the uttermost despair
And fled into the wilds and livd on bark
And found a cavern, once a hermit's lair,
And dwell'd there raving for that lovely thing
Gone from him, back to Cornwall and her King.

And in his madman's rage, he fashion'd bows,
And pointed arrows in the flame, and slew
The red stags of the mountain and their does,
The wolves of the mid-forest and their crew;
He killd, and flung their bodies to the crows,
But took their skins, and pricking with a thorn
Wrote on them in his blood his love forlorn.

Then, shrieking like the she-wolf gaunt and dire,
He would run raging like a fiend in hell,
Thro' berry-bramble, gorse and forest-fire,
Hunted by love remember'd but too well;
Love gone and living torment of desire:
Then dropping wretched he would rock with pain
Weeping for Isolt gone to Marc again.

Thus in a madman's misery he dwell'd
More than a year, then, on a summer night,
He wander'd from his cavern and beheld
The moon in heaven beautiful with light,
And saw the glowing dog-rose many-stell'd,
And joy return'd to him: he wept that things
So beautiful should bless this world of stings.

And as he wept, his spirit was aware
Of joy within him, lightening his mind
To marvels that had lain un-notic't there;
Custom had made him deaf and passion blind.
But now the universe was riven bare,
The very grass was singing from the ground,
The life within him carroll'd at the sound.

The sallow clover-clusters ting'd with red
Were rooted in immortal life and spoke
Of earth and living beauty, wine and bread,
That yet are starry in their mortal yoke;
The hairy and dark-crimson basil shed
Wisdom and peace: a moth with jewell'd eyes
Percht on his hand and sang of Paradise.

And all the glittering dusts upon his wings
Expanded and contracted singing too
Their unison and joy as living things,
The unison and joy that Tristan knew.
Life flow'd within him from eternal springs.
'O Heaven,' he cry'd, 'I am so gulft in bliss
Burn me away and let me live in this.'

But, in his joy, a flash of sorrow came:
'This, being dream, will vanish with the night.'
But lo, the morning toucht the East with flame
The forest tree-tops shiver'd and grew bright
Cocks from the little tofts without a name
Cried, and the blackbirds leapt out from the thorn
Intenser rapture came with day new-born.

For every waking bird and opening flower
And leaf upon the tree and four-foot beast
Cried out his exaltation in the hour
And brighter and still brighter grew the East
Then the great Sun strode up into his tower
And lookt and laught upon this world of men
This world of joy for all was singing then.

169

Then, from the forest of old, lichen'd oak
That had so often bow'd before the blast,
Leaf-crown'd immortals in procession broke;
Tristan beheld the spirits who outlast
Men, ravens, trees; they smil'd on him, they spoke
Those spirits of the waters and the woods,
Whose presence sanctifies the solitudes.

Brown-limb'd and starry-ey'd the Queens of hills
And Kings of glens came, and the Nymphs who rule
Brooks, lipping pastures glad with daffodils,
Or water from the chalk up-bubbling cool;
And spirits of the Peace whose beauty fills
Shy places, that the comer kneels in pray'r
That the eternal felt may bless him there.

And lesser spirits, lovely or austere,
Came from the summer bracken and the heather,
The speedwell, harebell and the mouse's ear
And water-guarding reeds with tossing feather
And fox-gloves, that the humble-bee holds dear
All these he saw, all Summer's queens and kings,
Followed by mortal troops of forest-things.

The red-tongue-lolling wolves out of the rocks;
Badgers that root the wasp-nests and the bees;
The kindreds of the poultry-murdering fox;
Stoats from the barren, squirrels from the trees:
And solitary birds and birds in flocks,
Curlews, and little snipe that in the spring
Make heaven noisy with their whinnying.

And there were otters from the mere, and voles
Out of the brooks, still nibbling at the cress,
The herons who stand fishing in the shoals
Watching the shadows in the glassiness;
And Kingfishers as bright as blazing coals
Burning blue skimmings where the minnows rise
And glittering wing'd green-gleaming dragon-flies.

All these went pressing up the Ancient Way
And Tristan follow'd, for a Summer King
Said, 'Follow, Tristan; all rejoice to-day,
The lost make merry and the broken sing.'
Within the rampart on the hill-top lay
A shelterd field, stone-mossy, scantly grasst,
To this those singers and rejoicers passt.

There they form'd circle, but as waiting still
For something greater that should crown the hour;
Joy made the spirit within Tristan thrill
Rapture was his again and peace and power
And all were singing on the holy hill
Bird, beast and spirit, grass and mossy stone,
Joy, yet foretelling greater joy unknown.

And then upon the summit of the year
So burning blue, so crooning with the dove,
Nature herself swept thither with her spear
Nature the naked swiftness, fierce as love,
With mad eyes full of lightning, striking fear,
Hawk-wing'd she was, wing-footed, antler-helm'd,
Compact of joy that drew and overwhelm'd.

'Spirits and subject creatures all,' she cry'd,
'In this mid-summer hour the ruling sun
Sends rapture into every heart, full tide,
Even now his glory quickens every one.
Sing for mid summer and the full year's pride
And sunlight flooding.' At her word they sang
Bird, beast and spirit till the forest rang.

Then Tristan, leaping to her, caught her hand,
And cry'd, 'O passionate swiftness, strike and kill . . .
I cannot care, being so sown with sand,
But, lovely fierceness, first declare your will;
Null me to dust, but let me understand . . .
What are you, fiery beast or goddess? Tell.'
Then Nature's voice made answer like a bell.

171

'I am so swift, that mortals think me slow;
I am so patient, mortals think me dead;
I am too little for men's eyes to know,
Too vast for what I blazon to be read;
Too jubilant with energy for woe;
Too truthful in my justice to be fierce.
All men must suffer, or annul, my curse.

But you, forsaken soul, by passion burn'd
Into one hunger, being daft and driven,
Bitten by watch-dogs, outcast, outlawed, spurn'd,
To mortal nothingness, shall now have Heaven.'
Then Nature told him all and Tristan learn'd.
The tale of Changing, never young nor old,
Dust into man and angel, clay to gold.

Then, having told, she sped, and Tristan went
Back to his cave, but trembling with such peace
As made his spirit seem omnipotent . . .
He wrote what Nature told, he could not cease
Though the moon rose, and southt, and westward leant
And morning stars beheld him as he wrought
Burnt into beauty by consuming thought.

All summer long, from day dawn until night,
The glory of the poem kept him glad,
So that he heeded neither wet nor bright.
Nor the rank chitch, the only meat he had
But beauty well'd from out him in delight
As from the hollow in the chalk the cool
Water comes bubbling to the sunny pool.

Till, when the summer waned and leaves were dying
To brown and red, and evening mists were chill,
And yellow crabs had fallen and were lying,
And morning frosts were white upon the hill
And heaven sighd with flocks of migrants flying
On Summer's heel, Tristan arose and said
'Isolt must hear these poems I have made.'

172

So forth he went, a ragged, starving thing
Gaunt as a famine, staring as an owl,
His matty hair and beard like tangled string
His body burnt like brick, his tatters foul.
On Severn bank he heard a church-bell ring
For the first time for months, the sound of man.
Then in the dusk an evening hymn began.

Then, lowing as they loiter'd home, the cows
Came swaying up the lane before a hind
Who whistled ballads of the milking house,
And tears of very joy made Tristan blind.
His living soul was come out of its drowse
Of love and madness, he was Man again,
Who had been mad as any fiend in pain.

Southward he went, until, behold, ahead
The river and the palace of the King,
The courtyard and the staghounds being fed,
And horses on the cobbles clattering
And Isolt, too, and Marc, like lovers wed
That morning, there together, entering in
After their gallop in the windy whin.

He knew them, but none present recognized
Himself, the wreck with bracken in his beard,
Him the dogs barkt at and the cats despised
And women shrank from and the children fear'd.
The porters markt him closely and surmized
He came for scraps, they watcht he did not steal
A bone from any stag-hound for his meal.

Then Kai, the steward, flaunted to the gate
To bid the porters close it on the throng;
And, seeing Tristan, askt, 'Why do you wait?
You, dirty gangrel? Off where you belong.'
And Tristan said 'I come to supplicate
Leave to approach Queen Isolt, and to sing
One poem to her from this pack I bring.'

173

Kai lookt upon the written skins, and frown'd
And said 'But that His Majesty has bidden
That poets shall find Cornwall friendly ground,
Such skins as these should go upon the midden,
And you, yourself, be hunted by the hound
Over the border . . . I will take your pack
In, to King Marc. Await my coming back.'

Soon he return'd and said 'The King has glanc't
At some of all this scribble: your request
To see the Queen cannot be countenanc't.
She sees no lazar smelling of the pest.
The prospects of your verse might be enhanc't
Were yourself cleaner; but the King, ev'n so
Dislikes it. Take your rubbish. Kindly go.'

Marc passt upon the instant and said: 'Stay,
You Severn poet, though I cannot care
For what you write, you must not go away
From this my palace, guerdonless and bare,
Give him a cloak and wine and victuals, Kai;
And for your journey westward, take this purse.'
Then Tristan flung it from him with a curse.

'No, Marc,' he said, 'I am Tristan, come again
To win back Isolt to me if I can.
Let Isolt tell me if I come in vain.
Let Isolt choose between us, man and man.'
'Tristan,' Marc said, 'I vowd you should be slain:
Hunted and torn to pieces by the hounds
If you were seen within my Kingdom's bounds.

You have wrought harm enough in Isolt's life;
You have disgrac't her, you have brought her pain.
She has renounc't you and is now my wife.
You shall not look upon her face again.
If you attempt it, boy, the hangman's knife
Shall have you into quarters in the yard.
Now you shall leave this Kingdom under guard.'

174

Then the guards, closing on him, dragg'd him thence,
Bound him, and flung him in a cart, and drove
Over the frontier to the forest dense
Where slink and savage wild wolves us'd to rove.
Then, flogging him, they left him without sense
And so return'd: the rime-frost striking cold
Reviv'd their victim lying on the mould.

PART II

When morning came, he gather'd up the sheaf
Of poems flung beside him: like a deer
That limps into dark covert for relief
Being sore hurt, so Tristan trod the drear
Dark, water-dripping forest full of grief
Not knowing where, but wandering amiss
Towards the camp where Isolt had been his.

And limping on, at dusk he reacht the place
So beautiful when it had held and shrined
Their summer love together, Isolt's grace,
And all the ecstasy of being blind
To all things but the beauty of a face.
Autumn had wrought her change, the bower now
Was sodden grass and leafless hawthorn bough.

There, with a flint and rags, he lighted fire
And burn'd his poems, all, except the last
That was the song of Nature and Desire,
And of Eternity and Time long past;
Of Doing, Good and Ill, and of its Hire
That never sleeps, but waits, and has its Turn;
This, being Isolt's song, he could not burn.

Daylong he crooned it until even-fall,
Praying for Death to come to give him peace;
And Autumn chill'd, until the oak trees tall
Had droppt the last brown shred of summer's fleece,
Then the snug dormouse curld into a ball

175

Deep under knotty roots in nibbled wool
And silent-footed snow came beautiful.

All winter-long he wander'd, living hard,
On roots and dulse and mussels of the rock
And grain forgotten at the thrashing-yard
And barley-porridge that the fattening stock
Left (or the upland swineherd did not guard)
And green cow-parsley thrusting from the snow
And other pasture such as thrushes know.

The Spring began again and at the stir
Of Earth's green fire thrusting into leaf
Again old passion prickt him with the spur
And April's beauty only added grief
April was only beautiful through her,
But rocking in his woe the tune took power
Nature and he were knitted for an hour.

And living beauty ridded his despair
Till joy compelld him to arise and sing
The song that Nature taught him to its air
That pierct like the green fire of the Spring
Clear as a challenge rang his singing there
The rabbit-bucks crept cock-ear'd out of holes
And stags came tip-toe upon velvet soles.

Still louder rang the challenge of the song
The great, white, black-eared cattle rowsd and came
The bull's chin chiselling as he lickt his throng
His brooding eyes alight with sullen flame
The stallion, whickering answer, snappt his thong
And ran to hear: and from the marsh the geese
Trumpeted out to birds the end of peace.

And ducks out of the pond, and cock and hen
Flappt and took wing at hearing of the call
Sheep from the moors turnd thither, hogs from pen,
Horses at ploughing, hunters in the stall,
And now it arrow'd in the hearts of men

It struck in Isolt's heart the while she wove,
In King Marc's palace, tapestries of love.

And at the sound she said: 'That song of power
Is Tristan calling me: I inly know
That here begins the striking of the hour;
The ebbing ends and here begins the flow,
To sweep us on its crest.' She left her bower
And caught her horse and galloppt to the cry
That seemed to draw the winds out of the sky.

And in the forest beast and hurrying beast
Throng'd to the singing; birds from bough to bough
Flitted like blackbirds to the cherry feast;
Rapine and mating both forgotten now.
There she found Tristan singing, facing East
Ring'd by the birds and beasts that croon'd and sway'd,
As Nature's song went ringing down the glade.

Then, flinging from her horse, she passt the throng
And cry'd: 'O Tristan, I have come again . . .
Forget that we have wrought each other wrong
We are as one as western wind and rain.
Forget my cruelty and teach your song
And let us sing together, you and I
And be away together in the sky.'

And then they sang together until space
And Time were over for them: Dinan's son
Rapt by the song to that enchanted place
Heard their two voices merging into one
And saw the lovers drawing face to face,
Shining with beauty such as seldom shines
On faces, here, where roses have such spines.

And then, lo, they were one, and all was over
Their rags and robes were fall'n and gleaming things,
Spirits, a lover wing in wing with lover
Were laughing in the air and spreading wings
Shining like stars and flying like the plover

177

Laughing aloft and singing and away
Into some Summer knowing no decay.

*   *   *

Men never say them more, but Dinan's son
Gathered those relics of the fallen gear
And bore them to the Saint within the Dun
Who sent for precious woods and wrought a bier
Inlaid with goldwork gleaming like the sun
And laid the relics on it and with pray'r
For those two lovers' souls displayed them there.

They lie there still within the holy shrine
And lovers sick with loving go to pray:—
'O God of Love, be such love hers and mine
As to touch Life that nothing can decay
And be at one forever and so shine
Singing forever, blessing sorrowing men,
Like these immortal ones, Amen, Amen.'

Simkin, Tomkin and Jack

Before old Tencombe of the Barrows died,
He called his sons, and said, 'Simkin, and you,
Tomkin and Jack, I am at Jordanside.
When I have passed the river you shall have
Each one, a thousand pounds, and this thereto,
This farm and downland where the Barrows stand;
Share it; all happy virtue is in land.'
He died, the three sons carried him to grave.

Then the three sons debated how to spend
Each one, his heritage; first Simkin spoke:
'I'm not for farming, here at the World's End:
The bailiff can do that; myself am fixt
On Science, to attempt some happy stroke
To make synthetic Man's Flesh which will do
Whatever menial jobs we put it to.
Flesh is but hydrogen and carbon mixt.'

Then Tomkin spoke: 'A beautiful resolve,
And yet less beautiful than what I plan,
I hope to catch the electrons that revolve
Within the excited brains of splendid men
And make an Essence of the Soul of Man
Injecting this will make the silly sane;
The normal splendid: it will kindle brain.
That done, perhaps I'll think of farming then.

Jack said, 'And I, who am a Business Man,
Reject your plans, and farming, which will leave
The practisers more poor than they began.
I shall go Citywards to Stocks and Shares
To venture at a profit and achieve.
Then, having money, haply I'll finance
Your Flesh and Spirit ventures, and advance
This farmstead for week-enders with cheap fares.'

179

They went to work: then, on a holiday,
Spent at the ruin'd farm, Jack said, 'The Press
Mentions our Barrow on the Roman Way,
And quotes the old Wives' Fable that within
There sits a giant in a golden dress.
Let's dig the barrow open to make sure.'
'Right,' said the brothers, 'Practice is the cure
For theories of all sorts: let's begin.'

So, out upon the Antient Way they drove.
There was the Barrow forty feet aloft;
Beeches were green about it in a grove;
Rabbits had burrowed deep into its sides.
The brothers settled on a site and dofft
Their coats and collars, then their swinging picks
Rang on the scattered flints with little clicks.
Blisters made bubbles on their fingers' hides.

Three days they dug into the barrow's heart
The shepherd on the downland thought them mad
Then, upon sunset, roofing fell apart
The Sun shone in upon a central cave
There sat a mighty Bone Thing, golden-clad
A skeleton, gold-helmeted, who grinn'd
Sitting below the beech-roots and the wind;
Kingly, tho fifteen centuries in the grave.

Then Simkin said 'So the tradition's true. . .
Cro-Magnon skull . . .' And Tomkin: 'He is big.
Look, on the bone, the markings of the thew'. . .
And Jack, 'This gold will speedily be ours.
A happy end to a successful dig.'
Then Simkin said: 'Synthetic flesh would go
Well, on these bones: a looker-on would know
The kind of chap he was, and all his powers.'

Then Tomkin said 'If you would clothe his bones,
I'd squirt Synthetic Spirit in his veins,
Then he would speak, I think, in monotones,
And tell us something precious about dates.'

But Jack said 'Brothers, after all our pains,
Let's cover him until the morning: then
Have in the Press and Moving-Picture men
And also charge admission at the gates.

But first, our duty is to take the gold,
It is not safe to leave it as it is.'
He took the armour, fold on gleaming fold
Leaving the rib-bones open to the air.
He said 'Collectors will be mad for this
Authentic armour fetches any price
And no such armour will be offered twice.
To-morrow we'll be famous everywhere.'

That night he clamour'd to invite the Press,
Simkin and Tomkin checkt him as they toil'd
Making in test-tubes many a smelling mess,
Or at a wire-end a spitting spark,
Or violet glowings from the wires coil'd.
They met at breakfast-time with amplest store
Simkin had outer husking, Tomkin core;
Jack was by much less cheerful than at dark.

'You know,' he said, 'this making flesh and soul,
Is going far: I'm not a squeamish man . . .
But in the play the Robots took control. . .
Besides, it's witchcraft, which is counted wrong
By every people since the world began.
The Witchcraft Statutes are not yet repealed. . .'
'Rats,' Simkin said, 'The plough is put to field.'
'Bunkum,' said Tomkin. 'Up, and come along.'

So out they went along the dewy grass
Up to the Barrow where the giant sat
Bone upright like the warrior that he was.
Tomkin took off his jacket, rolled his shirt,
Simkin upon the skullbones set his hat.
'Come, Father Noah,' Tomkin said, 'At last
We'll get authentic datings of the past.
First body, Simkin. Then the Soul with squirt.'

181

So Simkin wrought his wondrous chymic clay.
The figure, like an image made of wax,
Stared listlessly along the antient way.
'You've made him like a warrior,' Tomkin said.
'Now for the soul, to stir him in his tracks.'
But Jack in terror cried, 'No, not the last . . .
This creature is so awful and so vast. . .
If once you give him life he'll smite us dead.'

'Rubbish,' said Simkin, 'If we give him life
It will be elemental in its form;
If fractious you can stick him with a knife.
Go on with Spirit, Tomkin, fill the gland.'
'No, no,' Jack pleaded, 'you will raise a storm.'
'Bosh,' Tomkin said. 'Now for it . . . Look at me.'
'Mercy,' Jack pleaded, 'Let me climb a tree
I would not watch it for all English land.'

'Get up your tree,' said Tomkin, 'And be still.'
Jack climbed a little beech tree: Tomkin took
Transmitting wires for the vital thrill
To make the giant lively: Simkin helpt.
'When I count Three,' said Tomkin, 'You can look.
One . . . No, the wire's jammed. Two . . . There's a short.
Now the thing's working . . . waken up, old sport,
Three . . . there she goes.' Jack cower'd down and yelpt.

And lo, a marvellous thing, the figure stirr'd
It trembled, then its mighty jointings crackt,
Bones grided in their sockets, as they heard.
Then the thing stood upon its feet and breath'd.
Nothing of living man his glory lackt. . .
He strode into the sunlight, facing east,
At every pulse his majesty increast
He stood like light in something glowing sheathd.

Then, looking at the Sun, the figure spoke
Meanings, not words: his hearers understood.
Like morning in their minds his meaning broke:
'O Sun that I have worshippt: Sun that brings

The living green upon the wintry wood,
Sun that brings thought into the barren mind,
Sun that puts beauty into hearts unkind,
Lord of all life and Order, King of Kings,

I once more look upon you and obey
The call to Likeness with the Force that sends
Power in the shining of the ray
And Wisdom in the summer of your touch.
All Energy and Beauty are your friends
Your fires shout for rapture but confess
A power supreme above their mightiness
Who captains Heaven and many millions such.

I have been buried long and now awake,
I who was Arthur's comrade long ago.
Man is no longer manhood but mistake.
O spirits of the Morning, come like fire
Come, Arthur, from the dead; let trumpets blow.'
Then, lifting to his mouth his mighty hand,
He cried 'Come, comrades to this holy land
O Light breathe Light upon this land's desire.'

Once he called thus, and all the trees stood still;
Twice he called thus, and all the air grew tense;
Thrice he cried thus, and over Barrow Hill
A rush came, like the coming-by of birds,
As spirits never seen by commonsense
Gatherd, and gazed, and gleamd upon the view
Waiting, calm-eyed, for orders what to do
From some great trumpet call transcending words.

The brothers saw their many colourd wings
Fold, on their breasts: their beauty was so calm
Each spirit seemd a King of many Kings.
They came to carry light to human souls.
None of those victors carried sword, but palm.
The brothers knew that Arthur's comrade's cry
Had called to England lights that cannot die
Beauties and powers wearing aureoles.

And then . . . what then? . . . the warrior's figure died.
The body droopt, as all the aged bones
Droppt into dust upon the downland side.
Nothing was there except a chymic mess
The barrow's tumbled earth and scattered stones.
Then the three brothers heard a cry begin
'Open your doors and let the new life in.'
And skylarks rose and sang in nothingness.

Tristan and Isolt

The King and Queen debate with eagerness
What King shall marry Isolt the Princess.

On Marc, the Cornish King, the pair agreed.
Then, the Queen said 'But first we must take heed.

She seems to like this Prince, Sir Tristan, here;
The lad with love-songs ever at her ear.

Can you invent a plot to speed him hence
A week or two, and yet without offence?'

'Yes,' said the King. 'Ask Tristan to attend.'
'Ah, noble Tristan, trebly welcome, friend . . .

You are the huntsman whom I long to see.
Will you attempt a forest-quest for me?

But, ere I ask it, let me first declare . . .
No quest more perilous is anywhere . . .'

'Speak on, O King, and make my blood run cold . . .'
'You have a lion's heart, as I was told . . .

And this, the favour that I have to ask
Matches your soul: it is a lion's task . . .

In the far forest where wild cattle go,
A mad bull ranges, working bitter woe.

You may have heard of him from knight or ranger . . .'
'Truly, O King, and understand the danger.'

'I trust my woodmen, not the common tongue.
This bull is not an aged rogue, but young;

Young, but full-grown, and raging against man.
Mens' terror gives him horns of seven span.

White, with black ears, and as my rangers tell
Bitten by some mad wolf and mad as hell.

So mad, that any hound, hurt in attack
Upon him, maddens, and infects the pack.

Men dare not hound him now, nor venture near
The green wood grim that hides that bull of fear.

They think he is an evil spirit come
To terrify men back to devildom.

Secret he lurks along the forest marge
Till beast or careless mortal makes him charge.

His frightful horns have tattered many a limb.
O Tristan, will you rid the woods of him?'

'Sir, I will gladly try.'
                            'But go on foot,
With heavy arrow nocked, ready to shoot.

Horses he hears, and hounds are no more use.
Creep up to windward, matching guile with ruse.

A man on foot alone has better chance
To snatch one shot with arrow or with lance,

And you, men say, are deadly with both tools.
The many whom he kills are not all fools.

The quest brings cruel danger, Tristan mine.'
'O King, if Fortune cherish my design,

Perhaps I may destroy him, ere he me.'

Away, into the forest ways, is he

Then off the ways into the wildwood grim
Where every thicket might hide death for him.

'Whichever wins,' the Queen said, 'We shall thrive.
The bull or Tristan will not be alive.'

The King and Queen bade Isolt to attend
'Isolt, your days of singleness must end

We (and the Kingdom's need) alike decide
That you must be the King of Cornwall's bride.'

'I cannot, Sir: I love King Tallorc's Son,
The poet Tristan, Sir, that lovely one.'

'That is but childish fantasy and blind.
Royalty ever has the realm to mind.'

'My love for Tristan must be more to me
Than royalty or realm can ever be.'

'Girl, you talk folly, and you disobey.'
'Sir, I love Tristan; threaten as you may.'

The King bade build an earthen tower,
And in it shut Isolt the Flower.
He said 'Love soon succumbs to power.'

They shuttered her, and barred her fast;
Each day was sadder than the last.

Slowly, the weary hours fell
From cock-crow to the evening-bell.

Imprisoned Isolt hardly heard
The May cry of the Cuckoo-bird.

And saw no gleam of the May sun.
But, ere the seventh day was done,

187

On the grim prison's barry sill
A chaffinch tapped her tiny bill.

'O Little Mimi,' Isolt cried,
Fly to my Love, ere I have died,

Tell him, that I, who hold him dear,
Am shuttered up in prison here,

And here must perish sorrowing
Unless I wed the Cornish King.

But, tell him this . . . and, oh, attend
To each word, Mimi, little friend . . .

Say, that I have, and mean to try,
A drug that makes men seem to die,

That whitens cheek and lips, and nulls
The life-long comment of the pulse.

This, when I take, will lay me white
Dead to all touch, as to men's sight.

The King and Queen will come to see,
And sigh, (though scowling) 'Dead is she . . .

The Princess Isolt: let her have
Mourners to sing her to her grave

The yard where gannets' plumes are shed,
The sea-shrine, on St Dinas Head.

Bury her there . . . and let her lie,
She flouted our authority.

Then, Mimi darling, tell my lover
How he can make my corse recover . . .

188

Bid him attend, three mornings hence
Beside the chapel's seaward fence

Where the wild apples cluster close
Pure blossom, all, as April goes.

There let him loiter, till he hear
My singing ꞏꞏ ꞏꞏ ꞏꞏ ꞏꞏ ꞏꞏ ꞏꞏ

And let him stop them ere they pass
From All Saints Way onto the grass.

He need but beg to see my face
For certain they will grant the grace

And more, for knowing his despair
They'll stand aside and leave us there.

When they are gone, he can revive
My seeming death to girl alive.

First, he must kneel beside his love
And sign a cross; then, let him move

The poison-crystal from my lips
That holds my spirit in eclipse,

Then, let him doubt not, I shall smile
As living, in a minute's while.

And, Mimi, bid him have at hand
A ship to take me from the land

Or else, good horses, that will bear
Into some liberty of air

Two lovers, such as he and I
Who can but love until they die

And need no other gift from Fate
Than each the other, early or late.

189

In such green happiness, in Spring
I will be lover to my King

And you, beneath the hawthorn thatch
In lichen-silvered nest, shall hatch

Thy Arab-scripted eggs, and preen
All May to us, Love's King and Queen.

Such solitude, with Love for friend,
Will blur this bitter time, and mend

The curse called 'living' by the dull.
O Mimi, find my Beautiful,

There in the forest as he waits
By waters where the red stag baits.

O Mimi, hasten . . . tell him true . . .'

Away the pretty chaffinch flew.

Westward the happy Mimi drove
With all the energy of love

And after search, found Tristan tense
Eyeing new hoof-prints stamped immense

In mud, where Alan Water spread.
The bull had stamped those marks of dread

Not seven minutes since, and lay
Hidden, ahead, some yards away.

Perhaps within a javelin-shot. . .

But Mimi told . . . and he forgot
The mad bull and his hunter's zest
The plighted promise of his quest

All he could think of was his sweet
Dead, truly, in a winding-sheet,

Borne to the grave, and he, too late
There by the sea, to change her fate.

What if but one of Life's delays
Should shush him on the forest ways?

Check him, one little fatal hour
Till earth had hidden the white flower?

Five fatal feet of earth stamped close
Shutting the sunlight from the rose?

Doubt not, the anguish tortured him
There, as he ran the forest dim.

Within the prison, Isolt heard
The gossip pass from bird to bird,
'Mimi has told the Prince, and he
Runs through the forest to the sea.'

'No . . . he is there. And runs a ship
Into green water from the slip.'

'No . . . he has hoisted sail, and sped
Into that nook at Dinas Head.'

'No; he has left her there, and goes
To find some knowledge of his rose . . .

O listen, Princess, he has crept
Close hither, as the sentries slept . . .

And now will sing: O listen . . . Hark
Tristan will save you from King Marc.'

(The Song)

'Isolt, my share of all things good,
What the bird told, I understood.

In the green channel of cool sea
A swimming sea-swan waits for thee.

Deep in the apple-blossom bower
Tristan awaits the laggard hour

And prays, that it may make him meet
Isolt, his share of all things sweet.'

Then Isolt sang: 'Then, now, I take
A cold road for my lover's sake,

And lift the drug, whose presence stays
The red blood's currents in its ways.

And hope that it may swiftly bring
This eager subject to her King . . .

If not, that it may null to naught
The every longing of her thought,
That is but Tristan, everywhere.
I lift the eastern drug . . . and dare.'

At sunset, when the wardress knocked
And none replied, the guards unlocked

And peering-in upon the bed
The wardress saw the Princess dead.

And cried, 'O, she is dead, past cure.
Her loving heart has broken, sure.

O tell the King, for pity's sake . . .
Even his iron heart will ache.'

192

They told the King. 'Indeed?' he said
'She brought her death on her own head.

At dawn tomorrow, let her be
Borne to the chapel near the sea,

And buried . . . Bid the priests prepare
 ⸻ ⸻ ⸻ ⸻ ⸻ ⸻

And sing a psalm and let her lie.
She flouted our authority.'

    So the night passed while lady dew
    Danced the long grass with her wet shoe.

    Now through the grass on the sea's verges
    The priests bear Isolt, singing dirges.

    Tristan, in cover near the chapel
    Snowed on by blossom of wild apple

    Waiting, in lover's anguish, heard
    That song too sad to be by bird.

    Then the lone bell upon the Head
    Tolled, for the coming of the dead.

    And on the wayward winds there come
    The fragrances of burning gum.

So, moving forth, Prince Tristan cried
'O stay; sweet bearers of my bride.

Stay but a moment, till I see
The dear face dead for love of me.
    And let me be alone, to pray
    For one so darling rapt away'.

The bearers stopped: the singers ceased
'So be it' said the Warden Priest.

'Look on the empty case, whose soul
May now be bright with aureole

Where sorrow of love is turned to bliss,
And no parting of lovers is.

Look, then, and pray, two minutes here.
To God, all human love is dear.

Leave them together . . . we will go
Down to the holy well below.'

Tristan knelt down, and gently drew
The white silk from the face he knew.

Then, as the footsteps died, he quaked
Lest the still form might not be waked.

Then from her lips he plucked the dark
Death-crystal that had laid her stark,

And saw her eyelids tremble open
And Isolt stir, like one awoken.

He felt her pulse beat in her wrist
Her life spread like the sun through mist

Then with a smile, she waked; she stood.
They crept together through the wood

They clambered down to the green cove
Wherein the sea-bird galley hove.

There, thrusting forth, they cleared the rocks
And felt the water's slapping knocks

Yield to a purr along her rail
When once the wind had filled the sail.

Meanwhile, the mourners, having left the well,
Found the bier empty, so the stories tell,
Yet, in the dew, the lovers' footprints showed.
The priests and mourners hurried the same road.

And after them, the King and Queen came riding
The King all curses and his consort chiding.

'Show us this Tristan and his trickster girl.'

They saw a bright white water-furrow curl
Under the vessel's bow as Tristan steered;
Star-glittering gems of spray her going sheared.

The gannets plunged for fish and rose in glee.
Wind-hurries ruffled ripples on the sea.

Safe from pursuit the flying lovers drove
Ahead was liberty; beyond was Love.

My Library: Volume One

Fifty-five years ago, as impulse led,
I crossed by Patchin Place, and turning thence,
Heard the loud railway roaring overhead,
And felt the City's kindling excellence.

Knowledge was what I sought; to inly know
All wisdom, truth, past, present and to be . . .
There, in Pratt's Store, was Knowledge, in a row.
Which, of those thousands, should enlighten me?

What spirit guided me to Volume One,
The Story of King Arthur? So it fell
That summer morning on Sixth Avenue.
I had gone shopping better than I knew,
Returning friend to Bors and Lionel,
Cousin to Tristan and Romance's son.

(I hope that my memory does not play me false. In memory, I crossed Greenwich
Avenue from Christopher Street and entered Sixth Avenue by a road leading close
to the eastern end of Jefferson Market. This road may have been Patchin Place; it
was at least near it. – J.M.)

Caer Ocvran

There are some ramparts in the distant West,
A heave of hill, once castled for a king,
But now a sheep-walk where the curlews nest,
And Wild bees hive, and many skylarks sing.

Once, a heart beat here in a Queen of fable,
Child of a King here, still in people's tales,
Beat in a pulse that made her crown unstable,
But pardoned now, where beauty still avails.

Now, where she lived and rode, the curlews call
Their marvellous cry, that opens doors unseen,
Into a world wherein no sinners fall,
But Destiny sets crowns on King and Queen.

And though the realm fell and the hearts were riven
The heart that beat to beauty is forgiven.

Tristan and Isolt

A Play in Verse

First performed by the Lena Ashwell Players at the Century Theatre, Archer Street, Bayswater, at 8.15 p.m., on Monday, 21st February, 1927, with the following cast:

(Characters in the order of their appearance.)

Destiny	AGNES LAUCHLAN
Tristan, *a Pictish Prince*	JOHN LAURIE
Dinan, *His Steward*	OSWALD D. ROBERTS
Kolbein, *a Scandinavian Pirate*	HAROLD PAYTON
Marc, *King of Cornwall*	KYNASTON REEVES
Kai, *His Steward*	PATRICK GOVER
Bedwyr, *His Baily*	DONALD FINLAY
Sowkin, *the Swineherd's Wife*	OLIVE WALTER
Pixne, *betrothed to the Swineherd's Son*	RACHEL HILL
Thurid, *Kolbein's Queen*	AGNES LAUCHLAN
Isolt, *Her Daughter*	ESME CHURCH
Brangwen, *Her Waiting Gentlewoman*	LUCILLE LORNE
Arthur, *Captain of the Romano-British Host*	HAROLD PAYTON
Hog, *King Marc's Swineherd*	NORMAN CLARKE
Pigling, *His Son*	THOROLD DICKINSON
Attendants	BETTY BEARDMORE
	VICTORIA PARKER

198

(From Front Stage.)

DESTINY. I am She who began ere Man was begotten,
I am deathless, unsleeping; my task is to make
Beginnings prosper to glory and crumble to rotten
By the deeds of women and men and the ways that they take.
I am apple and snake.

I show Tristan, the prince, in glory beginning,
And Isolt, the maid, in her beauty: I show these two
Passing from peace into bitter burning and sinning
From a love that was lighted of old. I display them anew
And the deaths that were due.

(Full stage. Tintagel.)

TRISTAN. You have brought me over the sea, far from our home,
To a castle percht on a crag at the world's end,
Yet never said why. Then here, in the castle, father,
Nobody speaks, but all go still as the grave,
As though they were under a curse. What is this castle?
DINAN. This is Tintagel, the court of the Cornish kings;
It is under a curse, for Kolbein, the pirate,
My enemy and yours, is a tyrant here.
TRISTAN. Why do you call him 'my enemy and yours'?
DINAN. Tristan, my son, it is time that you learned the truth.
Twenty years since, Meirchyon, King of Cornwall,
Lived here with Olwen, his daughter, and Marc, his son.
Kolbein the pirate killed King Meirchyon here,
Seized all Cornwall as his, seized Marc as a prize,
Would have seized Olwen as well, to serve his lust,
But that my master, King Tallorc, chancing to come here,
Saved her, by bearing her hence and marrying her.
Kolbein became our enemy thus, son Tristan.
He gave pursuit and killed King Tallorc, my master;
And the Queen, my mistress, died. After twenty years
I bring you here to a Cornwall under a curse:
Marc, a slave-King, Kolbein a tyrant still
Bleeding the groaning realm.

But stand aside; here Kolbein comes with King Marc:
We shall hear what new exaction the pirate claims.

(KOLBEIN *enters with* MARC.)

KOLBEIN.   Marc, I ordered a tribute of thirty lads,
The sons of nobles: are they here to be paid?

MARC.   No.

KOLBEIN.   Then why not?

MARC.   Because I beg you to spare them.
A tax, of the sons of nobles, is tyranny.

KOLBEIN.   Being the tax I need, I bid you to pay it.

MARC.   But to drag sons from their parents is barbarous.

KOLBEIN.   To leave them to raise rebellion here is madness.

MARC.   Boys cannot raise rebellion; but outraged men may.

KOLBEIN.   I will deal with the boys now; with their fathers later.

MARC.   Will you not take instead some double tribute
Of copper and tin, or linen, or grain, or beasts?

KOLBEIN.   No.

MARC.   Then a threefold tax?

KOLBEIN.   Not a thousandfold.
I have things and beasts sufficient: I want young men.

MARC.   Remember, you, that the gods befriend the friendless.

KOLBEIN.   I have not found it so: your father was friendless,
So I clove his skull for him here in this very hall.
Your sister's husband was friendless; so I clove his skull;
And you are friendless and I will cleave your skull, too,
Spite of the gods, if you go running athwart.
Go, gather me here those thirty within five minutes.

(He turns to go, growling.)

You Cornish slaves must learn who is master here.

(He goes out.)

MARC.   What are you, strangers? What brings you to Tintagel?

DINAN.   I am a steward and harper, born in the north;
I come to speak with King Marc.

MARC.   You have spoken with him:
Now take his advice and go from this land accurst.

DINAN.   You do not remember me; but we met before,
I came here once with King Tallorc, the time he wooed
And wedded the fair princess, your sister, Olwen.

MARC.   I was then nine. I forget you. Stay! are you Dinan?

DINAN.   Yes, lord, I am.

MARC.   Why, welcome, Dinan, to Cornwall,
Now I remember well: and is this your son?
    DINAN.   Only a foster-son, lord: loved as my own son.
    TRISTAN.   Am I not your son, then, father?
    DINAN.   No, Tristan, indeed.
This lad is of royal stock, King Marc; your stock.
He is the son of King Tallorc and your fair sister.
    MARC.   Mind what you say, friend.
    TRISTAN.   I, the son of King Tallorc?
    MARC.   They swore to me that my sister died in childbed,
With the child dead, too.
    DINAN.   I spread that story, my lord,
Lest Kolbein or Kolbein's men should murder him.
The Queen, your sister, died, but her son survived,
And this is he, Prince Tristan, named from King Tristan,
King Tallorc's father: he is your nephew, King Marc;
Is he not like your sister?
    MARC.   Yes: but, by heaven . . .
This is a marvellous thing: proofs must be given.
    DINAN.   Here is Queen Olwen's ring: here is her brooch.
But on her death-bed she told me the rhyme unknown
To all but those of the blood of the House of Cornwall.
She said that that would convince.

                                  (*He whispers to* MARC.)
    MARC.   It does convince me.
You are Olwen's son, my nephew; welcome, then, home.
    DINAN.   My prince and king, I have loved you for all these years
Only for this great day. I kneel to my King.
    TRISTAN.   That you shall never do.
    MARC.   No, never, indeed.
Dinan, most faithful steward and loving friend,
You shall kneel no more to kings: I create you lord
Of my southern march.
            But, O good friends, I forgot. . .
You are in danger here, most deadly danger . . .
If Kolbein learns who you are, he will have you hanged . . .
If not, he may make you slaves. He is the pirate
Who killed your father and mine and governs Cornwall.
    TRISTAN.   I know about Kolbein, uncle.

201

MARC.   I hear him coming.
Go aside; be silent; lest he enslave you, Tristan.
     TRISTAN. I shall try not to be slave, being a King.
                    (KOLBEIN *enters*.)
     KOLBEIN. Marc, your minutes are past; where are the thirty?
     MARC. I have not gathered them, Kolbein.
     KOLBEIN.   You disobeyed.
Now I'll take sixty, with you for a sixty-first.
You shall pull at a bowman's oar aboard my galley.
                              (*He seizes* MARC.)
     TRISTAN. One moment, Kolbein! Take those hands from the
        King.
     KOLBEIN. God's sake, young cockerel, who are you that come
        crowing?
     TRISTAN. You shall soon hear. You boasted, five minutes since,
That you killed King Meirchyon and his daughter's husband.
I am Tristan, son of that husband and that daughter.
You are my father's and my grandfather's killer;
You shall pay me for their blood. Come out and fight.
     KOLBEIN. Tallorc's and Olwen's son! Why, they had no son.
     DINAN. This is their son. I nurtured him secretly,
So that you should not kill him.
     KOLBEIN.   Dinan, the steward.
     MARC. There are better proofs than that; he is my nephew.
     KOLBEIN. I see he is: he is Olwen's son to the life.
Boy, Tristan, son; I loved your mother of old;
I killed your father for love of her. It is hard
To fight you, who are so like her.
                    Listen, now, Tristan:
Let us not fight; but take your kingdom, and also
Ask what you please in settlement of our feud.
     TRISTAN. I ask for a fair fight to a finish with you.
     KOLBEIN. As you prefer. We will fight with swords then, at once.
This, being a blood-feud, I will swear my followers
To abide by what may fall. See there in the bay
A rock with standing for two? That's where we'll fight.
We two will row there alone and fight to the utterance.
You agree, that that seems fair?
     TRISTAN.   Most manlike and fair.
     DINAN. He is merciless to the beaten, fair to others.

KOLBEIN. So you will find me, Dinan, if I kill Tristan.
Marc, who says nothing, is doubtless thinking the more.
You will be happy with Kolbein killed and away?
    MARC. No: I do not wish you killed.
    KOLBEIN.   No, you speak the truth.
Though I killed your father and took your land, you like me.
Well, the cockerel has not killed me yet; far from it.
I am still King Conan down the rug to the laugh.
I have wisdom, you have youth: it is fair for each.

(They go out.)

    BEDWYR (entering). Kai, I have word that Arthur is coming to
        court
To ask for men for the war against the heathen.
    KAI. It is not likely that Kolbein will grant the men.
    BEDWYR. Not unless urged; but urge it, Kai.
I shall urge it.
    KAI. Urge it? That must depend upon Kolbein's will.
And Kolbein's will must depend upon events;
And events, good Bedwyr, depend on more than me.
But leave me Arthur's letter.

(BEDWYR goes.)

A good man, Bedwyr,

But narrow in view; no subtlety, no breadth.

(SOWKIN enters.)

What are you, good woman?
    SOWKIN.   Sowkin, Hog Swineherd's wife.
    KAI. Why do you enter here?
    SOWKIN.   Bringing our duty,
Our Easter duty of March black-puddings, lord.
There, sir, a love of a pudding, as black as medicine,
And thick and soft as a lady's thigh: do feel it.
There's something to lean on in a day of trouble.
There's a lordly life, to eat one of these at supper,
And lie awake all night feeling it doing you good.
    KAI. What vile beast's corpse did you desecrate for this?
    SOWKIN. A love of a pig, lord, who felt like heaven itself.
    KAI. Remove it into the garbage before it bursts.
    SOWKIN. But it is for the King, sir; all blood and onions.
    KAI. Go, bury it as I bid, and never again
Enter this hall. Your place is the gate or the sty.

203

(PIXNE *enters*.)

You, girl, what brings you here?

PIXNE.   O Sir Kai, a stranger
Is going to fight King Kolbein there on the rock.

KAI.   To fight King Kolbein? Quick, I must go: make way, girl!

(KAI *goes*.)

SOWKIN.   What are they fighting for?

PIXNE.   A blood-feud, the men said.
It is King Marc's nephew, they said. Oh, he is handsome!
He went just by me, with his eyes shining like stars.
Oh, I hope he will win.

SOWKIN.   You, think of no strangers;
Think of my son, my Pigling, whom you're to marry.

PIXNE.   So I do, Madam Sowkin; but this man is fighting
So that we shall be free, so the men were saying.
He may be all bleeding red. Oh, I wish we could hear!

SOWKIN.   Here's somebody come: who is it?

PIXNE.   The stranger's friend,
All white as a ghost.

(DINAN *enters*.)

DINAN.   You Cornish women, be quick,
Fetch balsams; and run for water and make a bed.

PIXNE.   Is the King's nephew wounded?

DINAN.   Wounded to death.

SOWKIN.   Run, Pixne, up to the spring; fetch water, quickly.

(PIXNE *goes*.)

If we bring this chair, it will serve. What happened, sir?

DINAN.   My boy, whom I loved as a son.

SOWKIN.   Did he fight the king?

DINAN.   Yes, he fought Kolbein: much as a young red stag
Might fight with a mountain bull: he attacked and attacked,
But Kolbein stood and pushed him off with his shield.
Then the lad, tiring, rusht and struck on the helm
And Kolbein tottered as though he were hurt. Our hearts
Leapt when we saw him totter. A good blow more
Might have ended Kolbein then: but the boy was spent.
Then Kolbein laughed and strode to him and smote him
Grovelling to the rock. So, seeing him down,
I came to ready his death-bed.

204

SOWKIN.   We'll help the lad.
You fly to a safety, sir, before Kolbein comes.
    DINAN.   No, I will stay with my lad. Listen. They're coming,
Bearing him up the steps cut in the cliff.
    TRISTAN.   Take care.
    DINAN.   Come, madam, help me.
                (TRISTAN *enters*.)
    TRISTAN.   I am only bruised, not hurt.
Help him into the chair; bring water and wine.
                (KOLBEIN *is helped in*.)
    KOLBEIN.   That is the last time Kolbein will climb that stairway.
Dinan, why do you gape? You thought I had killed him?
I had, too: only I slipped: it was too great odds.
Wisdom against man's youth, for youth has the luck.
I slipped as I went to end him: he ended me.

                                    (He *drinks*.)

Listen, you, Marc.
I have made your fiefs and mine one Kingdom only.
Let that be kept. I have a daughter in Ireland. . .
Isolt, her name is. Marc, you must marry Isolt . . .
My Irish fief shall be yours then; Cornwall, too.
Will you marry Isolt?
    MARC.   If she will have me.
    KOLBEIN.   Swear.
    MARC.   I swear to marry your daughter, if she consent.
    KOLBEIN.   If she refuse, may my dying curses blast her.
Now, Tristan, you. Hearken the rest.
When I am dead, carry my body to Ireland,
Tell my Queen Thurid and Isolt to take you to friendship.
The blood-feud is to end, on pain of my curse.
Bring Isolt back to Tintagel to marry Marc.
Swear you will do this.
    TRISTAN.   I swear I will do your will.
    KOLBEIN.   When you have borne my corpse home,
Bid my men bury me in my ship on the beach,
So that in gales the shingle will screech above me.
Now I'll die standing up.   (He *stands*.)
I am Kolbein, you dead, Kolbein Blood-axe, the King!   (He *falls*.)
    MARC.   He is dead, King Kolbein.
    DINAN.   Justice is done on him now.

TRISTAN. Cover his face.

KAI. All hail, King Marc of Cornwall!

BEDWYR. All hail, Prince Tristan, setter free of the land!

TRISTAN. King Marc, may this body be decked and carried to
ship?

Then I will sail at once for the Princess Isolt.

MARC. Shroud him and strew him, you women.

Follow me, men.

(*He goes out with the* MEN.)

SOWKIN. With a proud forefoot this ship rose to the sea,

But under all seas and ships are the dooms waiting.

CURTAIN.

(*Half minute's interval.*)

(*Full stage. Coisnafon.*)

QUEEN THURID. ISOLT. BRANGWEN. TRISTAN.

TRISTAN. I come as a herald from Cornwall. I say that Kolbein

Is dead of a wound I dealt him in fight.

QUEEN. What madness

Brings you to tell the news to his widow and child?

TRISTAN. My oath to the dead. I add: it is Kolbein's will

That you take me to your friendship, ending the feud.

QUEEN. Kolbein's will, do you say? What is my will, think you?

Mine, whom you widowed?

TRISTAN. Heralds are sacred to men.

QUEEN. To men, maybe, not to women: you shall learn, herald,

What kind of friendship the widow of Kolbein grants.

TRISTAN. Call up your people, have me flung to the wolf-hounds.

QUEEN. This kind of friendship I grant: my heart's best thanks.

You have freed me from the beast who murdered my lover.

My girl's best thanks: you have freed her from the threat

Of the lust of his pirate friend.

We take you to friendship;

There shall be no feud between us, Tristan the Prince.

ISOLT. As my mother says, we are slaves set free: we bless you.

TRISTAN. I thank you both.

I am charged by King Marc of Cornwall

(Under Kolbein's will) to offer this fair princess

His hand and crown.

QUEEN.   It is nobly offered of Marc.

TRISTAN.   While you debate the offer, it is my office
To bury Kolbein; will you attend his burial?

QUEEN.   I have longed for his burial more than twenty years.

ISOLT.   He killed my father the day before I was born,
It was that that made me his daughter. Bury him deep.

TRISTAN.   He killed my father also, before I was born.
He shall be buried deep.

(*He goes out.*)

QUEEN.   Here is the granting of twenty years of prayer,
Kolbein is dead; you are set free, with the offer
To be queen to King Marc of Cornwall, also set free:
He, too, was a slave to Kolbein; he is young, just, gentle.
What do you think of the suit?

ISOLT.   You are foretelling . . .
What do you think?

QUEEN.   I think he is worthy of you.

ISOLT.   Worthy, yes; but what will the end of it be?

QUEEN.   That which you make.

ISOLT.   Only a part can be made . . .
Something tells me that there is no quiet for women
Who come as foreigner queens into stranger courts.

QUEEN.   No fate is to be dreaded, but borne, or changed.

ISOLT.   Mother, what will my fate be?

QUEEN.   A strange and a royal.

ISOLT.   Happy?

QUEEN.   Much mixed with love out of the ages.

ISOLT.   There is no avoiding fate, going or staying.
And to go is royal and liker a queen than to stay.
So I will go to this Marc.

(TRISTAN *enters.*)

QUEEN.   Is the dead man buried?

TRISTAN.   His men have laid him in howe: I have scattered earth.

QUEEN.   The winter then being gone, let the spring begin.

ISOLT.   Prince, I accept Marc's offer of hand and crown.

TRISTAN.   In my uncle's name, I thank you for this great grace.

ISOLT.   And to you, who have brought the grace, I offer thanks.

QUEEN.   How soon will you rob me of my daughter, O Prince?

TRISTAN.   Now, if she will; the wind is fair, the ship ready.

ISOLT.   It shall be now.

TRISTAN.   I will order the ship brought near.

(She goes out.)

(He goes out.)

QUEEN. The day that Isolt was born, the spae-wife told me
That I had borne one knitted to tragical love.
What can love and knowledge avail, with Destiny?

(She fetches a casket.)

Is Brangwen there?

(BRANGWEN enters.)

Brangwen, you follow the princess into Cornwall.
Swear that upon her marriage day you will make
Occasion for Marc and Isolt to drink this.
It is a love-drink: those who drink it together
Are bound in a lasting love. See that they drink it.

BRANGWEN. I swear: they shall drink this wine on their marriage
    night.

QUEEN. Thank you, good Brangwen. I leave the flasket with you.

(The QUEEN goes out.)

BRANGWEN. Would I might drink it in love, that a King might
    love me!

(TRISTAN enters.)

TRISTAN. The ship is ready below; will you tell the princess?

BRANGWEN. I will go tell her at once.

(BRANGWEN goes out.)

TRISTAN. When I have landed her, I must leave Tintagel;
I dare not stay for her wedding, nor see her again.
I cannot look on her face without loving her.

(ISOLT enters.)

ISOLT. Since we sail at once, how soon shall we reach Tintagel?

TRISTAN. Sunset to-morrow.

ISOLT.   It is a leap into darkness.

TRISTAN.   But you bring light.

ISOLT. Shall I see you often in Cornwall?

TRISTAN.   No, lady; never.

ISOLT. Never? Why not?

TRISTAN.   Because I go to my Kingdom.

ISOLT. You mean that we may not meet, after to-morrow?

(TRISTAN nods.)

Not even there at my wedding?

TRISTAN.   I shall wish you joy.

208

ISOLT. Stay till then, prince, that at least one friendly face
May shine among all those haters of foreign queens.
    TRISTAN. No one who looks on you will ever hate you,
Save from jealousy or envy: but after to-morrow
I shall not see you. I shall not forget you, though.
    ISOLT. Nor I you, Tristan, because you have altered my life.
    TRISTAN. And you mine, Isolt, as I thank God.
        But come now
To the ship that strains to be gone, and the life beginning.
    ISOLT. Look, here is wine: will you drink to the life beginning?
    TRISTAN. With all my heart, but I see no wine-cup nor horn.
    ISOLT. There in the niche on the stair is a cup of crystal.
    TRISTAN. It is broken to pieces, see . . .
    ISOLT.   It was Kolbein's cup,
He called it his Luck: it is broken like Kolbein's self.
What can we drink from?
    TRISTAN.   The wine is fragrant as June.
                    (DINAN enters.)
    DINAN. I bring a gift for the princess Isolt, a shell
Drawn up but now in the bay with the anchor flukes.
We say that the sea-brought things bring fortune, lady,
So we cleansed it: it is strange: may it bring you fortune.
    ISOLT. I thank you for gift and wish: strange things drift hither.
    DINAN. Princess, your gear is aboard and the ship is ready.
    TRISTAN. We will come aboard in a few short moments, then.
                                    (DINAN goes.)
    ISOLT. Here is the fortunate cup brought by the sea.
I drink to your fortune, prince. Will you drink to mine?
    TRISTAN. To your fortune, Isolt, princess: be it ever happy.
O golden beauty, I love you so that I die.
If you cannot speak some solace, I am but dead.
    ISOLT. I cannot speak a solace, being so swayed;
But you are my one thought, you are my life, my love;
I care not what may happen so I have you.
                                    (They embrace.)
    TRISTAN. To-night at sea we shall be each other's, beloved.
                    (TRISTAN goes out.)
    ISOLT. I am sworn to Marc . . . what matter? Though the world
        end
I have drunken a queen's fortune, O love, O love!

209

(BRANGWEN *enters.*)

BRANGWEN.   Lady, the Queen your mother and all the house
Are there at the ship to see you sail.

ISOLT.   I come, then.

BRANGWEN.   O lady, my mistress, you have drunk of the wine.
It is magical wine, and I know not what may come.

ISOLT.   Can it matter what may come? I have been in heaven;
The joy of its beauty is over me like great flames.

CURTAIN.

(*Half minute's interval.*)

(*Full stage. Tintagel.*)

ARTHUR. Now that the wedding is over, I must be gone.
King Marc has a lovely bride.

KAI.   The wedding went well,
Save for young Tristan: a most rude, wild young man;
He thrust Queen Isolt ashore and would not stay
Even to wish his uncle joy. What could he mean?

ARTHUR.   He needed the wind and tide. Now I'm for the war.
King Marc is sending me men: farewell, good Kai.

KAI.   Farewell, Lord Arthur.

(ARTHUR *goes.*)

                        A good man, but no depth.
Why should this Tristan fly like that from the wedding?
He has offered Queen Isolt love and been rebuffed.
I know young men: it is that: she has boxed his ears.

(TRISTAN. *enters.*)

TRISTAN.   Where is Queen Isolt? I wish to speak with Queen
    Isolt.

KAI.   Her Majesty has gone to the bridal chamber.

TRISTAN.   The King's not there?

KAI.   His Majesty is in council,
Deeply concerned that you were not at his wedding.

TRISTAN.   I cannot help his concern. Where is the bride-room?

KAI.   You cannot go to the Queen of Cornwall's room.

TRISTAN.   Where is it? I wish to see her.

KAI.   My prince, consider:
She is unrobing now, on her marriage night.

(ISOLT *enters.*)

ISOLT.   Good steward, Sir Kai, will you find Sir Constans for me?
Prince Tristan, we thought you had fled. Welcome to Cornwall.

KAI.   I will find Sir Constans as Your Majesty bids.

ISOLT.   I thank you.

(KAI *goes.*)

Why did you fly before our wedding?

TRISTAN.   Fly, O Isolt, beloved!

ISOLT.   O Tristan, hush!

KAI. (*re-entering*).   May I bring commands to Sir Constans?

ISOLT.   We wish to see him.

KAI.   Your Majesty will pardon my asking more . . .
Is it your pleasure that he attend you here?

ISOLT.   No; at the robing-room.

KAI. (*going again*).   Madam, he shall attend.

TRISTAN.   Isolt, my darling, this marriage must not be.
Whatever we swore or promised to Kolbein or Marc,
Is burnt all blank by our love. Why are you shrinking?
Kai's gone.

ISOLT.   But he suspects; he is peering and prying.
No: he is coming back. Stand further away.

KAI.   Pardon my troubling, but at which robing-room
Shall he attend?

ISOLT.   The robing-room of the Queen.

KAI.   At the Queen's. I thank Your Grace.

TRISTAN.   Will you now leave us?

KAI.   Pardon, Prince Tristan, the Queen's will must be done.

ISOLT. The Queen thanks you, Sir Kai, for zealous service.

KAI.   I thank the Queen: may she never lack loyal servants.

(KAI *goes.*)

ISOLT.   You see that he suspects.

TRISTAN.   We are done with suspicion . . .
What they suspect or know is naught to the truth.
We are each other's, and this pretence that we tried—
That you could keep to your promise and I to my oath—
Is nothing, nothing, but false; it is false as hell.
And I am here. Look, darling, you know as I do
That we are each other's. You are mine, mine only.

ISOLT. Marc will be here, Kai said: somebody said . . .
Look at the door.

211

TRISTAN.   There is no one there.
ISOLT.   Not yet.
But I am Marc's wife, with a ring; in a few moments
I have to go to his bed.
    TRISTAN.   That you never shall!
    ISOLT. He has talked of it all day long; he is greedy for me.
    TRISTAN. Greedy? That scholar? Kolbein's slave? Take the ring
       off.
Look . . . we must get from this, back to my ship.
    ISOLT. Where is your ship? In the harbour below?
    TRISTAN. No, Isolt.
The harbour below is barred, with a chain across it.
My ship could not get in: she is there . . . to the south.
    ISOLT. How did you get here then? Through the gates?
    TRISTAN.   I climbed
From the sea, and over the walls, for the gates were locked.
    ISOLT. But the crag is rotten with wrack, and a slip means death.
    TRISTAN. It was to get to you. I have left a rope there;
I could lower you down.
    ISOLT.   I could not: it is too giddy,
To swing down there . . . I have seen that terrible crag.
TRISTAN. I would make you safe, with a knot.
ISOLT.   It is beyond me.
TRISTAN. You are the Queen . . . order the gates to be opened.
ISOLT. Kai holds the keys: he would suspect, if I asked.
TRISTAN. He dare not suspect the Queen.
ISOLT.   Even if I asked,
Even if I had the keys, if we climbed the stairway
Down to the beach, Marc or his knights would come, too.
We could never reach your ship.
TRISTAN.   Then I'll go to Marc,
Tell him our love and force him to fight for you.
ISOLT. No, for God's sake do not, Tristan; his men would kill you.
TRISTAN. What else can I do? We are knotted into the nets.
ISOLT. Brangwen has gone.
TRISTAN.   Gone where?
ISOLT.   For my mother's love-drink.
Marc and I are to drink it together in bed,
So that we love each other . . . O Tristan, I cannot!
    TRISTAN. I'll tear him in pieces rather!

212

ISOLT.   O quiet! quiet!

Somebody comes. . .

              (*Enter* MARC, KAI, BEDWYR.)

    MARC.   We have missed you, nephew, to-day, at our wedding
      feast.

Why were you absent?

    TRISTAN.   I chose it.

    M....   How do you come now!

Your ship was not in the port when the chain was drawn,

Nor were you yourself in the castle when gates were locked.

Kai thinks that you scaled the crag.

    TRISTAN.   I scaled it: what then?

    MARC.   Then this is your rope that you left upon the wall?

    TRISTAN.   It is my rope.

    MARC.   You need not have run such dangers,

Gates would have opened for you, my sister's son,

You are my heir, remember.

    KAI.   At present, my lord.

    MARC.   But I need you, nephew . . . And why did you not bring
      Dinan?

I need him, too. I cannot let this day pass

Without a sign of the love I bear to you both.

I have a gift for you: come.

                    (*He leads* TRISTAN *off.*)

    KAI.   Sir Constans attends in the robing-tower, madam.

    ISOLT.   I thank you. I shall not need him.

    KAI.   He shall be told so.

    ISOLT.   Sir Kai, you were charming in all your welcome to me.

    KAI.   You are gracious, madam.

    ISOLT.   Sir Kai, might a new-crowned Queen

Ride for one short half-hour into the moonlight?

I long to be quiet after the feast's tumult.

    KAI.   Take horse and ride alone?

    ISOLT.   Friends might come with me.

    KAI.   I will ask King Marc, who will doubtless gladly ride,

Though the horse-boys are off duty till to-morrow.

To ride in the moonlight doubtless would be quieting.

                      (KAI *goes.*)

    ISOLT.   He knows, that pryer and scraper; and Marc must
      suspect . . .

If we get horse, we will gallop: but shall we get horse?
                    (BRANGWEN *enters*.)
    BRANGWEN.   The cup of magical love-drink is made ready,
The bridal-chamber is deckt. King Marc has sent me
To bid you come to disrobe.
    ISOLT.   I have sent to the King,
Saying that I entreat a half-hour's quiet,
Riding into the moonlight.
    BRANGWEN.   Was it Sir Kai
That you trusted with the message?
    ISOLT.   Yes, it was Kai.
    BRANGWEN.   I heard him say to Sir Bedwyr there at the door,
Even as I passed, that he would not bring such a message.
They laughed and agreed.
    ISOLT.   Where is Prince Tristan, Brangwen?
    BRANGWEN.   But, my mistress, he sailed this morning, leaving us
        here.
    ISOLT.   He was here a moment ago. Where did he go?
Has King Marc put him in prison?
    BRANGWEN.   I know not, madam.
He is not now with the King, for the King sent me
To say he awaited you.
    ISOLT.   I must see Prince Tristan;
Must know where he is; must plan with him what to do.
    BRANGWEN.   Madam, I hoped that all that folly was over.
    ISOLT.   Over! my God!
    BRANGWEN.   But you have married the King;
Who loves you, madam, and now is expecting you.
    ISOLT.   Go back to him and say I am suddenly ill.
    BRANGWEN.   That he will know to be false.
    ISOLT.   I am so ill, Brangwen,
That to touch that creature will kill me.
    BRANGWEN.   O madam, no!
He is a good, just King, handsome and noble;
Trust to his love, Queen Isolt, and give him yours.
That was your promise and oath, and your mother's wish
As well as his own great longing. You shrink at first,
But a husband is God's gift as a help to women.
Besides, the magical wine will make you love him.
    ISOLT.   I have pledged Tristan in that: no wine, no magic,

214

No wonder more in the world can alter my love:
I am Tristan's queen, to the depths.
  BRANGWEN.   O madam, hush!
        (*Enter* KAI *and* BEDWYR.)
  KAI. Madam, I grieve to intrude. I come from the King
To ask that, graciously, you forbear your riding
Until to-morrow, an hour and day more fitting.
  ISOLT Say I am feverred, Sir Kai, and long to be out
  KAI. Madam, I said so. The King replied as I say.
  BEDWYR. He added, madam, that we might crave your consent
To light you hence to the King, who is much concerned
To hear of your fever and longs to comfort you.
  ISOLT. I am not ready to go. Where is Prince Tristan?
  KAI. Gone to his rest.
  ISOLT.   What, killed?
  KAI.   No, to bed, madam,
In the castle's landward wing.
  BEDWYR.   May we return,
To light you hence, in a moment?
  ISOLT.   Give me two moments.
  KAI. Thank you, Queen Isolt.
  BEDWYR.   We humbly thank you and go.
  ISOLT. See, I am jailed by this Marc; watched, wardered,
    turnkeyed.
Would I were like the wolf that, trapped by both feet,
Gnaws them both off and hobbles away alive.
Girl, there's some cranny or attic where I can hide?
  BRANGWEN. They would soon find you.
  ISOLT.   But there is the coil of rope;
I will tie that to the wall and let myself down.
  BRANGWEN. The sentries are on the wall now, going their
    rounds.
You would be stopped on the way! O beautiful mistress,
Your queenly destiny calls, accept it queenly.
  ISOLT. I cannot be queen to Marc.
  BRANGWEN.   But you are his queen.
  ISOLT. Only by word, never in heart.
  BRANGWEN.   Word suffices.
He has rights upon you: right to use force . . .

ISOLT.   I, too,
Have a little force, and a little knife, my Brangwen.
    BRANGWEN.   Queen, if you threaten yourself, I will cry for help.
                         (TRISTAN *enters*.)
    ISOLT.   O Tristan, save me, lest I be dragged to the King!
Where have you been?
    TRISTAN.   With the King . . . and seeking a way.
    ISOLT.   Can we escape?
    TRISTAN.   Not now, nor to-morrow, maybe.
    ISOLT.   You mean I must go to the King?
    TRISTAN.   That, or I kill him.
    ISOLT.   O Brangwen, save me! I cannot face it, I cannot.
    BRANGWEN.   My queen, take courage.
    ISOLT.   I will not go to him: no.
Girl, it is dark; for this night, only this night,
Go to the King in my place.
    BRANGWEN.   O my mistress, Isolt,
Never speak such things!
    ISOLT.   Only to pledge him the wine . . .
He will not see, will not know; will you do it, girl?
    BRANGWEN.   O hush, madam, hush! the very thought is such
        shame.
    ISOLT.   I saved you, body and soul, when you were a girl.
    BRANGWEN.   You stopped my being a slave, and I thank you and
        bless you,
And pray God bless you, for that; but this is a sin.
    ISOLT.   It's a service you shall perform when your princess bids.
Go, or I'll kill you.
    TRISTAN.   See, good Brangwen, we two
Are taken in nets; will you do this thing to save us?
    BRANGWEN.   I should be known, and whipped by the guards and
        spat at.
    TRISTAN.   No, girl, I promise not. I am asked by the King
To serve the love-drink there in the marriage-bed.
I have seen that the room is dark: I will make it darker
With but one taper, and that away from the bed.
You will be in the bed before him in almost darkness,
And stay till you drink the love drink: that's all we ask.
    BRANGWEN.   All! He will know that I am not the Queen.
    TRISTAN.   How can he?

216

BRANGWEN. He will want more from me than the loving-cup.

ISOLT. If we drug the wine with this, he will fall asleep.

BRANGWEN. You will not bid me do this terrible thing!

ISOLT. As soon as he is asleep, you may steal away.

BRANGWEN. Where shall I steal to, Queen, to hide and be
cleansed?

TRISTAN. Here, to our loves and our gratitude, good Brangwen.

BRANGWEN. Suppose this drug that you give should kill the
King?

TRISTAN. Girl, till your mistress had this thought, I had planned
To kill the King as he came to the marriage-bed.
That I will still do, if you do not consent,
And you, too, knowing so much.

BRANGWEN.   No, do not threaten me, sir.
I will do this for my mistress, to whom I swore.

ISOLT. Brangwen, the gods reward you.

TRISTAN.   We will reward you.

BRANGWEN. But, hark! here the Knights are coming: it is too
late.

(*Enter* KAI *and* BEDWYR.)

ISOLT. Sweet Knights, I am grateful for your loving care.
I will not trouble you now to light me hence.

KAI. Queen, the King charges us that we bring you to him.

ISOLT. Kai, the Queen charges you that you tell the King
That she, on her marriage-night, will now put off
All ceremony and claim; she is now going
To prepare herself for bed. Good-night, Prince Tristan.
Good-night, Sir Kai and Sir Bedwyr. Come, Brangwen, come.

(*She and* BRANGWEN *go.*)

KAI. Good-night, Queen Isolt.

BEDWYR.   Good-night.

MARC.   Is Prince Tristan there?

(MARC *enters.*)

TRISTAN. Yes, here.

MARC.   And the Queen?

KAI.   Just gone to her robing-room.

MARC. Is her maid Brangwen with her? Call her back, will you?

(KAI *goes.*)

Come, Bedwyr, go to your bed, you are bed-weary.

217

BEDWYR. I thank Your Grace: may to-night be a blessed night
To you and to Cornwall, King.

(He goes out.)

MARC.   I thank you Bedwyr.

KAI *(returning)*. The girl will be here at once.

MARC.   Thank you, good Kai;
Now you, to your rest.

KAI *(kneeling)*. I pray good-night to my King,
And joy, with a loving Queen, who will bring an heir,
May never a traitor come 'twixt you and the Queen.

MARC. Amen to that.

KAI.   Will Prince Tristan say Amen?

TRISTAN. I was praying, Sir Kai; I did not hear your prayer.

KAI. I will say good-night.

MARC.   Good-night, good steward.

TRISTAN. Good-night.

(KAI goes. BRANGWEN enters.)

MARC. A good, true servant, Sir Kai. I sent for you, girl,
To give you this jewel of gold. As my Queen's servant
May your life in this court be happy.

BRANGWEN.   I thank Your Majesty.

(BRANGWEN goes.)

MARC. Marriage is solemn, nephew.
I have been in the vaults where all our House is buried,
Each in his bed of stone with his mask of gold.
My father and his and his, eleven dead Kings,
Each felt as I feel now, and all are still here;
For a House is a tree of souls; some, roots in the earth;
Some, leaves in the air . . . all one.
                    Lad, you must soon marry.
Isolt and I will think of a wife for you.

TRISTAN. I am not thinking of marriage this yet awhile.

MARC. It is man's happiest state. Will you follow Brangwen?
And bring me word if the Queen has retired to bed?

(TRISTAN goes.)

Invisible spirits of all my ancestors
Who watch o'er the House ye made, help me to fortune.
O unseen helpers, who once were my forefathers,
Help, that the tragical fate which wrecked my boyhood,
May never return.

218

(TRISTAN *enters*.)

TRISTAN. Sir, Brangwen tells me that the Queen has retired;
She has darkened the bedroom for you.

MARC.   Let us then go.
I have not angered nor vext you?

TRISTAN.   Never, sir. Why?

MARC. You fled my wedding, and then you have wished me no
    luck

TRISTAN. I fled your wedding, indeed; being no courtier.
As for my wishes, I wish more than I can say.

MARC. I am glad that it is not anger, my sister's son.
Bring us the love-drink soon as I strike on the floor.
I will strike thus.

                                (*They go upstairs*.)

                    (ISOLT *enters*.)

ISOLT. This is the love-drink. Brangwen is in his bed,
Waiting his coming. What if he see through the cheat?
Or if she betray it? A whisper, a gesture's enough.
He's in his room there, undressing; this bridegroom and beast . . .
Not for me, thank God, not for me.

TRISTAN.   Queen Isolt . . . Isolt.

ISOLT. Hush Tristan; not so loud.

TRISTAN.   The girl is in bed.
It is dark, but I'll leave it darker.

ISOLT.   But oh, if she cry!

TRISTAN. She dare not utter a sound, even if he urge her.
Where is your sleepy drug to mix with the wine?

ISOLT. I have not mixed it already, because . . . ah! hark.

TRISTAN. It is the King.

                    (MARC *appears above*.)

MARC.   I am ready now for the love-drink.
Is that the girl?

TRISTAN.   It is. I will bring the wine.

                                (MARC *goes*.)

ISOLT. My mother asked that the bride and her groom should
    drink
This wine, on their marriage night. Pledge your love, husband.

TRISTAN. To our love, sweet wife, wherever it lead.

                                (*He drinks*.)

ISOLT.   To our love,
Sweet husband, with all my worship, now and for ever.
                        (*She drinks, they embrace.* MARC *strikes the floor.*)
    TRISTAN.   O my love, what was it struck then? That knocking
        sounded
Like laughter from outside life. All this trick with the girl
Does but delay our trouble, you are still his.
    ISOLT.   I will be yours on my marriage night, my Tristan.
Here is the sleepy drug, for Marc shall sleep sound.
When he wakes, I must be at his side; until then, yours.
                        (TRISTAN *takes the drink upstairs.*)
    ISOLT.   He will kill them, if they discover!
                        Yesterday morning
I had not seen him, and now he is all my world.
He must be serving them now.
                        (*A clatter above.*)
                O God, what was that?
Has he killed them? What was it that clattered? Who's there?
What if Kai knew it and killed him? Where is he now?
Why does he not come, or give signal?
                (TRISTAN *descends.*)
                        Is that you, Tristan?
What happened?
    TRISTAN.   Listen, love, listen.
    ISOLT.   All's silent.
    TRISTAN.   Quiet, still: do not you breathe. No; he's drugged: it is
        safe.
    ISOLT.   Why are you shaking so? Did he discover her?
    TRISTAN.   No;
But she was so shaking, she scarcely could drink: having drunk,
She dropped the gold cup on the floor.
I picked up the cup, but the wine was all spilled. What he drank
Was the bitter brown ooze from the drug: it has sent him to sleep.
    ISOLT.   Marc will not love her, then, but she will love him.
    TRISTAN.   It is a grim night for the girl: she was proud.
She shuddered.
    ISOLT.   To-morrow will be grim for us: we may shudder.
    TRISTAN.   Would God
To-morrow might never dawn.
    ISOLT.   It may never dawn.

The world may end. Listen. The lovers are quiet.
Now, for to-night, we have each other, beloved.
Will you not take me, Tristan?

CURTAIN.

(Three minutes' interval.)

(Same Scene.)

KAI.   You fellow, what are you doing here? Who are you?

HOG.   Hog, the King's swineherd, sir, that the King sent for,
About the killing of hogs.

KAI.   I am the steward.
I will consider what hogs shall be killed, if any.
Be off now, where you belong.

HOG.   May I speak to the King?

KAI.   To the King? No, certainly not. Get out!

(HOG goes aside. BEDWYR enters.)

Ah, Bedwyr, welcome.

The King will not believe that Tristan's her lover.
I gave him proofs, but he loves the Queen too well.

(TRISTAN appears above.)

Still, I made him promise to set a trap for Tristan.
The Queen has gone to stay at her summer manor;
The King has given out that to-day he will start
For a long week's summer-hunting out on the moor.
That is the trap: and Tristan has fallen into it.
He has told Marc that he feels too ill to come hunting,
He has sent Dinan to beg the Queen to return.
The Queen will return to-night: Tristan will court her:
Marc and we shall return, and catch them, and end them.

(ARTHUR enters.)

BEDWYR.   This is your plot, Kai, What does Arthur think about
    it?

ARTHUR.   I take no hand in't. It is no quarrel of ours,
It lies between Marc and Tristan.

Besides, these quarrels
Must be patched up; we need our strength for the war.

(He goes out. MARC enters.)

MARC.   We'll ride to this hunting, then. You, Bedwyr and Kai,

221

It will be ill for you if to-night's trap fail.
Swineherd, what is it?

KAI.   I settled his business, lord.

MARC. I see my swineherds myself. What news from the sties?

HOG. O my lord King, fine news:—

Farrowing came like the lily and went like the rose,
Beautiful; ten to the sow; and to-morrow's the year.

MARC. Ah, yes, I promised that if you could keep swine a year,
Not losing one from a wolf or a robber, I'd grant you
Freedom to you and to yours: so I will; have you lost none?

HOG. Not yet, lord; no.

MARC.   Have you hope of your freedom, then?

HOG. No, lord, none: that would be heathen, to hope.
I feel inside like a pan of eels being boiled,
But never let it be thought I dared to hope.

MARC. Who keeps your sties while you're here?

HOG.   My wife and son, sir.

MARC. Then to-night will be anxious watching for you three
    souls.

Well, come to me here to-morrow; if none has been lost
By then, you shall all be free, with something beside.

HOG. Thank you, my King.

MARC.   And, Kai, remember, my swineherds
Report directly to me, when their duty calls.

KAI. Certainly, lord.

MARC.   Bedwyr, come; we must ride.

                                (He leads BEDWYR *off.)*

KAI *(to* HOG). Never you dare presume to come here again.
Whatever the King may say, you report to me,
Or I'll give you cause to repent.

                                      (KAI *goes.)*

            (TRISTAN *comes down as* HOG *moves away.)*

TRISTAN. The trap has caught us unless I can warn the Queen.
What messenger can I send to stop her returning?
I have told them that I am ill; so I cannot go.
I dare not trust Marc's courtiers.

                         Perhaps this swineherd.

O swineherd!

HOG.   Sir.

TRISTAN.   Will you take a word to the Queen,
There in the forest, not to return to-night?
    HOG. That's a long way. I couldn't be back by midnight.
    TRISTAN. You shall have my horse.
    HOG.   No, lord, no horse for me.
Better not show it was you who sent the message.
But going on foot takes time,
And I must be guarding the swine to-night, my lord
    TRISTAN. No one will rob the sties.
    HOG.   Yes, many might rob them.
The slaves might do it to spite me. Sir Kai might do it
So as to keep me a slave; and if I'm away,
There's only my wife and son, to watch.
    TRISTAN. I'll guard your sties to-night, if you'll take the message.
    HOG. You, lord?
    TRISTAN.   Why not? Will you go, then?
    HOG.   Yes, lord, I will.
I tell the Queen she's not to return to-night?
    TRISTAN. Not to return tonight, whatever happens.
    HOG. I will not fail you, my lord.
                     But you'll bear in mind
It's a deal to us to have freedom near . . .
    TRISTAN.   I swear
I will guard your sties to the death. If I lose a hog,
I pledge my crown that I will buy you your freedom.
Now go, and for God's sake do not fail.
    HOG.   Trust me, lord.
                         (HOG goes.)
    TRISTAN. Will he be there in time? Will he miss the Queen?
Marc goes a-hunting, does he? The quarry is warned.
               CURTAIN.

             (The front stage.)
    ARTHUR. Have you not hunted, Bedwyr?
    BEDWYR.   Marc bade us return;
But he, meanwhile, has ridden to join the Queen.
The trap that was planned is not to be set.
    ARTHUR. I am glad that he scorned this trap: it was unworthy.
    KAI. It is not unworthy to watch over Cornwall's peace;

And I tell you, Arthur, what I have since discovered.
Tristan had word of the plot: someone betrayed it.
He has sent that swineherd to tell the Queen not to come.

    BEDWYR. No, truly?

    KAI. He has. And now, in the swineherd's absence,
Tristan, this King's son, Cornwall's nephew, our saviour,
Has gone to the sties and taken the swineherd's place.
He, the Queen's lover, is guarding pigs, while the herd,
Who is the King's servant, goes warning the Queen.

    ARTHUR. It is true he is guarding the sties, for I saw him there.

    KAI. Now let us teach both him and the swineherd a lesson.
Let us take his swine from under his nose to-night,
Ruin this swineherd's prospects of liberty
Which he plainly cannot deserve, and make this Tristan
Such a laughing-stock as will force him out of Cornwall.

    BEDWYR. Raiding the swineyard would be a pleasant frolic.
I will make one.

    KAI.   And Arthur?

    ARTHUR.   This is no frolic.
Tristan is dangerous with a spear in his hand.

    KAI. Dangerous? Grown men's wits are sharper than spears.

    BEDWYR. How do you plan to outwit him?

    KAI.   I, in disguise
As an old, old man, will wheedle him from the sties;
Then you and Arthur shall carry away a hog.

    BEDWYR. And suppose you fail?

    KAI.   I imitate old, old men
So that I cannot fail.

    ARTHUR.   No, Kai will not fail.
But Tristan may not be wheedled.

    KAI.   Then Bedwyr may try.

    ARTHUR. What will you do, Bedwyr, to outwit Tristan?

    BEDWYR. I will go to Tristan and say, 'I'm the swineherd's
      brother,
Come to relieve your guard.' I will take his place;
And when I have taken his place, you may take the swine.

    ARTHUR. Tristan may be less trusting than you suppose.

    BEDWYR. I imitate country-folk to the very life.

    KAI. That is true: he imitates country-people well.

    BEDWYR. What will you do, Arthur, if Kai and myself should fail?

ARTHUR.   In that unlikely chance, I should say 'Attack,'
Make an assault together. Three against one
Should make us masters at least of a virgin sow.
  KAI.   We might try that, if the other attempts should fail.
But they will ot fail.
  ARTHUR.   I do not think that they will.
Wait. If the night-guard hear us thieves at the pigsties
And come to the rescue and capture us red-handed,
We may be hanged at the nearest tree.
  KAI.   What nonsense!
The guard will know the King's steward, and the King's baily,
And the Captain of the Host. We will start from here, then,
An hour before first cockcrow?
  ARTHUR.   Agreed.
  BEDWYR.   So be it.
  KAI.   Since we rise so early, Bedwyr, we'll get to bed.
                    (KAI and BEDWYR go out.)
  ARTHUR.   Deliver us from old men who are old women!
And here is Tristan.

                    (TRISTAN enters.)
                    And why in such hurry, my Prince?
  TRISTAN.   I'm guarding the sties to-night, and I need a knife –
A broad sharp knife for a stab, instead of a spear.
  ARTHUR.   Take mine, my Prince; so you work for the swineherd's
    freedom.
  TRISTAN.   Yes, I take part. Will you come, too?
  ARTHUR.   No, I cannot.
  TRISTAN.   Why not? Do come.
  ARTHUR.   Do you think that you need my help?
  TRISTAN.   One never knows in these moonless nights of the
    spring.
  ARTHUR. True: but to-night I have work to do with some friends.
Are you going back to your kingdom soon?
  TRISTAN.   Not soon.
  ARTHUR.   Your father was on my staff in the Pentland war.
I stayed with him there: you inherit a goodly realm.
  TRISTAN.   It is a fair land.
  ARTHUR.   Why not go to it, Tristan?
  TRISTAN.   Men can only play one game at a time, Lord Arthur.
  ARTHUR.   Only one dangerous game.

                         225

But you must to sty . . .
'Look out before cockcrow' was your father's proverb.
I'll see that the night guard march that way. Good-night.

(ARTHUR *goes*.)

TRISTAN.   Something is plotted against me: that was a hint.
I will 'look out before cockcrow': I do not fear them.

(*He goes off.*)

(*Half a minute's interval.*)

(*Full stage.*)
The swineyard on the left of the stage, of wattled hurdles.
TRISTAN.   She got the message, thank heaven; I ruined their trap.
I wish the swineherd would come,
For this is a lonely watch on a night so dark.

> (*He hums*) When Uther lifts his one stone pin
> To drink at the brook below the whin,
> Down in the hold
> You will see gold,
> But be quick, boys, quick, or tombstone.

I wish that I had a dog: someone is coming . . .
Someone is coming, a light foot: is it the Queen?
No; it's a man, and sobbing. Halt there! Who are you?
KAI (*disguised*).   For the love of God, sir, mercy! Are you a
   robber?
TRISTAN.   Robber, sir? No, the swineherd. Stand where you are.
Who are you? Hold up your hands. What are you doing here?
KAI. For the love of God, sir, help me to save my daughter.
We've been set upon by robbers. Oh, I am faint!
They burst in a cloud upon us. You heard us scream?
My daughter cried: 'Run, fetch the swineherd, father!'
So, sir, I ran. Oh, sir, I am faint. Come swiftly.
My delicate daughter, prey to ruffianly men,
And she a cripple since birth and not quite sane,
Like her poor mother now at peace in the madhouse.
Come, my good sir. Oh, Christian swineherd, or pagan,
There, you can hear her screaming. Oh, come, sir, hurry!
TRISTAN.   Hurry! But hurry where? Where is your daughter?
KAI.   At the little copse in the dip, there, down the road.

226

TRISTAN.   Strange that I heard no scream.

KAI.   The wind was against it

And they choked the screams with a gag.

TRISTAN.   Run back to her.

I will call my mates, who are dozing here while I watch.

Shout as you go.

(KAI *runs off, shouting.*)

(KAI *returns at once.*)

KAI.   Alas, sir, lost, lost, lost! Good Christian swineherd,

You ought to have come at once when first I called.

TRISTAN.   Is your girl killed?

KAI.   Worse than killed; taken away.

Taken by ruthless ruffians in her beauty

To guilty splendour in a kitchen of thieves.

Pity a father's tears; an old man's weakness.

Feel my heart beating, like a dying bird waggling.

TRISTAN.   Run to Tintagel and borrow the King's bloodhound.

KAI.   Run? An old man like me. If you'd a mother,

For her sake, run.

TRISTAN.   I am sworn not to leave the swine.

KAI.   Then alas for a lonely old age walking the roads;

No daugher by my side, no filial prattle

Cheering the long tramp; ah! and no woman's hand

Lighting the fire of twigs to cook the supper.

O desolate old age!

TRISTAN.   You wander the roads then?

KAI.   A ballad-singer, sir.

TRISTAN.   Oh? Sing me a ballad.

KAI.   I am too broken with grief.

TRISTAN.   Say me one, then.

KAI.   I can say nothing but woe and alas my daughter!

TRISTAN.   Were you camped when the robbers came?

KAI.   No, sir, on foot.

TRISTAN.   Had you walked all night?

KAI.   All night and the day before,

Thirty long miles through Cornish bog in the rain.

TRISTAN.   Thirty long miles through bog in the rain! You lie,
   man.

Your shoes are as clean as a courtier's; not even dusty.

As for your daughter and robbers, they don't exist.

227

A nightingale was singing there in the copse
When first you brought the alarm. Get home to your daughter,
This cripple from birth who walks thirty long miles.
Be off!

    KAI. Then you don't believe me?

    TRISTAN.   I don't.

    KAI.   King Marc
Shall know who keeps his swine; he shall know the truth.
Then we shall see.

    TRISTAN.   That will be interesting.

    KAI. And the world will see.

    TRISTAN.   That will be clever of it.

    KAI. And King Marc will see what all of us see already.
                         (KAI goes.)

    TRISTAN. Which of the courtiers was it? It was likest Kai.
But I have not done with them yet. Who is that there? Halt!
                      (BEDWYR enters.)

    TRISTAN. Explain yourself.

    BEDWYR.   Be that you zwineherd?

    TRISTAN.   Who are you?

    BEDWYR. Old zwineherd's brother Pig, sent by old zwineherd.

    TRISTAN. I didn't know he had a brother. Where from, you?

    BEDWYR. I be Queen's pigkeeper, out by her zummer palace.
Hog come to me to-night when he'd talkt with the Queen;
Hog said 'I've cut my foot; I'll be late reaching sty;
Get you back, brother,' he said, 'and help young master.'

    TRISTAN. But Hog is coming? How soon can he be here?

    BEDWYR.   Dawn,
Or maybe an hour after. Anyone been here?

    TRISTAN. Nobody.

    BEDWYR. No? Then it was birds or the pigs.
I could be sworn I heard voices; an old man's voice.
But indeed all be still as a stound: no robbers and nowt.
Why, all be at peace and morning will be in a bit.
All's zafe as a church. I'll watch; you lie and be easy.
No need for two to be up. If a robber should come,
I'd give 'ee a call: you could be up in a trice.
Do'ee lie down, my young master, and sleep while I guard.

    TRISTAN. No. Since you said you heard voices, the thieves may
      be near.

BEDWYR. I think it was just the hogs grunting, or owls eating
mice.

TRISTAN. It's better be certain than sorry: we both will stand
guard.

How is your brother's hip?

BEDWYR.   Which brother's?

TRISTAN.   Hog's.

BEDWYR   Ah, Hog's!

His hip: yes.

TRISTAN. Didn't he mention it?

BEDWYR.   Not this time.

TRISTAN. You knew about it, of course?

BEDWYR.   Oh yes, indeed, yes.

All that he cared to tell.

TRISTAN.   He made no secret of't,

He gloried in't to me, for a hip like that
Not many men have; you haven't one, nor have I.

BEDWYR. Why, no: thank heaven.

TRISTAN. It's nothing to thank heaven for.

Many would give one hand for a hip like that.
That was an odd case of Hog's wife's brother's wife?

BEDWYR. Ah, very odd!

TRISTAN. It looked suspicious to me, Pig,

I don't know how it struck you, but I said and say
I shouldn't have liked the case to happen to me.

BEDWYR. Being out with the Queen's swine at the summer
palace,

I may not have heard the truth of all that story.

TRISTAN. Why, it was there that it happened; you must have
heard it.

BEDWYR. I heard it: yes, but I believe only half

The things that I see, and nothing of what I hear.
Hog said I wasn't to let 'ee watch. Lie down, man,
Sleep while 'ee can: to bed.

TRISTAN.   I enjoy our talking.

That's a pretty girl, Hog's daughter; with pretty hair.
Would you call the hair red-gold, or a copper-bronze?

BEDWYR. That's a hard question: I'd call it a sort of wryneck
Wryneck or partridge mottle.

TRISTAN.   Do you think the lad
Who is always with her, means to marry her?
    BEDWYR.   Yes.
    TRISTAN. What? Out of his mind as he is?
    BEDWYR.   I'm talking of Cador.
    TRISTAN. I'm not. I am talking of one who doesn't exist.
There is neither lad nor daughter, nor wife's brother's wife,
Nor hip; nor has Hog a brother, nor are you swineherd.
You are a courtier; I knew you from the first.
Out of it, Arthur: away!
    BEDWYR.   I am not Arthur.
    TRISTAN. Then whoever you are, be off. Take that direction,
And make no signals.
    BEDWYR.   All right, I'll go: good-night.
You won't have long to wait ere you see us again.

                                           (BEDWYR goes.)
    TRISTAN. I have not done with these knaves; worse is to follow.
Now is the time for a raid, now the East grows grey.
Here one comes creeping – or is it an old dog-wolf?
Halt, there, or I strike! Stand!
    HOG.   Hist, young master, it's Hog.
    TRISTAN. Let me be sure: open your hands; so. Welcome.
    HOG. Have they been raiding, master?
    TRISTAN.   They are all about.
Two, and their mates are coming; now is the hour.
    HOG. I knew they'd come, so I've brought my son and my wife.
Come in, my Sowkin and Pigling.

                                       (They come in.)
    TRISTAN.   You are both most welcome.
    SOWKIN. Good-morning, sir, and our thanks for your kind
      watching.
    PIGLING. I hope you'll find some use for my holly ballow.
    TRISTAN. You come in the nick of time. They'll be here in a
      minute.
    HOG. Well, sir, we're four; I say 'Get into the pigsty,
In with the pigs': then, if they come to steal pigs,
They'll be into our clutch before they know we are there.
    SOWKIN. Trust to my Hog, sweet sir, he's a King at this game.
    TRISTAN. In with the pigs, then. Give me your hand, good
      madam.

SOWKIN. Thank you, kind sir; that's it. And don't be afeared, sir,
The hogs won't hurt 'ee, and though they smell a bit flighty,
It's good for the lungs if you breathe it deep in down.

PIGLING. How about that supper, mother?

SOWKIN.   First make all snug.

TRISTAN. Come along, Hog.

HOG. That's that. Now, Pigling, my son.

SOWKIN. Now we'll all sit out of the wind and eat our supper,
That's cheek in that, and this is cider in this.

(*They settle to supper.*)

(*Enter* ARTHUR, KAI, BEDWYR.)

ARTHUR. So you have not thriven? How came it that you failed,
   Kai?

KAI. The ruffian was suspicious and most astute.

BEDWYR. I did not see round his questions; he trapped me fairly.

ARTHUR. What shall I do, then?

KAI.   These are the pigsties, Arthur . . .
He is not here . . . he has gone. Look yonder, Bedwyr.

BEDWYR. No, there is no guard here.

KAI.   O treacherous peachick!
Is that not like one of these sprigs of to-day?
Take a poor swineherd's place and then break faith with him.
He has gone to his doxy, or else to his bed of ease,
Leaving the swineherd's freedom to shift for itself.

ARTHUR. What shall we do; climb over and take a hog?
Or pull a gap in the paling and drive them out?

BEDWYR. I should say drive them; but what is it Kai most wants?

KAI. To bring this whipper-snapper into disgrace.

ARTHUR. Pull down the pales, then, and the herd will be ours.

KAI. The herd is the King's, Arthur; so are these palings.
I as the steward will act here for the King.
I will not risk the loss of a hundred hogs:
We will step inside the pen and choose one hog,
Evidence to King Marc of his swineherd's slackness
And of Tristan's want of faith.
                        We will take this hog,
Call King Marc from his bed and hand it to him,
Saying 'Thus do domestic traitors guard your swine.'

ARTHUR. You are very bitter about this young man, Kai.

231

KAI. Medicines are bitter. I will be first to lay hand
Upon a pig.
    ARTHUR.   Have you had much dealing with pigs?
    KAI.   No; but I'm competent to handle a pig.
    ARTHUR.   A pig is a big strong beast.
    BEDWYR.   But only at first.
They tire at once; shut up like this they are fat.
    ARTHUR.   You have dealt with pigs, then, Bedwyr?
    BEDWYR.   Once at the Fair
I wrestled a pig at the good old Cornish game
Of putting a pig into pen: and I put him in.
    ARTHUR.   Then you and Kai are designed to capture him now;
I will stand outside the pen and help as I can.
    KAI.   Come on then, Bedwyr; Arthur shall hold our clothes.
There is my cloak; my cap; my tunic; no, strip, man,
Keep our things clean: we shall go from here to the King.
    BEDWYR.   True. I'd forgotten that. Well, there is my tunic.
    ARTHUR.   You cannot enter the swine pen in those shoes;
Take off your under things: that's better, much better,
Now are you like those heroes, whoever they were,
Who wrestled the what's-its-name in the how-d'ye-call-it.
    BEDWYR.   Won't you strip, Arthur?
    ARTHUR.   No, for I am the guard.
If Tristan should reappear or the swineherd come,
You will need defence; but the coast is clear; are you ready?
    BEDWYR.   Take a cruise round, Arthur; I doubt that the coast is
      clear.

                                        (ARTHUR *goes*.)

    KAI.   No need for Arthur to go.
    BEDWYR.   It is safer so,
For these young devils, like Tristan, are full of tricks.
    KAI.   Where on earth has Arthur gone? We shall catch our
      deaths.
We might have caught twenty hogs and have gone by this time.
    BEDWYR.   He has just gone to the pen's end to make certain.
    KAI.   I am not going to freeze to death in my shirt
While Arthur looks at the moon. I am going in,
Into the pen. Come, give me a leg over.
    BEDWYR.   There you are, then. What is inside? Can you see at all?
    KAI.   It is all safe. Come over, Bedwyr, I'll help you.

BEDWYR. Where are the pigs sleeping?
KAI.   In the corner yonder.
BEDWYR. Whereabouts, Kai? I do not see them.
KAI.   Be quiet!
They are sound asleep: we must do as the lion does,
Leap upon one, before the rest are awake.
Those dark masses below the pales are the pigs.
BEDWYR. Lace them now. Spit on your hands, Kai.
KAI.   The big one,
The fat hog nearest the wall, that is our quarry.
BEDWYR. Come on: not another word.

* * *

HOG I'll learn 'ee steal King's hogs!
SOWKIN.   Down with un, husband!
PIGLING. Ballow one, and ballow two, and ballow dree!
BEDWYR. O I am killed! . . .
TRISTAN.   One of them's down!
PIGLING. Hold to him, mother, until I give him ballow.
SOWKIN. Quick, son, he's slippery as an eel in sin.
PIGLING. I'll slippery him with ballow; ballow 'ee Bong.
KAI. Alas, alas, my country!
SOWKIN.   Here comes another.
Get your sling, Pigling, and blast him like Goliath.
PIGLING (opening the pen and coming out). No, mother, it's
       someone running. Well might he run!
TRISTAN. There were only two, then?
HOG.   Two. Here they are, both corpses.
KAI. Oh, water, water! cold water!
BEDWYR.   My neck is broken!
PIGLING. It hasn't been broken yet; you haven't been tried yet.
He's wandering: mother, he thinks he's hanged already.
BEDWYR. I'm one of the King's household.
KAI.   So am I.
BEDWYR.   We both
Are knights of King Marc's court: eminent courtiers.
SOWKIN. Look at this raiment here. Courtiers indeed!
Not courtiers; robbers, who robbed all these fine clothes.

233

Hog. And thought to rob his sacred Kingship's hogs.
And might have, too, but for unprospering pride.
    Bedwyr. We are not robbers.
    Hog.   You are. We heard your words;
You meant to take the fat hog nearest the wall.
    Bedwyr. Take us before the King.
    Pigling.   We'll take you to him
As soon as it is light: then, cord to the windpipe,
To save your wives the expense of cooking breakfast.
    Kai. I tell you, lout, I am Kai, the King's steward.
    Hog. Now, quiet, quiet; remember your latter end;
Don't take the name of the Lord in vain.
                    (A horn is heard.)
    Tristan.   A hunting horn!
King Marc is coming a-hunting: here is the King.
                (Enter MARC, with ARTHUR.)
    Marc. I come to ask if a hog were lost this night.
But what and who are these?
    Tristan.   They are thieves, King Marc,
Caught in the pen red-handed a moment since.
    Marc. And what brings you here, Tristan?
    Tristan.   I came to help guard,
So that your swineherd might save his hogs to the end.
    Marc. Bring the two thieves before me. What plea can you urge
That you be not hanged at once?
    Kai.   My lord, I am Kai.
    Bedwyr. And I am Bedwyr, the Knight.
    Marc.   Bedwyr and Kai!
What brought you into the swine-pen?
    Kai.   We saw no guards . . .
We got into the pen to defend the herd;
Then all these set upon us before we could speak.
    Marc. But why get into the pen to defend the herd?
Defend them from whom? What brought you here in the first place?
    Sowkin. He came to take the fat hog nearest the wall;
We heard him say so. But that fat hog was my husband.
He wasn't a wise choice.
    Marc.   Did you want a pig, Kai?
    Kai. No, not to steal; but we heard that Prince Tristan here

234

Was guarding the pen, and we thought that to take a pig
From him, would be held good fun.
    MARC.   But the very thought
Of taking a King's pig, why, it is treason, Kai.
You, as my steward, surely know that?
    KAI.   My master,
We would have spilled our bloods to the last to defend
Your swine from any but Tristan.
    MARC.   Do not say Tristan, nor even Prince Tristan, steward;
He is a King.
    KAI.   I had not heard he was crowned
King Tristan, lord.
    MARC.   It is a serious matter
When stewards and knights break laws, even in game.
You have been hurt.
    PIGLING.   I gave them a palt with ballow.
    KAI. I am cold from my wound, lord; may I put on my clothes?
    MARC. Why did you take them off? It is Cornish law
That any man taking a thief may have his gear.
These clothes are Hog's and Pigling's; take them, they're yours.
And, Hog, I give you your freedom and rank you here
My master swineherd.
                Be off, you two, to the castle;
Quick, ere the women be up to see you pass.
                          (KAI and BEDWYR go.)
Arthur, go with them: fetch them a couple of cloaks.
You swineherds, move from earshot a little space.
                              (They move off.)
Nephew, there is much talk, which I never heeded;
Now there is much ill-blood which I have to heed.
I cannot have my courtiers poisoned with rage
By you, who have no place here.
                     I have been too tolerant.
Your Kingdom cries for your rule.
    TRISTAN.   I say let it cry.
    MARC. It shall not cry in vain while Cornwall demands
That you be gone from Tintagel. Therefore, my nephew,
I order you to take ship and leave this Kingdom.
    TRISTAN. Order me to leave Cornwall!
    MARC.   Order you strictly.

Banish you, if you choose, on pain of slaying
By the first man who meets you: go before noon.
    TRISTAN.   You drive me out; you dare; drive me, who killed
      Kolbein!
Why, uncle, you are King because of this hand!
(ARTHUR enters.)

    MARC.   Arthur has orders from me to see you aboard.
    ARTHUR.   Come, Tristan, I have a sword and you but a knife.
There are twenty spearmen here.

Must I call them, Tristan?
(TRISTAN goes with him.)

CURTAIN.
(Half minute's interval.)

(Full stage. Tintagel.)

    MARC.   You asked for Tristan. I said that he is not here.
That was not the whole truth, Isolt; I sent him hence;
Banished him hence, on pain of slaying, in short.
He has sailed to the north, never to come back here.
    ISOLT.   May I know your reasons for forcing him hence thus?
    MARC.   Yes. His own good first, since his kingdom needed him.
Then, since this folly of Bedwyr, Kai and the swineherd,
I would not have him in Cornwall: so he has gone.
    ISOLT.   He was my friend, King Marc; he wooed me to Cornwall
Ere ever I looked on you; could you not wait
Until I had said farewell to my banished friend?
    MARC.   Isolt, I wished him away before you returned;
Evil tongues bracket your names together in gossip.
Such talk must cease.
    ISOLT.   Is a Queen to be ruled by talk?
    MARC.   Yes, madam; yes, if she will not rule herself.
Tristan, a King, was keeping the swine while he sent
The man with a message to you. I am ashamed
That a friend of yours should have so little esteem
For you, as the Queen, as to send the swineherd to you,
Whatever the message was, which I do not ask.
Filthy, no doubt, having such a messenger.
    ISOLT.   It was not filthy: it was a love message.
    MARC.   Love message! Do you dare say it?

236

ISOLT.   I do dare.
It was a message of love from a man who loves me,
Warning me of a trap for the Queen of Cornwall
Set by her loving husband at his Knight's bidding.
    MARC.   Now I will ask a question I meant to spare.
Why did he send the swineherd? Had you intended
To meet last night, if I were away?
    ISOLT.   Yes, we had.
    MARC.   You have met before, in secret?
    ISOLT.   Ask your court spies.
    MARC.   I ask my wife, beautiful Isolt, my wife,
Who pledged me her troth last week, the love of my soul.
Ah, my beloved, whatever the young man is,
Let it not weigh with a husband's love: I love you
More than a boy can. And we are married. Besides,
I have heard it said that often, when people marry,
In the first days they shrink from each other. It's true.
So he seems much to you?
    ISOLT.   There is no question of seems.
    MARC.   Love is a blindness full of seeming, my Isolt.
    ISOLT.   There is no seeming in my love and no blindness.
Nothing else is, or matters, or means, save this.
And against this shaking and transfiguration, you
Plot with a steward and lie to ensnare the Queen.
    MARC.   That passionate sin is done. You are married to me,
And I love you so that I will permit no rival.
    ISOLT.   I love him so that I am all his, to the spirit.
    MARC.   Keep him from Cornwall, then: he dies if he come here.
You are my wife till you die.
Love me or not, I will not share you, believe me.
                                        (MARC goes.)
    ISOLT.   How was the secret known? Which courtier learned it?
What did we do to betray it? Or was it Brangwen?
Brangwen alone knew all, and the King knows all.
                    (BRANGWEN enters.)
    ISOLT.   Brangwen, come here to me. Have you betrayed me?
    BRANGWEN.   God forbid, mistress.
    ISOLT.   You lie; you have told the King.
    BRANGWEN.   O Queen, I had rather die than tell of my shame.

237

ISOLT.   You have loved King Marc since you pledged him in the
     wine.
BRANGWEN.   That is true, madam; may God forgive me the sin.
ISOLT.   You have told him all, hoping to win his favour.
BRANGWEN.   Sweet mistress, do not kill me. I swear to heaven
That I have not breathed a word. Only this hour
Marc's men took me and threatened me with their swords;
Said they would kill me if I would not accuse you.
I said 'that you harboured me, who am spotted and base,'
That that was the only fault you had, sweet mistress.
That is the only betrayal I have betrayed.
ISOLT.   Marc's men? Which? Bedwyr and Kai?
BRANGWEN.   Yes, and others;
With swords at my throat swearing I hid your love.
ISOLT.   Who has betrayed me, Brangwen, if not you? Traitress,
It was you!
BRANGWEN.   Madam, it was not: this I can prove.
ISOLT.   Prove it then, swiftly.
BRANGWEN.   Queen, at this very moment
Tristan is there in the glen. I have not betrayed him.
ISOLT.   Here, with a price on his head?
BRANGWEN.   Disguised as a harper.
He is in a hut by the brook; he sent me to you
To say he will clamber the rocks up to your window,
Now, or some minutes hence.
ISOLT.   O my God, as we talk
He may be there! O girl, forgive my suspicion,
I know not where I am led.
BRANGWEN.   Sweet mistress, my lady,
I will deck you for him and make you fair for your love.
                                        (*They go upstairs.*)
               (MARC *and* KAI *enter.*)
MARC.   You say he is here, dressed as a harper?
KAI.   And plans
To enter the Queen's room, clambering up the rocks.
I heard him telling the maid.
MARC.   He shall die, if taken.
KAI.   After my humbling the other day I am loath
To labour with zeal for the King; but to get proof
I have laid rye-meal upon the rocks and earth

238

Under Queen Isolt's window, and in her room
From the floor beneath the window up to her bed.
If a man step in the flour, his track will show.
It will be dark; he will not notice the meal.

    MARC. How soon will he come?

    KAI.   At once: even now, my King.
You will hear him come, for Queen Isolt's window hinge
Is rusty and creaks.

                  (*Enter* BEDWYR.)

                       I posted Bedwyr to watch.

    BEDWYR. The harper went to the rocks by the Queen's window;
He started to climb up.

    KAI.   Listen.

    MARC.   That was no hinge.

    KAI. Tapping with finger-tips; she is going to open.
There is the window, my lord.

    BEDWYR.   He is wearing a sword.

    MARC. Call Arthur hither.

                    (BEDWYR *goes to fetch* ARTHUR.)
That it should be my wife and nephew who wrong me,
Those nearest to me, my sister's son and my heir!

    KAI. It is always the nearest who deal the cruellest blows.
Here is Arthur, my lord.

                (ARTHUR *and* BEDWYR *enter.*)

    MARC.   Tell him; I cannot, Kai.

    KAI. Arthur, it is thought that the banished Tristan is here
Now, with the Queen, in her room.

    BEDWYR.   He is in the room;
My guard saw him clamber up and tap at the window,
And the window opened and white arms helped him in.

    KAI. He is with the Queen at this moment and we shall take
      him.

    ARTHUR. Why am I bidden to this assembly, King Marc?

    MARC. Because if I take my Queen, as I fear, I wish
To put her to trial before you.

    ARTHUR.   You, as the King,
Are the law, not we.

    KAI.   We will bear witness, Arthur.
Shall we proceed, King Marc; bid the Queen open?

BEDWYR. My guard are ready with spears below the window;
He cannot escape as he came.

MARC.   Summon the Queen,
Bid her to open her door that her room be searched.

ARTHUR. One moment, Marc. I am bidden here as accomplice
To the trapping of a woman, a Queen, my hostess.
I take no part in a trap. Therefore: Take heed, you!
Danger! a trap is set! danger! Look out! Look out!
Here come King Marc and his men to murder you!

                                    (*He raises a loud alarm.*)

KAI. You devil, Arthur, to give them warning! Be silent.

                                    (*He knocks at the door.*)

Is the Queen within? King Marc bids Queen Isolt open!
If the Queen be there, let her answer the King's summons.

ISOLT. Who is there, calling the Queen?

KAI.   It is I, Sir Kai,
Charged by the King to bid you open this door.
Will you open, or else compel us to use force?

ISOLT. These are strange words to use to the Queen, steward.
Go tell King Marc, 'I will open to none but him.'

KAI. King Marc, she says 'she will open to none but you.'

MARC. Wait, then, until I come.

                                    (MARC *goes to the upper door.*)
                                    Open, I command you.
                                    (*She opens.*)

ISOLT. Why do you rouse me thus in the dead of night?

MARC. Because I must search your room. Light candles, Bedwyr,
There at the brazier.

ISOLT.   Why do you bring your soldiers
Thus to my room, to search? What think you to find?

MARC. If you know not, madam, I know not and will atone.
Thrust through the curtains, Bedwyr; look in the corner.

KAI. King Marc, will you take this light and see for yourself
The footprints marked in the meal. Did you see, my lord?

MARC. I have seen with my own eyes.

KAI.   Bedwyr's watchers
No doubt will have caught him as he tried to escape.

MARC. Madam, I ask you to have the goodness to cloak
And join me there in the hall: I would speak with you.

                (ARTHUR, KAI, BEDWYR, MARC, *in the hall.*)

Did your watchers kill him, Bedwyr?

BEDWYR.   No, lord; they failed.
In the dark, he leaped among them, laid Corvus dead
And so escaped in the dark, none can say where.

MARC.   Corvus, my guard, laid dead! You, Kai, and Bedwyr, saw
The footprints marked on the floor in the Queen's room?
No need to speak; you saw it and therefore know.

ARTHUR.   This is no quarrel of mine, but I ask to remain,
Lest one, my hostess the Queen, should need a friend.

(*Enter* ISOLT.)

MARC.   Sit you down there, madam; I have something to say.

(ISOLT *sits.*)

A man was watched to your window and seen to enter.
The marks of his feet are plain on your room floor.
But that alarm was given, we should have caught him
In your room with you. You are the Queen of Cornwall,
Quit of the forms of law, but bound to a choice.
Either you shall declare what man was with you,
Or drink the water of test to prove your innocence.

ISOLT.   Dismiss these men from the presence: is it not enough
That you bring them into my room in the dead of night
But that you, the King, must arraign the Queen before them?

MARC.   I bring three witnesses as the law prescribes.
What man was with you?

ISOLT.   A man who came in and went.
Being dark, I could not see his face: the flour
Wastefully spilled by your steward on the floor
Will show his footprints.

MARC.   You expected him, you knew him;
Who was he?

ISOLT.   Nay, your steward expected him,
You and this bevy of knights expected him;
I should ask you: Who was he?

MARC.   God's passion and death!

ISOLT.   Will you repeat? I could not distinguish the name.

ARTHUR.   Beautiful Queen, and you, King Marc, may I speak?
Life will have to be lived when this is settled.
Do not make life more hard by bitterness now.
Marc, may I counsel the Queen apart one moment?

MARC.   Yes, if she care to hear.

ISOLT.   I will gladly hear him.

(MARC, KAI, BEDWYR, *go up stage.*

ARTHUR *and* ISOLT *come down.*)

Did Tristan escape when he leapt from the window, then?

ARTHUR.   Yes; he killed Corvus and got away unwounded.

ISOLT. I thank you, Arthur, for giving me the alarm.

ARTHUR. I do not care for trappings: but now to peace.

Cannot this trouble be mended, or ended, lady?

ISOLT. Mended? I am as may-blossom in a flood,

Or a straw in flames; when the flood has run to sea

And the flames burnt out, I may be mended or ended.

What is this water of test?

ARTHUR.   A drink of ordeal.

ISOLT. Poison?

ARTHUR. The innocent drink it without harm.

ISOLT. What chance is there of Tristan reaching his ship?

ARTHUR. No great chance, madam.

ISOLT.   Has he any?

ARTHUR.   Not much:

They are beating the countryside with a hundred men.

ISOLT. Thank you, good Arthur. I have been blest this night:

I have had a lover and found a friend, a true one.

May the gods bless you, Arthur.

ARTHUR.   You, too, Queen Isolt.

ISOLT. Tell them that I will drink this poisonous brew.

ARTHUR. The Queen does me the honour to bid me say

That she will drink your water of test, King Marc.

MARC. I am thankful that she, being innocent, accepts

To drink this drug, which the guilty dare not drink.

Truth, which mortals may hide, is revealed by the gods.

ISOLT. It is safer to be in God's hand than in man's.

MARC. Bring me the flask from the casket in the aumbry

On the gospel side of the altar in the chapel.

(BEDWYR *goes.*)

ISOLT. Poison like this is a useful drug to a husband,

He can murder his wife, yet lay the blame upon her.

KAI. None but the guilty are poisoned by it, Queen Isolt.

ISOLT. Have all you innocents drunk it?

MARC.   It is your privilege,

Should you desire, to see a priest ere you drink.

ISOLT.   The drink will shrive me enough; let the priest sleep.

(*Sings.*)   A ship came west from the eastern kings,
            With a cargo aboard of three good things:
            She had gold to change and spice to sell,
            And a beggar in rags with news to tell.

(BEDWYR *enters.*)

BEDWYR.   I have brought the flask and a cup, so please your grace.
MARC.   Hold the cup, Bedwyr. I call you all to witness
That the seal on the sacred flasket is unbroken.
I break the seal. Show that the cup is empty.
BEDWYR.   Bear witness, the cup is empty; a clean glass.
MARC.   I empty the hallowed water that shows the truth.
May this bright water declare your innocence.
Take the cup, Bedwyr; offer it to the Queen.
BEDWYR.   Madam, I offer the cup as the King bids.
ISOLT.   I am your Queen, fellow: offer it on your knees.
BEDWYR.   I offer it on my knees.
ISOLT.   I take it from you.
This cold, bright poison, like to my husband's love
Will soon declare the truth: no, I will declare it.
I am Tristan's queen, not Marc's: I was Tristan's love
Before ever I saw King Marc: I am Tristan's now.
I drink to the setting free of the soul within me,
That it may follow my love, my Tristan slain.

(TRISTAN *enters.*)

TRISTAN.   I am not slain yet. Fling down that poison, Isolt.
See there, it burns like quicklime: and you stood by
Making this lady, your Queen, drink of this death!
Here is one for you, my poisoner, one for you!
Come with me, Isolt.
BEDWYR.   Come all you King's men, help!
KAI.   Come, rescue, help! Tristan has seized Queen Isolt.
MARC.   Stand back, Bedwyr and Kai. Tristan, hark to me.
Your godless and lawless path leads to destruction.
TRISTAN.   Your godly and lawful road was leading to murder.
Keep clear of me, I warn you: keep your men clear.
I have horses below and I am going with Isolt,
And the man who tries to stop me shall die on the spot.
ISOLT.   I am going with Tristan; he is my lover; I, his.

243

This is your Cornish crown; this, your Queen's wedding ring.
I go with my lover to a den in the forest,
Or a wet rock by a brook, or a tilted deck,
And the infamy of the world; and I go with joy.

(*They go out together.*)

CURTAIN.
(*Three minutes' interval.*)

(*Full stage. The forest, near the Alan.*)

DINAN.   My lord and master, your subjects send me to beg
That you leave this living here in the wood with your friend
And come to your kingdom at once.

TRISTAN.   And I reply:
Will they take the queen of my choice?

DINAN.   No, my prince, no.
They ask you to leave this lady, since we in the North
Demand an unspotted queen.

TRISTAN.   Then inform my subjects
That I am filled with beautiful thoughts, and will not
Trouble my joy with a realm.

DINAN.   Son, they risked their lives,
And starved their bellies, to help you, for twenty years.

TRISTAN.   Then say I will come in a little while: not yet.

DINAN.   But the heathen are pressing in with fire and sword:
We ask for our King to lead our host to the war.

TRISTAN.   War is an unreal thing to a man who has love.

DINAN.   It is not an unreal thing to your friends and comrades.
Hoel is killed, that you used to hunt with: and Ambrose,
Your friend, little Ambrose, was captured and murdered
By heathen raiders: only last week.

TRISTAN.   What, Ambrose?

DINAN.   He was heard saying 'You wait till Tristan returns.'
He thought you would come.

TRISTAN.   And I have said that I will . . .
And soon, when I choose.

DINAN.   Come now; there can be no soon.

TRISTAN.   I, who am King, have stated my will: my subjects
Must wait, as I bid.

DINAN.   I am your subject, Tristan,

244

Only a subject; but your future and fame
Are dear to me as my blood. Fling off this fever,
This ruin and rot of an unchaste, forsworn trull.

 TRISTAN. Take back those words!

 DINAN.   I will not, because they are true –
You know that they are.

 TRISTAN.   That ends it, Dinan: now, go.

 DINAN. Will you come to your realm?

 TRISTAN.   When I think it fitting.

 DINAN.   But now?

 TRISTAN. No; I will not come now.

 DINAN.   Then your subejcts tell you,
Through me, that they cast you out from kingship and kingdom,
And brand you traitor and choose another as king.
I have declared their bidding.
I'd have been wiser to have let Kolbein spear you
When you were a little baby.

       Farewell, Tristan.

           (*He goes out.*)

    CURTAIN.
    (*No wait.*)

     (*Front stage.*)
    (*Enter* MARC *and* ARTHUR.)

 ARTHUR. So, Marc, as I have said, the pagans have marched.
Will you come, with the Cornish army, to fight them with me?

 MARC. I will muster my men at once: we can march forthwith.

 ARTHUR. With those and the Mendip men we shall beat them
  back.
But who comes here? It is Dinan, Prince Tristan's man.

 MARC. You were promised death if you came to this land again.

 DINAN. You may kill me if you wish: here is my dagger.

 MARC. Where are your master traitor and mistress quean?

 DINAN. They are in hell, King Marc.

 MARC.   You mean, they are dead?

 DINAN. They have not yet the luck to be dead; they linger.

 MARC. Do you serve them here?

 DINAN.   I have no service with either.

 ARTHUR. Grant him your pardon, Marc; he may give you news.

        245

MARC.   Here is your dagger, fellow: I shall not harm you,
No, nor those others; I am too sick at heart
To wish to make others as wretched as myself.
Only, you said that they are in hell . . . I would grieve
If I thought that they needed help.
    DINAN.   They need the help of the gods; they are past men's help.
There is no peace for those two under the moon,
Nothing but horror of heart from their greatness ruined.
They live in a den by the brook, like the fox or otter.
They dare not face the daylight: they hunt by night
And at dawn they sleep with a drawn sword laid between them.
    MARC.   Are you sure of that?
    DINAN.   Yes, I will take my oath on it.
If you will swear to spare them, I'll show them to you.
    MARC.   My sister's son and my wife; they are safe from me.
    DINAN.   Are they safe from your men-at-arms?
    MARC.   Yes, on my oath.
    DINAN.   Come this way, then, King Marc: you shall see them.
Softly.

                                   (They move off.)

(The curtains, opening the full stage, discover TRISTAN and ISOLT asleep,
a sword between them. Enter MARC and DINAN.)
    DINAN.   There are the two as I said. Are they not lovely?
    MARC.   Ay, they are lovely. Leave me alone with them.
    DINAN.   Step quietly, lest you wake him and he kill you.
    MARC.   Our cups are not yet drunken, our three cold draughts.
                                   (DINAN goes.)
Youth had to turn to youth, I was too old for her.
She is so beautiful, she would damn a saint.
I could strike them dead; many would strike them dead.
Killing them will not bring me quiet again.
He is more of a man than I, my sister's son.
He would kill me, were I thus.

                        They are unhappy,
So Dínan says. They are happier than the King.
They shall see that I found them sleeping and pitied them.
                        (He lays his glove between them.)
Lead me out of this, Dinan, back to Arthur.

                                   (He goes out.)

246

ISOLT. Yes? Who is there? Who goes there in the thicket?
Someone was here.

TRISTAN.   Where? When? There is no one, Isolt.
It was some bird or beast going by on the leaves.

ISOLT.   Someone stood looking down, with thought to kill us.

TRISTAN.   You have been dreaming.

ISOLT.   No; this was not a dream.
I knew it, but could not stir. Look! What is this glove?
Tristan, while we were sleeping, Marc has been here.
This is his glove.

TRISTAN.   It is true. That is the King's.
But had he been here, he would have killed us, surely . . .

ISOLT.   It is not Marc's way, to kill.

TRISTAN.   No, not by himself;
But he dropped this glove in his hurry to call his men.
He will be here with his knights to take us, Isolt.

ISOLT.   Tristan, he did not drop the glove in a hurry,
He laid it carefully on the hilt of the sword
To show that he might have killed us and did not kill.
He spared us.

TRISTAN.   I should have guarded while you slept.
We two must go upstream to the secret cave;
And start at once; we cannot trust to his mercy.

ISOLT.   I am not sure that I can go to the cave.

TRISTAN.   You must: it is not safe here.

ISOLT.   No; unsafe henceforth.
I am unsafe henceforth to you, my Tristan.

TRISTAN.   I welcome the risks you bring.

ISOLT.   That is not what I meant.
I meant that I have been harsh, he has been generous.
He has taken the ground from beneath my feet.

TRISTAN.   How so?

ISOLT.   I cannot forget this. Tristan, if you had been Marc,
And had seen us lying, would you have spared me?

TRISTAN.   Yes.

ISOLT.   And my lover?

TRISTAN.   Yes, asleep. I'd have roused him and fought him.

ISOLT.   He is greater than we two, Tristan.

TRISTAN.   He plotted

247

With Kai, to trap you; he tried to poison you.
Had I been awake when he came, I'd have laid him dead.

    ISOLT. Yes, he risked that, too.

    TRISTAN.   Yes, the first risk of his life.

    ISOLT. Sorrow has nobled him; he has done such a deed
As none but a great man could. Therefore I'll show him
That I see his greatness.

    TRISTAN. I've shown that I see his weakness.
I have not killed him: that is enough for Marc.
And now you are mine.

    ISOLT.   I was till to-day: not now.

    TRISTAN. Isolt, where are you going?

    ISOLT.   Back to Marc, barefoot.

    TRISTAN. You shall not! What? to be pelted and put to death?

    ISOLT. Will my lover bar my way?

    TRISTAN.   No. Let us use reason.
I see your mood. This living here in the wilds
Has been too hard for you: you want to go back
To a world of women and friends and fires and homes.
We will go to my kingdom.

    ISOLT.   Your subjects have cast you out.

    TRISTAN. We will go to Arthur, then.

    ISOLT.   He has gone to the war.

    TRISTAN. Then we will go to your home.

    ISOLT.   I have no home now.

    TRISTAN. Your mother's house is a home.

    ISOLT.   Nevermore to me.

    TRISTAN. Because of me?

    ISOLT.   Partly.

    TRISTAN.   You could go there alone.

    ISOLT. I could not go there.

    TRISTAN.   Why not?

    ISOLT.   I should not dare.
This love, that I thought was great, is blindness and greed
And I am unclean, unclean, till I drive some nail
Right through this passionate heart.

                          If he scourge me, well.
If he kill me, well; he shall have his chance and choice.
If he cast me out, I will come again, perhaps;
But until then, I am a thing.

TRISTAN.   So am I, Isolt.
A young thing, much in love, who saved you from death,
And flung his kingdom away for the love of you;
Weigh that with creeping in like a thief with a glove.
      ISOLT.   Marc, who is cruelly hurt, is great in his pain.
      TRISTAN.   Meaning that I am little?
      ISOLT.   O Tristan, beloved,
See it as I do.
      TRISTAN.   I cannot see it as you.
Either you have gone mad or you never loved me.
      ISOLT.   Never loved you, Tristan? Do not let us be bitter.
We have trodden the depths, let us rise to the heights.
      TRISTAN.   By heights, meaning that you return to your husband?
      ISOLT.   I'll pay a great deed with another.
      TRISTAN.   Yes, raiment and women
Are what you want, not me, who am ruined for you.
Get to your Marc; and tell him I'll tear him piecemeal
If once he touch you. Go, get to your heights and depths . . .
I'll follow deer, not women, henceforth, and stab them,
Stab them and stab them dead. Out! get to your husband.
                         CURTAIN.
                         (No wait.)

                    (Front stage.)
                 (MARC and ARTHUR.)
   ARTHUR.   We will march at dawn, then, Marc. We shall give
        them battle
About full moon. I'll come with your horse at dawn.
      MARC.   Till dawn, then, Arthur: good-night.
      ARTHUR.   Good-night.
                              (ARTHUR goes. ISOLT enters.)
      MARC.   Who are you, lady?
      ISOLT.   I am Isolt, your wife, come to return your glove.
I say that I have sinned in act and in thought,
Broken all vows, all pacts, tricked you, betrayed you.
Now, toucht to loyalty by the greatness in you,
I stand ashamed by your generous deed, my King.
I come to atone, or to bear my punishment.
      MARC.   Isolt, my queen, we have been harsh to each other.

                         249

ISOLT.   You do not know my worst.

MARC.   You have suffered from mine.
Let us put by the past; for I love you, Isolt,
More than words tell. I march to the wars at dawn.
The knights who poisoned your peace from hatred of you,
Have marched already: you have no enemies here;
None but dear lovers now. Go: robe you and crown you,
I will declare you the Queen and the ruler here
While I am east at the war.

ISOLT.   I will atone, Marc;
I promise. God bless you, lord.

MARC.   And you, too, Isolt.
I shall be home from the wars by the summer's end,
Please God, my Queen. Our life shall be different then.
Come, Queen of Cornwall.

                                                        (*They go out.*)

                    (*Half minute's interval.*)

                    (*The main stage. Tintagel.*)
                    (HOG *and* SOWKIN.)

HOG.   Our Queen has kept great state since King Marc went
    warring.

SOWKIN.   She should not wear this black; King Marc isn't dead.

HOG.   She wears the black because King Marc is away.

SOWKING.   Many might say she wears the black for another.

HOG.   Now, Sowkin, now! whatever the other was,
He is not now. She has shut her doors upon him,
Turned her thoughts from him, and all is for King Marc.

SOWKIN.   The more's the pity, I say, for our poor daughter.
She thinks of nothing but this Prince Tristan in sorrow.
Run mad in the woods, they say.

HOG.   He is crazed from love,
And our girl Pixne is right to be sorry for him;
But for his friendship we wouldn't be free to-day.

SOWKIN.   Set free. Ah, husband, many a time and oft
I'd have given much to be back among the swine;
It was so homely among those dear kind creatures;
They weren't like courtiers: they loved you for what you were.

HOG.   The Queen says, after the war we're to be rangers;

250

Which means I'll have a horse and a red stomach-piece,
And you'll be mistress ranger and carry keys.
Think of that! carry keys on a dingle-dangle.

SOWKIN.   I hope these glories will not turn us from truths.
I fear for you, my Hog, as I fear for Pixne.
You were always ones for the world.
                        When will the wars end?

HOG.   Here comes the Queen, our mistress; God save you, lady.

ISOLT.   You were asking about the war's end. There is news.
The Cornish men have come to the dyke with Arthur,
They expect to fight the heathen at once. Perhaps
They have already fought and ended the war.
We shall have more news during to-day, no doubt.
Tell Constans he must go with the horses to-night.

HOG.   He shall be told, O Queen.

                              (HOG *and* SOWKIN *go out.*)

ISOLT.   Would I were a man, to be out there in the battle,
Instead of a woman, toiling to keep from brooding
On the fierce memories which are woman's portion.
Out there in the forest, where the river runs,
And the soft-foot deer go, and the otter plays,
And the partridge calls, my lover waits for me.
He waits in vain; I have bolted the bars on love.

                              (BRANGWEN *enters.*)

BRANGWEN.   The hunter speared you a salmon in the river.
He said that he saw a young man in the forest.

ISOLT.   I have no wish to hear of what man he saw.

BRANGWEN.   This man was running frantic among the trees,
Beating his head, that was all crowned with flowers.

ISOLT.   There are many masterless men, and madmen, too,
In the great wood.

BRANGWEN.   This man wore all the flowers
That you most love: June flowers, sweet dog-rose buds,
Big ox-eye daisies, that children make old men of,
And clover cops that are partly red, part white.

ISOLT.   If he be mad, he is happier than some sane.
If the hunter go again to that forest place,
Let him not look at such madmen, nor bring tales
Back to this house about them. My madness is dead.

                              (*She goes out.*)

251

BRANGWEN.   You are she who forced me into your husband's bed
So that you might love this madman. Now you have Marc
At the war, because you fled him; and Tristan mad.
Had Marc but drunken the wine, he would have loved me.
Ah! woe to you if you turn again from the King.

(TRISTAN *climbs in by window.*)

TRISTAN.   Where is this Marc, this so-called King of Cornwall?
BRANGWEN.   By the Severn mouth, at the war, with Arthur, my
     prince.
TRISTAN.   You lie! Marc goes to no wars. Where is he hidden?
BRANGWEN.   You know me, Prince; you know that I do not lie.
TRISTAN.   How many miles to his camp?
BRANGWEN.   A hundred at least.
TRISTAN.   It is not a hundred.
BRANGWEN.   It's over the moor and the plain,
And over the Mendips beyond.
TRISTAN.   O God! O God!
He is out of my reach. When does he plan to return?
BRANGWEN.   Not till autumn.
TRISTAN.   Ah, God, I cannot get there to kill him,
Nor live till he comes; but I'll kill his steward at least.
BRANGWEN.   He too has gone to the war. O Prince, you are
     bleeding,
And fevered and broken and starved.
TRISTAN.   Yes, I stumble and hit things.
BRANGWEN.   I will have a bed prepared.
TRISTAN.   No bed for me here.
No; they strew flour about the beds, for traps.
After those traps, all's fair.
                    I've been running the forest . . .
The moon was there and the deer and the grey wolves . . .
Pitter-patter, pitter-patter, with fangs gleaming . . .
But a moor-man told me that Marc had murdered her,
So I'll break his neck across and tear out his heart.
But a hundred miles, you said: I haven't the strength.
Brangwen, sweet Brangwen, I want to kiss the ground
Where that most beautiful thing lies buried, at peace.
BRANGWEN.   Sir Tristan, Queen Isolt is not dead, but alive.
TRISTAN.   Mind what you say, girl; I am unable to bear.
BRANGWEN.   She is well.

252

TRISTAN.   Then where is her prison?
BRANGWEN.   She is the Queen.
TRISTAN.   And here? In the castle? Take me to where she is.
BRANGWEN.   Sweet Prince, you must wait.
TRISTAN.   I am mad from waiting. Take me,
Or I'll kill you.
BRANGWEN.   Oh, you are hurting! Loose me, Prince.
You will frighten her as you are, I will bring raiment
You shall bathe and dress; then see her.
TRISTAN.   I'll see her now.
BRANGWEN.   She thinks you dead. For pity's sake let me warn her.
TRISTAN.   Tell her at once then, girl.
BRANGWEN.   Yes; but you make ready.
Come with me, Prince. What bliss for you both to meet.
This way, Prince Tristan. While you dress I will tell her.
                        (*She leads him off.* ISOLT *enters.*)
ISOLT.   Tristan is mad, she said. He is saner than I.
O I would that we loved like the birds, and then fled south!
What is this hunting spear? It is Tristan's spear.
Yes; it is Tristan's spear. Did the hunter find it?
Or did Tristan bring it here? Yes, Tristan is here,
To take me back. They'll think that I sent for him.
Where is he now? Who is there?
                        (HOG *enters.*)
HOG.   It is I, my Queen.
Sir Bedwyr brings news of the war: he asks to see you . . .
He is all foundered from riding.
ISOLT.   Bring him in, Ranger.
But, Ranger, wait. Have you seen Prince Tristan to-day?
Or heard of his being here?
HOG.   No, madam, indeed.
ISOLT.   Do you know who found this spear, or brought it hither?
HOG.   No spear like that came in at the gate, Queen Isolt.
ISOLT.   It has been brought here, within the last five minutes.
HOG.   It was brought through the windows then: not by the
    doors.
ISOLT.   Bring in our people. Let Bedwyr tell us the news.
                        (ALL *enter.*)
BEDWYR.   God bless you, Queen. I bring you news of the battle.
ISOLT.   God bless the bringer of news: may the news be good.

253

BEDWYR. Good news and bad: things given by God and taken.
Hear all, Queen Isolt and all the Cornish court,
Sir Arthur the leader, bids me to tell you this:–
(*Enter* TRISTAN *from above.*)
BRANGWEN.   O prince, keep away!
TRISTAN.   Stand aside, Brangwen. My Isolt, beloved Isolt,
I thought you were dead. O my beloved, sweet saint,
Angel of God, dear darling; O my heart's best.
Come to me. I have been frantic for want of you.
ISOLT.   Hold this man, Ranger; help to secure him, Bedwyr.
Hold him away.
                              (*He is caught.*)
TRISTAN.   Isolt, for God's sake, give me
One little word. Loose me, friends, let me speak to her.
Loose me! I'll cut your throats else. Isolt, my Isolt!
ISOLT.   Can you come again, after your uncle's mercy?
Could you think I should greet you in my husband's absence?
You are outlaw, sentenced to death: I could have you hanged.
TRISTAN.   He told me that you were murdered and buried. O
      God!
Give me your hands. I will have your hands. Let me go.
ISOLT.   Carry that frantic madman into the court,
Deliver him to the guard as a cast felon,
And let the marshal flog him with fifty stripes
And drag him upon a hurdle out of the bounds.
Remove him.
TRISTAN.   Isolt, remember; think what I am!
ISOLT.   Think, you, of what you are; and of what I am.
BEDWYR.   Away with him, as Queen Isolt bids.
TRISTAN.   O gods!
            (*He is dragged out, struggling and raving.*)
ISOLT. You harboured that creature, Brangwen.
BRANGWEN.   Yes. I love lovers
And I pity sufferers; life having taught me so.
ISOLT.   And I hate madness and trample it underfoot.
                (*Enter* BEDWYR.)
Did you hand that man to the guard?
BEDWYR.   As the Queen bade.
            (*The others enter.*)

ISOLT. You, take your places; give good heed and be silent.
What news of the war, Sir Bedwyr?

BEDWYR.   We fought the heathen
At Badon Hill; we fought all day and all night,
And at dawn we fought them again: twelve times we charged them,
Not seven heathen escaped alive: they are ended.

ISOLT. Thank God, who has given victory to our men.

BEDWYR. Let us also thank the men whose lives bought victory

ISOLT. Ah! doubtless many most precious have paid the price?

BEDWYR. Many: and one most precious of all to Cornwall.
King Marc lies dead at the thorn tree by the brook,
Killed as we broke them. He being dead, I salute
Isolt, the Queen of Cornwall. God save Queen Isolt!
Our hearts and swords are Queen Isolt's to command.

ISOLT. I thank you for this loyalty to our House.
I pray God help me to govern Cornwall rightly.

BEDWYR. (to the household). That Tristan, whom we have flogged
        out of Tintagel,
Was King Marc's heir, and still may claim to be King.
But we have turned him out for ever and ever,
Understand that. Queen Isolt alone rules Cornwall.
The man who kills that outlaw shall be rewarded.
May we take our leave, Queen?

ISOLT.   Yes, dismiss to your tasks.
                              (BRANGWEN stays; the rest go.)
Did that prince talk with you before he came down?

BRANGWEN. Only to say how loving you made him mad.
Thinking you dead, he has lived upon leaves and grass;
No diet to withstand flogging from marshal's men.

ISOLT. What I have done, I have done. Where is he living?

BRANGWEN. He is not living, but dying. There's a hut on the
        moor
Where Pixne, the Ranger's girl, leaves comforts for him.
There he will speedily die from grief and shame.

ISOLT. It is no great pain to die, the heart being dead.

BRANGWEN. No, madam, you utter truth: it is no great pain.
May I take your orders, madam?

ISOLT.   Orders? For what?

BRANGWEN. For the funeral feast for your royal husband killed.

ISOLT. There will be no funeral feast.

255

BRANGWEN.   For his burial, then.

ISOLT. There will be no burial save what his comrades gave him.

BRANGWEN. Surely his body will be borne from the field
And brought with flowers and lights here to Tintagel,
To be laid in a sacred place with his father's bones.

ISOLT. God made the earth where he lies: he will sleep sweeter
Under the milkwort and the larks of heaven
Than in this charnel of bones and dead Kings' sin.

BRANGWEN. He laid his glove beside you in noble mercy,
Yet you will not lay a flower upon his corpse,
Hacked as it is, in saving you from the heathen.
You could not love this royal man who is dead;
I could, and do, as the noblest, gentlest King
That ever was famed in Britain. Therefore, my Queen,
I at least shall go till I find where my lover lies.
He was my lover for once; thank God therefor.
What worship these hands may render to the dead,
I will give, madam, being more his wife than you.

ISOLT. May your last duties comfort your widowhood.

                                        (BRANGWEN *goes.*)

              (ISOLT *comes forward to the front stage:*
                  the curtains close behind her.)

ISOLT. So this one triumphs over me as a lover,
Thinks that she loves if, after sighing in secret,
She lays a daisy upon a dead man's body.
She has never known what it is.

                              Love is so terrible,
A love like mine. I have killed Tristan, my lover;
Killed him as though with a sword.
I have been perilous to Tristan and Marc.
What have they had from me but fever in the bones?
Marc was dead all the time: no need to have scourged him.
I was the virtuous wife; see where it sank me.
It is ended: nothing can bring it back. I have
This little knife of mother's. Poor mother afar,
Who was thoughtful for me before I thought, and will feel
After I cease to feel. The brook will run down
Over the shingle to sea; and the corncrake call;
And the honeysuckle, up in the glen, drowse sweetness:
And the moon come over the hill: mother will have them,

256

Not I: I shall not have them. What shall I have?
Some sky for the two wild swans to be wing in wing,
Some holly thicket for the stag and his deer,
Some space in heaven, where I, the comet, will seek
My mate, past withering orbs and moons gone blind,
For centuries to come. I am following, Tristan;
Wait for your cruel killer, a little hour.
You shall be my death as I have been yours, beloved.
We who have flooded like the Severn, will ebb
To the great sea together like tides going out.

(*She moves off.*)

(*No wait.*)

(*The full stage. The forest scene.*)

PIXNE. Why, you are better, sir; you have come to yourself.
Now drink this apple-water: it's sweet and cooling.

TRISTAN. You have been good to me like an angel of God.
But I shall never be better: I'm dying, Pixne.
What did you mean by 'come to myself'? Myself;
I had a self once: destiny interfered.
I was a prince once, girl; but I loved a queen.
Before this life I was somewhere linked to her life;
After this life, God knows she will be at my soul,
Either my thirst in hell or my light in heaven.

Isolt the sweet, Isolt the bright,
In you my day, in you my night.
Isolt my love, Isolt my own.

I am fevered and faint. I have loved that lady, Pixne.

PIXNE: Sir, do not think of her: it was that that harmed you.
You must not talk, lest your coughing begin again.

TRISTAN. The coughing is over; like me.

Isolt my hope, Isolt my star,
In you my share of things that are.

I cannot rhyme as I did. Pixne, if you loved me
And I were dying, even if we had quarrelled,
You would come to say good-bye?

257

PIXNE.   You know that I would.
So every woman would.
        TRISTAN.   Not all. It is hard
For some, when they choose a path, to be thought mistaken.
But something here in my heart speaks of her coming
To say good-bye to her love.
        PIXNE.   O my prince and master!
Whoever is coming, it is not to say good-bye,
But to heal your cruel wounds and your broken lungs,
And take you to some nice home with fire and wine
And good food fit for your health.
        TRISTAN.   Look on the road, girl.
Is there anyone on a black horse crossing the moor?
        PIXNE. Nobody, sir.
        TRISTAN.   She would come on the horse, Black Eagle,
Because I gave him to her.
        PIXNE.   There is no black horse.
        TRISTAN. Not yet, perhaps; but look for a brown horse, Pixne:
She would send Brangwen first to say she is coming.
Is Brangwen there, on a brown horse, with a message?
        PIXNE. There is no horse at all on the moor, Sir Tristan,
But the carrier's blind white pony, moving away.
        TRISTAN. Brangwen was faithful. Brangwen, a Welsh king's
                daughter,
Enslaved in a raid: a life of hell, which I worsened.
Brangwen, good Brangwen, a brown horse, or Black Eagle.
                                        (He lapses, muttering.)
        PIXNE. What are you muttering, Prince? Hush! I think he is
                sleeping.
If he can rest now, he will throw off this cough.
I will creep out while he sleeps, to pray at the cross.
The prayers will help: I dare leave him for so long.
He is so weak, he must sleep, poor lovely man.
                                        (She goes out.)
        TRISTAN. There was no horse on the moor, no horse at all,
Save a rider with a spare horse drawing nearer.
I shall mount and ride with him and not return.
But there is a horse upon the moor: I hear him.
I will look to see: alas, I am so weak
That I cannot stand, nor see. But on the moorland

258

A horse is at a gallop heading hither. . .
It is she . . . yes . . . it is she . . .
But she cannot know my dwelling, she will pass me.
Isolt, I am here! Isolt, Queen Isolt, Isolt.
No, no, no, she has passed: she could not hear me.
What time of year is it? are the harebells come?
It's the end of the year with me, Tristan, the Prince.

Isolt the maid, Isolt the Queen,
Isolt the April, budding green.

Those are Black Eagle's hoofs. Eagle, boy, Eagle!
Yes, it is Eagle, he hears me: Isolt is coming.
It is Isolt coming to see me before I die.

(*The voice of* ISOLT *is heard.*)

Isolt! come to me, Isolt!
ISOLT.   Tristan, my Tristan!
O my beloved Tristan, where are you hidden?
    TRISTAN.   I am here, Isolt: I knew that you would come.
Ah! I shall not see her face: my death is on me.

(ISOLT *enters.*)

    ISOLT.   O Tristan, my heart's own darling, take me again.
    TRISTAN.   Isolt my blood, Isolt my breath,
                In you my life; in you my death.

(*He dies.*)

    ISOLT.   He has gone from me for ever from this shell,
This broken body that my cruelty killed.
I will come with you, Tristan; stay but a moment.
We two will journey together whatever ways
Bodiless spirits travel in the heaven
Of being set free. You were more beautiful, Tristan,
Than the young stag tossing tines near the holly thicket.
You were dearer to me than anything else on earth.
Take pity upon me, darling, though I took none.

(*She stabs herself.*)

Tristan, my captain, my love; my only love.

(*She dies.*)

(*Enter* PIXNE, DINAN, BRANGWEN, ARTHUR.)
    PIXNE.   It is here, sir; they are here. O Sir Tristan; dead!
    DINAN.   Dead: we're too late: the birds have flown from their
        cages.

ARTHUR. We will bury them together, here where they lie.
If they have sinned, they have loved with a love exceeding:
Now they are spirits of love, not bodies bleeding.
                         CURTAIN.

                         EPILOGUE.
DESTINY. Not as men plan, nor as women pray, do things happen.
Unthought of, unseen, from the past, comes the ill without cure;
By the spirit of man and the judgment of God it is shapen;
And its end is our pride in the dust: it is just: it is sure.

                    THE END.

Stage. This play was written to be played in two hours and twenty minutes upon a stage without scenery, hung with back cloths. It was written for a theatre with a fore-stage, or apron, and a main-stage on a somewhat higher level. At the back of, and above, the main stage, there is a gallery or balcony, approached by stairs on each side.

Some of the scenes of the play are designed for action on the apron, when the curtain between the two stages is drawn.

Costume. Should be that of Romanised Britons. Arthur should wear golden Roman armour with the scarlet cloak of a general. All the costumes, without exception, should be of bright and vivid colours: that of Kolbein should be the most barbaric and the gayest.

Decorations. The shields of King Marc's household bore a golden horse upon a blue field. The men of his household wore white satin scarves with black borders. His banners were white, with black points.

The ages of the characters:

TRISTAN and ISOLT . . . . about twenty years.

MARC . . . . about twenty-nine years.

THURID, ARTHUR, and KOLBEIN . . . . about forty-five years.

DINAN, KAI, and BEDWYR . . . . about fifty-five years.

HOG and SOWKIN . . . . about sixty years.

TRISTAN, MARC, KOLBEIN and ARTHUR should be clean-shaven.

Part II

UNPUBLISHED POEMS AND PLAY

The Aftermath

Kol brought the news of Uther's murdering
To Iddoc in the East within few days
He, the bloodsbrother, suffered no delays
But manned his dragon-ships and sailed and brought
Merchyon the Cornish King
East, into Kent, and hung him till he died
Caged in a cresset on the rampart side
But Breuse whose traitorous hand the killing wrought
Breuse was still scatheless, having taken wing.

Breuse was on foray with King Merchyon's son
There in the south when Merchyon was made prize
And at the news he thought in heartless wise
'This boy being prisoned, I might have the crown.'
No sooner said than done
He seized the youth, usurped the Cornish throne
Swore that the girl Elaine should be his own
And thought that all the barriers were down
Twixt him and Kingship and the struggle won.

When Ban of Benwick heard how Uther died
He, too, set forth to bring the killers down
And finding Breuse had seized the Cornish crown
He fought him in Tintagel man to man
And thrust him through the side
Killing him dead, and crowned young Merchyon King
And wed Elaine the golden with a ring
(A Queen well fitted to the golden Ban)
Then home to Benwick with his bride.

And there the next year, in the Keep of Joy
Their son was born, Prince Lancelot the bright,
Known in his manhood as the peerless knight:
'The fairest manchild ever seen by men'
They called that glorious boy.

265

And at his birth a shining one of those
Who dwell within the changing seas arose
And signed him with a blessing beyond ken
That no man's steel should maim him or destroy.

But at the birthfeast held for Lancelot
Young Merchyon the Second wooed and wed
Ban's sister Helen in that Joyous stead
And bore her home to high Tintagel keep
That lovely pair begot
Olwen, whom Tallorc married, and King Marc
To whom the portioned destiny was dark
Queen Isolt's sinning made his spirit weep
In ways his happy childhood reckoned not.

And meanwhile Queen Ygerna bred her son
In white-walled Sarum in the downland wide
O'er which, all day, the singing larks abide,
And wind makes ripples gleam along the slopes
There Arthur was begun
By Kol and Guy in every manly play
Of gentle dealing: there he learned the way
Of horse and battle – there he raised the hopes
Of those who taught him, as a likely one.

There, too, when he had grown, he came to know
An older man, Sir Ector of the Marsh,
There where the sea makes Parret water harsh
Often with Ector he would sail that fief
The brown sail loitering slow
Through thickets of dense reeds, and pools, and ways
By islands fortified in ancient days,
To spear the pike beneath the lily leaf
Or drop the flying heron with the bow.

There Ector taught him war as practised then
By Roman soldiers, there he grew apace,
Dark haired, immense of bone and calm of face
When he was hardly twenty he was sent
To rule his western men

Beyond Caerleon, for the country seethed
Destruction poisoned all the air men breathed
Destruction of all stable government
Down to the roots that man might start agen.

So, in Caerleon town he made his seat
Keeping his father's league with other Kings;
Wales and the islands hummed with mutterings
Of some great storm of pirates soon to break:
When they had reaped the wheat
Of that hot summer, lo the pirates came
Throughout the west the farms went up in flame
Into each haven thrust the fiery drake
Up to each wall the wolves came seeking meat.

And in that foraying of many packs
Though Arthur kept the coasts of southern Wales
The heathen reddened ocean with their sails
And held their course beyond him to the south
King Kolbein, Bloody Axe
A chief among them stormed Tintagel tower
Killed Merchyon, took his kingdom for his dower
And settled there and ruled to Helford mouth
Making men slaves with loads upon their backs.

King Merchyon's daughter would have been his slave
Had not King Tallorc come and borne her forth
To be his Queen in Pictland in the North
Where she soon died in giving Tristan birth,
Soon like a broken wave
The furies of the heathen onslaught slackt
Their ships drew homewards leaving much unsackt
'When next they came,' they said, 'they would leave
      dearth
From Tyne to Wight one desecrated grave.'

267

Brother Lot

When Merchyon murdered Uther in the glen
King Lot was roving with his Orkney men.

Far on the Irish coast his dragon's beak
Struck in the living flesh of men more weak.

Then having plundered well, he came ashore
East of Red Headland betwixt Mull and Gore.

There, he speared salmon for his winter keep
And rode the moorland for the moormen's sheep.

There Kol of Sarum came to him with news
Of Uther murdered by the King and Breuse.

Lot called his men about him on the sand
Beside the brook, and stilled them with his hand.

He said 'You recollect how we were cast
On Swanage Beach the winter before last.

How the ship broke to staves and how we froze
In withered bent-grass starving in the snows

Waiting till men should see our broken crew
And ring us round with spears and run us through.

You recollect how Eirik said 'Standby.
Here comes the King to kill us; here we die.'

And how Prince Uther came as Eirik spoke
And all we death's-heads waited for the stroke

And how that young Prince came with open hand
Saying 'You come unhappily to land,

But shall not want for welcome, being come'
And how be brought us to his Wareham home

Within the Roman wall to food and fire
Warmth and dry clothing, life and heart's desire

And when the storm abated sent us forth
In a new ship to our beloved north

You do not marvel that so great a friend
Should be remembered by us till we end

You did not marvel when I took the oath
That made a brotherhood betwixt us both

Mixing our blood, with promise of support
As each might need or Destiny assort.

You were as proud as I that one so good
Should be allied to us in brotherhood.

Now that great friend my brother has been killed
His seeing quencht, his heart of kindness stilled,

Stabbed as he lay asleeping with his bride
In some green valley by a waterside.

Stabbed by King Merchyon and heartless Breuse
Himself asleep unarmed among the dews

Stabbed on that very morning when we sackt
King Dermot's castle for the gear we lackt

While we were feasting then our brother lay
Dead, with his heart's blood drying on the clay.

Though he be dead, alive within me still
His blood is quick, that Merchyon did not kill

269

That blood cries out for vengeance and shall have
Both Breuse and Merchyon in a traitor's grave.

We will begone, adown the shrieking Mull
Tintagel gates shall carry each a skull

Breuse's to westward, Merchyon's to east
Their flesh shall give the corbie crows a feast

Them or the pilchards plucking with wet mouths
Their corpses as the loit'ring ebbing souths.

Run down the great Red Dragon to the sea
And then away, my brothers, come with me.'

The rollers splintered as the Dragon drave
Across the beach and flashed into the wave.

The billows shattered as she ran the Mull
Past holy Ailsa, nest-rock of the gull.

The billows shred to brightness at her bows,
Past sacred Mona where the puffins house,

The north wind held, the crying gear complained,
A mile astern her gleaming pathway waned

Past Ramsey and past Lundy in dim dusk
Her bow-wash whitened like a dragon's tusk

Thence, hauling shoreward, she came gently in
To beach, beneath a headland bright with whin.

She came too late, for Uther's killers lay
Unknowing, recompounded into clay.

Already judged, the country people told,
By Bran and Iddoc, dead and under mould.

270

They came too late, but Lot the pirate said
'We never yet went empty from a raid.

We will fill water while our fellows try
What fortunes wait us in the glens near by

For something tells me that a treasure comes
Well worth the bringing northward to our homes.'

Arthur's Youth

Arthur was born within Tintagel hold
And grew to boyhood taller than his peers
And left his mother's fold,
While still a boy, to join the British host,
Who kept the dyke with spears
As they had kept it now for thirty years,
Spite of the heathen's forays, threat and boast
And valorous captains giving up the ghost.

There daily, yearly, Arthur helped to keep
The white, chalk-burrowed, palisaded line,
Now grazed on by the sheep,
Then a fierce frontier, where at any hour
A trumpet would give sign.
Then on the down the heathen spears would shine
And sling-bolts twanged and arrows in a shower
In all the tumult of a border stour.

Or sometimes in the midnight he was roused,
After a weary day, to leave his bed,
To mount his horse half drowsed
And cross the wall into the no-man's land,
Where heathen riders fled,
Driving the booty from some plundered stead
Of cattle herded by the fleeing band
Or girls, mouth muffled by a pirate hand.

But after certain times the pirates grew
Stronger and surer in their kingdoms here,
For many thousands drew
Westward to join them from the northern lands.
The time grew daily near
When all their myriads, flooding with the spear,
Savage as wolves and many as the sands,
Would whelm like a spring tide that breaks all bands.

There in the north they mustered, thousands strong,
In islands and in branches of the sea,
Made rich by doing wrong,
Nourisht by dead men's food, by dead men's fires,
Singing in drunken glee
Of cruel murders done in treachery,
Counting no men as statesmen but their liars
And nothing good save glutting of desires.

And to confront this overwhelming ill
The West and Wales and nothing more remained,
But with divided will,
Due to the jealousies of petty kings,
Whom pirates' gold had gained.
Everywhere else the Roman strength had waned.
Her eagle-birds had long since taken wings,
Her walls were grave-mounds of forgotten things.

For always in his youth the pirates presst
Westward against the still unconquered plain
That barred the fertile west.
Sometimes a summer passed without attack,
Then they would come again
Unwearied and as many as the rain,
The places filled of those who went not back
And spoil-fed spearmen eager for the sack.

And sometimes in their long-ships they would sail
Round to the western coast and come ashore
And hurriedly assail
Some outland farm or shepherd with his sheep
And then be gone once more
With yet another slave to tug the oar,
Leaving but flames and widows, who would weep
A man who sowed but now would never reap.

So in this troubled boyhood of alarms
Arthur became a champion, strong and tall,
Hardened to acts of arms,
Ready upon the instant with a plan,

273

Whatever fate might fall,
So that his rulers took him from the wall
And sent him westwards as a trusted man
To keep the marches where the Severn ran.

There at Caerleon upon Usk he held
The passages of Severn, Usk and Wye,
Where petty kings rebelled
And gave the pirates welcome and support.
But with King Arthur by
They lived like slaves beneath their master's eye.
There Arthur's splendour made that frontier fort
Known throughout Gower as the golden court.

Before the Darkness Came

As on some westward fronting crag the sun
At sinking casts a coloured light that glows
(Although the mountain line) with a longing one
Which makes each jutting of the quartz distinct
Before the day is done
So in that hour before the darkness came
On Roman Britain all her peaks were flame
Like brother crags her captain kings were linkt
Fronting the ruin which they knew begun.

The Coming of the Pirates

This year the pirates came
In many thousands from their Eastern shores
They linkt with Arthur's enemies, they presst
Wherever ships might beach
City and farm alike went up in flame.
As flooded water at a river pours
They thronged along the valleys to the west
Camelot city's self was in their reach
Camelot, Queen unsackt in many wars,
Camelot Red Rose Crest.

The Dyke was Arthur's fort
There looking north and east the sentries stood
Shading their eyes and seeing now the smoke
Of some burnt town or farm
Now, the red sails of pirates nearing port
Now, a horsed outpost boding nothing good
Now, men and women fleeing from the stroke
A widow with a child upon her arm
A handless victim of the pirates' sport
Old men with bundles snatcht out of the flood
Before the barrier broke.

All Hallow Night

Before the fight with the pagan men,
Who were fifty thousand strong,
King Arthur came to the moor lake,
Led by a curlew's song.
He passed the shore of the moor lake,
Where the summer's reeds lay dead,
The thought of the pagans made him ache
For the too few men he led.
The fish leaped in the lonely tarn,
The curlew mewed in the sky,
The owl called as he left the barn
To make the field mouse die.
The moon came up above the lake
In a white track glimmering clear
And a lady stood in the white track
And bade Arthur come near.
'I have loved you all these years,' she said,
'In the dark mere all alone.
I bring you a sword for your fight,' she said,
'Lest you be overthrown.
Draw it tomorrow, when you fight,
And the pagan hosts shall flee.
Then each year on All Hallow night
Come here to speak with me.'
King Arthur took the lady's sword
And smote the pagans stark
Till the thousands of them lay in horde,
Killed between dawn and dark.
And he kept the sword about his side,
But he never kept his day
And the lady came at All Hallow tide
And took the sword away.

The Hunt is Up

Arthur the King has gone to hunt the deer
Sir Lancelot has gone to Guinevere
There in her room the lovers have no fear
But love each other as these lovers use
Then Modred gathers Agravaine and Breuse
Colgreve and Kai and telleth them the news
'Now we will take this traitor with his dear'.
The dew drips from the leaf
The red-felled stag goes by.

Modred and all his gang have taken swords
Their mail, their shields each painted like a lord's
'We'll bind these lechers face to face with cords'
Thus braggart are they as they climb the stair
They knock the door, the Queen asks 'Who is there?'
'King's men who come to lay a treason bare
And give a royal harlot her rewards.'
The stag steps like a thief
He treads no leaf awry.

'You, Lancelot, come out', they shouted then
'Put by your doxy: come and deal with men.
Surrender straight, we shall not call agen
But break the door and drag you from her bed.'
Sir Lancelot was mail-less torse and head
'O misery,' the Queen wailed, 'We are sped.'
The hounds had caught the lion in his den.
The tufter hounds come in
The dewy covert green.

Sir Lancelot had neither sword nor shield
Nor had the Queen a bar that he could wield
The plotters beat the panels shouting 'Yield.'
'O Queen,' he said, 'They hack the panels through
Wrap thickly round my arm this cloak of blue

Unbolt the door, but, lady, shut it to
The instant I have dealt what must be dealed.'
Dew where the spiders spin
Makes all the down one sheen.

Queen Guinevere, that beauty golden-red,
Round his left arm the mantle thickly spread.
The knights beat on the door with malls of lead
'Leave beating on the door,' said Lancelot,
'I will undo: you need not be so hot.'
'Undo, sir traitor with your royal trot'
Cried Colgreve, 'Yes, unbolt,' Lancelot said.
The dainty nostril tries
Through the green thickets close.

The Queen drew back the bolt: Sir Colgreve thrust
Into the room, crying 'You two who lust . . .'
Lancelot smote him on his brain-pan-crust,
'Shut-to the door,' he cried: then in the face
Of all those strugglers at the opened space
He and the Queen drove back the bolt to place
Colgreve lay quiet as the summer dust.
There where the warm taint lies
The questing nostril goes.

Lancelot took Sir Colgreve's coat of mail
Of bullock's leather fenced with iron scale
He took his sword and said 'This may avail'.
'Come out, you traitors two,' Sir Modred cried.
Then once again the braggart party tried
To burst the door: the lovers flung it wide
Lancelot rushed upon them like a gale.
And now the tufters find
Where the light foot has sped.

Lancelot burst upon them like a squall
He beat them down the stairway to the hall
They struck at him with axe and sword and mall
Wounding each other, being all too close,
There Lancelot dealt Agravaine two blows

279

So that he stumbled sideways, rolled, half-rose
Then dimmed and fell and knew no more at all.
Gone like the startled hind
Across the heather red.

Lancelot charged them like the boar of Thrace
He struck Sir Breuse a slash across the face
Kai flung away his shield and screamed for grace
Modred who ran was wounded in the back
The stag at bay had scattered all the pack
They had no lust for any more attack
Lancelot took the Queen in his embrace.
Across the heathery moor
Purple against black sky
The great stag lifts his brow
And snuffs the moor's expanse.

'Lady,' he said, 'our love is at an end,
None here, henceforth, can ever be my friend
Nor can one doubt what Modred will intend
Death to us both, so therefore come with me
To Joyous Gard my castle by the sea.'
'Ah lovely friend,' she said, 'that must not be
Break nothing further, rather try to mend.'
By tor and combe and howe
His way is and his chance.

'And yet,' she said, 'tomorrow they will bring
Agravaine's death against me to the King
That and our love, and cry for punishing
That I be burnt at stake: if I be cast
Then rescue me and bear me northward fast.'
'I will defend you until death and past'
Lancelot said, 'I pledge you with this ring.'
He sets his eye to point
And leans into the air.

Modred the Messenger

Arthur was in his hunting lodge at rest.
Modred came crying 'Treason manifest.
Lancelot was your lady's secret guest
We broke upon their guilt and caught them there
Lancelot leaped upon us unaware
And, O Gawaine, for pity's sake prepare
For bitter new of him you love the best
Your brother Agravaine

Lancelot killed your brother Agravaine
By two great cruel blows into the brain
But for that death the traitor had been ta'en,
But, seeing Agravaine and Colgreve fall,
And we being slasht, fear came upon us all;
The madman beat us bleeding to the hall
And then returned to love your Queen again.
Lord, see the traitor killed.'

'Now I foresee the breaking of our guild,'
King Arthur said, 'The league we built and build
The candle dwindles and the cup is spilled.
But for the Queen, so wanton and so light,
She shall be burned before tomorrow night.'
'Lord,' Gawaine said, 'such hurry is not right.
Be not so angry nor so hasty-willed:
Lancelot and the Queen

Are friends, you know it, as they long have been,
Because friends meet it surely need not mean
That both are wicked traitors and unclean
As Modred says being savage at his shame.
Modred has been maligning the Queen's name
For years, and now gets payment for the same
And Agravaine deserved his death I ween
For sorting with such mates.'

281

When morning dawned the King in justice sate
Dooming the Queen as cast from her estate
And to be burned as traitor at the gate.
And to Sir Gareth, Gawaine's brother, he
Gave instant order to proceed and be
Chief of the guard that did this cruelty
'When she is shriven let her perish straight
Burn her to ash and then report to me.'

Gareth's Wake

Gawaine the Kind,
The golden-hearted
Was broken-hearted
At Gareth's bier.
The lad lay slain
In the Queen's room
Three candles blowing
Cast strange shadows

Modred stood
In the dark door
Tiptoed there
To watch Gawaine
As a ghost waiting
To drink black blood
His face showed
In the candle-light.

White-armed Queens
Sat beside Gareth
At candle-watch
By the bread and wine
One said, 'Ill
Is the fruit man beareth
By grief he fareth
From life to death.'

One said, 'Ill
Is the fruit man beareth
But this our Gareth
Was good not ill,
As good as light
After a darkness
As sweet as April
After March.'

One said, 'Ill
Is the fruit man beateth
But this our Gareth
Was never fruit
But a green blade
In the April waving
Or an apple blossom
That frost slays.'

Then all three Queens
Sang together
A song of death
By Gareth's bier
Such a song
As the swans dying
On raddled Severn
Sing in death.

'Now the wind is changing,
Now the tide is turning,
Now the sun is setting,
And I, too, change:
I turn seawards
To the red sun sinking
To the unknown waters
There beyond.

What sun dawns
On the night of dying?
What cock crows
To the waking soul?
What branch of peace
To the bird homing?
Song that I sing
Light thou my way.'

Gawaine looked
At his dead brother
'Gareth,' he said,
'Young brother mine

You are but a boy
And now have trodden
Through a dark gate
Still barred to us.

Look, O Queens,
At his maiden's mouth
At his grave brow
Where the thoughts were gentle
The little birds
Would perch on his shoulder
Man-killing stallions
Ate from his hand.

Only last year
He first saw battle
On the windy down
Where skylarks sing
His eyes were bright
As they lookt at danger
The spear-points' line
Below the helms.

Only last month
We sailed together
To the summer island
Of the Sea-Queen
His eyes were bright
At the Queen's beauty
As she sat and sang
Under golden boughs.

Only yesterday
You sat your hunter
At the covertside
When the red stag broke
Your eyes were bright
At the hounds' crying:
Brown September
Upon the beech.

285

Now you are away,
An ache in the heart,
A want unending
Daylong, nightlong;
The ear missing
Voice and footstep;
The soul alone
With no companion.

And he who killed you
Was one you loved,
Nay almost worshipped,
As boys will:
One in the rage
Of love-blindness
Foe a red-gold Queen
With her honour gone.

Here I take oath,
Gareth my brother,
I will be avenged
On Lancelot
I will go seek him
Till I find him
I will kill him
Or he me.'

Modred turned
From the dark door
He muttered 'Well
Is the game beginning
Gwenivere gone
And Arthur broken
His two best knights
At each other's throats.'

The white-armed Queens
By the three candles
Heard horse-hoofs stamp
On the castle yard

One said 'Here
Is the Lone Rider
With the led horse
For Gareth's soul.'

One said 'No
It is Arthur's Fortune
Riding away
To come no more.'
One said 'No
It is Modred riding
To bring in Death
And to wreck the realm.'

When Good King Arthur
An Unpublished Play

[First cast list:]

Howell.	Phipps. Helen. J.M. [Judith Masefield]
Kynon.	Maunder.
Geraint.	Davey. [Leslie Davey*]
Owain.	May. [W.E. May*]
Arthur.	Knips. [or possibly 'Knipe'?]
Merlin.	O.H.
Math.	G.D.B. [G. Dudley Barlow*]
Erbin.	Vincent. [C.E.J. Vincent*]
Odyar.	Brooks.
Lear.	Wood.
Wallt.	Lew. [Lewis Masefield]
Boy.	A.B. or ['B.C.'? or 'E.C.'?: two initials have been written over two others]

[Second cast list:]

When good King Arthur.

A play in ['two'>] three Acts.
by Alfred Jones

Persons

Olwen.	E D D.?
Merlin.	F. Maunder
Math.	G D. Barlow
A ships boy.	N B
Helen.	J. [Judith Masefield]
Geraint	H. Chester

288

Arthur.   Davey. [Leslie Davey*]
Owain.   W May   [W.E. May*]
Odyar   Owens
Wallt   Walsh
Erbin   Hooper
Lear   Bell?
    Sailors. Courtiers.

* Name appears in cast list for the performances of A *King's Daughter* by the
  Hill Players on Friday 25 May and Saturday 26 May 1923 at the Oxford
  Playhouse (English ed. 1, p. vii): all identifications are presumptive.

[Act I.]

(A ship's deck. OLWEN *and* MERLIN.)

OLWEN.   Well met, friend Merlin. Have the poets come?

MERLIN.   Not yet, nor has King Arthur; but the ship
Is ready, as you can see, to take the winner.

OLWEN.   Will you explain exactly what's to happen?

MERLIN.   Yes, it is this: today King Marc of Cornwall
Is holding a contest of poets at Tintagel.
Each kingdom in the country sends one poet
To speak his poetry against the rest.
King Arthur's realm, more fortunate than most,
Has two great poets, Owain and Geraint.
As only one can go, they will compete
Here in this ship to settle which.

OLWEN.   And which,
Do you suppose, will win the right to go?

MERLIN.   I think Geraint; but I am Owain's friend
And certainly prefer his poetry.

OLWEN.   I do myself. And everywhere I go
Men prefer Owain's poems, yet all say
Geraint will win the contest: why is this?

MERLIN.   This is not Gaul, good Olwen; this is Britain.
Owain, dear fellow, is a stranger here,
Wheras Geraint comes from a grandfather
Who had some post around Ambrosius' court.
The world does like a man to have a grandfather.
Besides, between ourselves, both these poets
Are paying homage to King Arthur's ward,
The Princess Helen; this their contest here
May have some bearing on their suits to her.
You must admit that it would not look well
If Owain, sprung from none knows where, should win
The hand of a princess.

OLWEN.   I come from Gaul.
To me, great talent is the only rank.

MERLIN.   But hush . . . here comes the captain of the ship.
Observe him well; he is the type we call
An old sea-dog.

290

OLWEN.   He seems a mad sea-dog.
Would he were muzzled.
                    (Enter MATH, *the ship's captain.*)
    MATH.   Condole with me, friends, on this doleful day.
I call it hard that a God-fearing man,
Who has paid his way these forty years and more,
Should now be ordered by the king, God bless him,
To make his ship a stage for two mad poets
To fight on with their muses and their moonshine,
Not only that, but, when the moonshine ceases
And one bard bull-frog has out-croaked the other,
I've got to take the winner to Tintagel,
Wait till the contest's done and bring him back.
I call it risking ship and good men's lives.
    OLWEN.   It is an honour to carry poets, captain.
    MATH.   May I be saved from all such honour, then.
I know what comes from bringing bards to sea.
I'd rather take a woman, I'd rather take
One of those Finns who raise the wind by whistling.
I know what comes of it – watery sepulchres.
Where's that young devil of a boy of mine?
    BOY.   Here, sir. I'm here.
    MATH.   What use is being here?
You should be there. Get down where you belong.
You dirty young scoundrel, when did you wash your hands?
                    [(BOY *goes down below.*)]
    MATH.   Next to a woman, a Finn or a great poet
A boy's the thing to drive a sailor mad.
(*goes down below after the* BOY) What is that dirty young scoundrel
    doing now?
(*below*) You dirty young scoundrel, you come here not there.
                    (*Whacking and cries are heard off.*)
    MERLIN.   Here comes the Princess Helen. Let us go
To bring the poets to the contest: come.
                    (*They go. Enter the princess* HELEN.)
    HELEN.   How my heart beats to think that in a moment
This contest will be held.
Oh how I hope that Owain will succeed,
[Owain who comes with the sea's strangeness on him,
With poetry as lovely as the sea.]

291

Oh that Geraint, that dull ambitious poet,
Might slip and sprain his ankle, as he comes here.
Geraint to vie with Owain! Nay, some think
[Those judging may prefer him before Owain.]
Geraint with that fat, gloomy brow the winner!
Oh heavens, here comes Geraint. There is no escape.
                    (*Enter* GERAINT.)
    GERAINT.   Oh Princess Helen, omen of success!
I see my inspiration ere I speak.
    HELEN.   Is this the ship in which the court is held?
    GERAINT.   This is the ship, princess, this is the stage,
This is, if one may style it so, the court
In which a scoundrel of base life and birth,
Who dares pay homage to your excellent beauty,
Will be denounced in public to the king.
    HELEN.   No scoundrel has paid homage to me, poet.
If he had, my guardian, being king in Camelot,
Would know how to protect me from his suit.
    GERAINT.   Princess, if I presume, forgive me for it.
My fault is that I love you far too well.
I will not watch a scoundrel trifle with you.
    HELEN.   I cannot listen to such speech as this.
    GERAINT.   But you must listen to a man half-mad
From love of you, princess. This scoundrel tricks you.
Even if I die, I will protect you from him.
This is a letter from the King of Winchester,
My friend, to whom I wrote for information.
(*reads*) 'Owain the poet came here from the East,
Where he left debts, a wife and family.
He disappeared from Winchester last year
Under suspicion of a felony.
Instantly urge King Arthur to arrest him
And send him here for trial.'
    HELEN. Your letter does not move me. Put it away.
Owain the poet did not come from Winchester,
But came from Lympne.
    GERAINT.   It is true he came from Lympne.
Here is a letter from Lympne's governor.
(*reads*) 'The poet Owain was here some months ago . . .
He won the esteem of an old, wealthy lady,

Who made him heir and told him of the fact.
Within a week she died, as was thought, poisoned.
Owain, seizing her goods, made all haste hence.
If he should dare return to Lympne again,
He will be tried for murder. If King Arthur
Should find him in his realm or jurisdiction,
He is besought to seize him in this cause.'
     HERMIT. Yiu are a jealous man and speak from jealousy
    GERAINT. I thank my God I am above such smallness.
But set aside these words from foreigners.
You ask in Camelot here at the Bunch of Grapes
Whether the girl knows Owain, so-called poet.
    HELEN. I will do nothing of the sort, Geraint.
    GERAINT. Ask her to sing the songs he sings about you.
    HELEN. I have heard enough. I will listen to no more.
    GERAINT. You need listen to no more. I have told you all.
    [HELEN. Then tell the king, my guardian, if you dare.]
       (*Enter* MATH *and the other* SAILORS *with the ship's* BOY.)
    GERAINT. Here is your guardian, Merlin and the court.
What I have told to you I dare tell them.
           (*Enter* ARTHUR, MERLIN *and* COURTIERS.)
    GERAINT. Welcome, your Majesty, to this court of poets.
    ARTHUR. Friends, as you know, Geraint and Owain
Meet here to speak their poems before us
Who sit in judgement on them.
Geraint is here. Where is the poet Owain?
    MERLIN. Not at his lodging, lord, I called for him.
Owain is famed for more than poetry.
He is skilled in setting bones and healing sprains.
They told me that he had been called this morning,
To set the broken leg-bone of a child
But left a message that he would be here.
    ARTHUR. He should be punctual to the time appointed.
    GERAINT. I am ready to begin, if you desire.
I will wait till Owain comes, if you prefer.
    ARTHUR. Thank you, Geraint, I do not like to wait
But in a contest the competitors
Should be in presence pitted 'gainst each other.
What say you, Merlin, shall we start or wait?

MERLIN. I am an old, old man with little time.
I say, proceed. But what does girlhood say?
    HELEN. I say, delay.
    ARTHUR.   It is against the rules.
    HELEN. But you as King can make and unmake rules.
Owain is constant to his word, I know,
And for this brief delay a poor child's suffering
Excuses him. He had to help the child.
    ARTHUR. These children govern us.
    MERLIN.   Wait for five minutes.
    ARTHUR. Five minutes seems too much. I will wait three,
If in the meantime you can keep us smiling.
Tell us a story to beguile the minutes.
    HELEN. Once upon a time before the Romans came –
    ARTHUR. Another time, my Helen: here is Owain.
    OWAIN. Forgive me, king, for being late in court.
    ARTHUR. How was the child, whose bones were broken, Owain?
    OWAIN. Lord, I was tricked, for when I reached the house,
Which the man told me of, there was no child . . .
And the messenger slipped from me in the crowd.
    ARTHUR. What a base trick. Enquiry shall be made
Into this matter, for it nearly spoiled
Your chances, Owain, since you were not here
At the time named. Now, Owain and Geraint
Cast lots for which shall speak his poem first.
    MERLIN. First let me call upon the spirits of poetry,
Those muses of delight, whom poets serve,
That they may help our judgements in this case.
Here are the sacred lots. Geraint, throw first.
    GERAINT [(throwing)]. Seven, the luckiest number.
    ARTHUR.   Geraint seven.
    MERLIN. Here are the sacred lots.
    OWAIN [(throwing)].   Three, the blest number.
    ARTHUR. Geraint, having won the throw will speak the first.
Make offering to your muses and begin.
    GERAINT. Spirits of earth and air by whom man lives
Give me your strength and fire that I may prosper.

When Kador came to Stone-on-the-Heath,
He heard the bones talk underneath.

Betwixt owl's cry and fox's bark
He saw the Stone rise up in the dark.
It hove itself to the pit's brink
It stumpt downhill to brook to drink.

Kador peered at the Stone's Lair
Seven Queens were in prison there.
Each of the seven cried to Kador loud
'Save me, and I will be your bride.'

Kador crept to the Queens in the dim
Their white arms entangled him;
Stone-on-the-Heath came back to hole
And crusht Sir Kador body and soul.

    ARTHUR. Geraint has spoken. It is your turn, Owain.
    OWAIN. Oh source of life, oh waters that nourish life,
I call upon your powers to help me speak.

Pendragon Ruthercock
Chained me upon his rock
In the mid sea;
Unhappy me.
          And there for many years
          Sorrow and I were peers,
          Grief was my food,
          And solitude.
Over my head, the mewing
Of gulls; below, the strewing
Of seaweeds flung
By the sea's tongue.
          Until my lover came
          With lithe sword like a flame;
          Those years, that isle,
          Were made worth while.

    ARTHUR. All who were privileged to hear these poems
Are privileged to vote.
    MERLIN.   Spread out the beans.
Here are white beans and black. Each is entitled

To drop one bean, according to his judgement,
A black bean for Geraint, a white for Owain,
Within this urn. Come one by one, but all
Must close their eyes while a man votes:
The ballot must be secret.
[(*All close their eyes, then they vote, by* MERLIN *leading all present,
except the poets, one at a time in silence to the urn; when he comes to
lead* HELEN, *she silently indicates her refusal to vote.*)]

MERLIN.   Now all have voted we will count the votes.

ARTHUR.   The voting is equal, black and white alike.

GERAINT.   The princess did not vote.

MERLIN.   How did you see?

GERAINT.   I did not see, I listened, and am sure
She never left her place.

ARTHUR.   Did you not, Helen?

HELEN.   I did not vote, because I had decided
Before the contest; it would not be fair.

MERLIN.   But you must vote and give the casting vote,
The voting being equal as you see.
Two such great poets must not speak again.
We must decide by this that we have heard.

HELEN.   Oh Guardian, must I vote?

ARTHUR.   As Merlin bids.

GERAINT.   But is it lawful for a woman to vote
In contests of the kind?

ARTHUR.   Do you, a poet,
Ask if men's inspiration should have votes?
Poetry is for all: vote therefore, Helen.

HELEN.   It is not fair that I should vote alone.
Let all revote and I will vote among them.

ARTHUR.   Friends, you can change your choices: vote again.
                    (*They vote.*)

MERLIN.   Five for Geraint, and six for Owain. Therefore
Owain has won the right to go to Cornwall
To today's contest of the British poets.

GERAINT.   Victor by one vote given by a girl.

MERLIN.   You would not have been vexed at the girl's vote
Had it been cast for you.

ARTHUR.   Come with me, Owain,
For you must bear a letter to King Marc.

And bring me back an answer without fail
When you return this evening.
  OWAIN.   I will do so.
  ARTHUR. Good fortune to you. Listen, friends; tonight
When Owain has returned, meet here again.
Another matter must be settled then.
Captain, make ready to set sail.
  MATH   All's ready, lord.
  ARTHUR. Come then, my friends.
       (*All go except* GERAINT *and* MATH.)
  MATH. What other matter must be settled here?
  GERAINT. He means the Laureateship. Curses and furies
Follow this fellow Owain. You heard his poem?
The thing he called his poem?
  MATH.   I liked yours better.
Yours had some sense, but his, good Arthur, his –
All about mewing and spewing and weathercocks.
  GERAINT. At first vote we were equal.
  MATH.   That's what I said.
  GERAINT. Both of us should have gone: the second vote
Was most unjust, and I am cast by a girl.
  MATH. Being King Arthur's ward she is always favoured.
  GERAINT. That is how things of the mind are judged in Britain,
Decided by a little mad princess
Whose head is turned by this stranger and his folly.
You saw him posturing and casting sheep's eyes.
  MATH. I heard him praying to waters and to the seas.
That was enough for me. A sailor's god
Is good dry land, the devil take the fellow.
  GERAINT. That's what I say, the devil take the fellow.
And, if the devil were to take the fellow,
Take him quite soon, take him this evening, captain,
On his way back from visiting King Marc.
You would find me a very steadfast friend.
  MATH. How much is steadfast friend in good hard cash?
  GERAINT. I have a little farm out on the hills.
  MATH. Has it got cows?
  GERAINT.   Three red cows and an orchard.
  MATH. All of my life I've dreamed of having a farm.
  GERAINT. Well, you shall have a farm.

297

MATH.   Yes, but besides,
My sailors would want something, they would want money.
    GERAINT.   I am a poet. I have not much money.
    MATH.   Them that can't pay, friend, didn't ought to break.
I am willing for the farm. But hands need money
And without money I'll not bruit it to them.
    GERAINT.   They would obey your bidding.
    MATH.   Maybe they would,
But they'll not get my bidding without pay.
    GERAINT.   I cannot pay, but listen. At the contest
He will be loaded with rewards: gods curse him.
Golden and silver cups, crystals and jewels.
They will be brought aboard – take them for yours.
No one will know you have them in the ship.
I will declare that Owain stayed in Cornwall
To court another princess in the south.
If that excuse seem insufficient to you,
Say he fell overboard.
Or better still, go for a southern cruise
And don't return here for a year or more.
    MATH.   The king commanded me to return here.
    GERAINT.   You must obey then. We will, therefore, say
That he preferred to stay behind in Cornwall.
    MATH.   And will the cups be mine?
    GERAINT.   All his rewards,
To pay the crew to silence. Can you trust them?
    MATH.   Yes, all but one, perhaps, and him I'll settle.
    GERAINT.   For certain?
    MATH.   Yes, for certain, more than certain.
    GERAINT.   Now, what is your opinion of the plan?
    MATH.   It seems more likely.
    GERAINT.   Likely? What can thwart it?
    MATH.   Nothing that I can see, but in these cases
The things one doesn't see are the main things.
It is the sunken rock that splits the ship.
    GERAINT.   What sunken rock might split us in this case?
    MATH.   Why, that I do not know.
    GERAINT.   Well, what can you imagine?
    MATH.   I leave imagining to poets, lord,
But since you wish to know, I will say this:

298

It's easy to take cups, but to take life
And have no questions asked is not so easy.
    GERAINT. Then take him south and sell him as a slave.
    MATH. Slaves may escape, and bring a story home.
No, there must be no chance of his escape.
'Better be sure than sorry' is our motto.
    GERAINT. 'Better be sure than sorry': a good motto.
But how would you be sure?
    MATH.   Leave that to me.
It's ill luck to talk about these things
Till they are done, with no more need for talk.
But let him come aboard after the contest
And if he come again to Camelot
He'll come by a wet road from a far land.
    GERAINT. Then all is understood?
    MATH.   Yes, watery sepulchres.
    GERAINT. The wet way home and from a far land, captain.
    MATH. The winds blow enough air without your words.
Promise is pretty in the face but Pay me
Is more the man for me.
Before we venture farther in this matter
You give the parchments of the farm to me.
    GERAINT. No, when the deed is done you have the parchments.
    MATH. Not so. No deed is going to be done
Until I have the parchments in my hand.
    GERAINT. Yes, but suppose you do not do the deed?
    MATH. Yes, but suppose I do not have the farm?
    GERAINT. You will have the farm, of course you will have the
        farm.
    MATH. Of course I will have the farm. Give me those
        parchments
Or I will go straight to Arthur here and now
And tell him of your devilry. So choose.
    GERAINT. Who would believe you, captain, if you do?
    MATH. He would believe me, telling it as I'd tell it.
    GERAINT. Well, talk like this between a pair of friends
Leads nowhere, captain. You shall have the parchments.
They are here. They are yours.
    MATH.   Right, sir, I thank you, sir.
I always knew a gentleman when I saw one.

And now your friend, this poet who likes water,
Water, the stuff the cows drink, your friend likes it –
Sir, he shall have enough of what he likes
Up to the chin.
    GERAINT.   Yes?
    MATH.   Watery sepulchres.
    [GERAINT.   That's the idea, but many miles from land,
So that no tide shall cast him on the shore.
    MATH. Better than miles from shore is what I'll do.
I'll put him in the herring shoal down channel.
Measles and chickenpox are child's play to it.
When he's been in the herring shoal an hour
He'll have less meat upon him than a monk
On Easter Saturday.
    GERAINT.   O excellent Math.]
    MATH.   You see this hand? A good hand, is it not?
    GERAINT.   A right good hand.
    MATH.   And there's my hand upon it.
                      (*Curtain.*)

[Act II.]

[(*The ship's deck.* MATH *and* ODYAR.)]

    MATH.   Now that that Owain is at supper below
Tell me about the contest that he won.
    ODYAR.   It was a contest, sir, of seven poets
Chosen by all the kings within this island.
His poem was the best and the best spoken.
I never heard such cheering in my life.
The other poets, who had been competing,
Took off their crowns and laid them at his feet
And then King Marc himself gave him a crown.
    OATH.   You mean he won seven crowns for speaking poems?
    ODYAR.   Yes, seven crowns, but only one is gold.
The rest are made of that green kitchen stuff,
Which they cook pork with in the eating-houses.
    MATH.   He had more than a crown and kitchen stuff. Look here.
Look at these bales and boxes and this gear,

Caskets and barracoes and kilderkins
Stuffed with I know not what. All these are his.

   ODYAR.   These were from all the people whom he pleased.
They flung him jewels, brooches, ear-rings, necklets,
All they were wearing. Then they ran indoors
And fetched out linens, woollens, furs and silks,
Out of their cupboards or their beds or any place.
But that was not enough — no, down they went,
Down to their cellars and got wine for him.
[Gold-work and silver-work and oil and victuals
And precious cloths from Egypt, spices and coral.
And that thing there, sealed up inside the pot,
The greatest treasure in the land, they said,
A lock of hair, they said, from Homer's forehead.]
But there are all the things, as you can see,
[They brought to him.

   MATH.   For saying just one poem.

   ODYAR.   He made the poem first before he said it.]

   MATH.   Why, it's enough to keep a working man
In luxury for all his whole life long.

   ODYAR.   Well, sir: they're landsmen: you know what landsmen
      are.

   MATH.   They never earn their jewels, as we do,
So they fling them away to the first comer.
[It's waste like this which causes revolution.]
[What will he do with it, when he has it, Odyar?
I know these poets. Light come, light go with them.
What men don't work to earn they never value.]

                   (Enter WALLT, [LEAR] and ERBIN.)

   MATH.   Look at these pretty things given to Owain,
Because he spoke a poem – gold, silk, scarlet,
All these for stringing twenty words together,
While men like us, who do the work of the world,
Go in our rags and sunburn.

   WALLT.   That's the truth
And it's a cruel shame, that's what I say.

   ERBIN.   These landsmen should be just before they are generous.

   MATH.   Here is a helmet, Here's a sort of tunic
And here's a sword.

   ODYAR.   Put them on, captain.

(*He puts them on.*)

LEAR. They become you better, captain, than that fellow.

MATH. I hope they do. I'd be sorry if they didn't.

Now here is something to give your girl in port

And here is something for you and something for you.

ERBIN. But, captain, all these things belong to him.

MATH. They don't belong to him. Has he worked for them?

No. Has he pulled and rowed for them? Not he.

Could he have gone to get them without us?

No, he'd have drowned. Would he and they be here,

But for our bringing them? Of course, they would not.

Is he entitled to them, therefore? No.

Are we entitled to them then?

    ODYAR.   Of course, sir.

WALLT. Yes, if we had our rights.

    ODYAR.   We are entitled.

LEAR. Better entitled than he is, anyway.

ERBIN. I am not so sure. I like to go by rules.

The rules say they are his and, if he chooses

To give me one of them, then I will take it.

Till then they are his and I will do without.

MATH. So Brother Erbin obliges with a sermon.

Get forward out of this and, when you're forward,

Shove your head down between your knees and keep it down

So I don't see it or hear it, for, if I see it

Or hear it, I tell you I'll hit it with my stick

So quick and hard you'll think the fish are singing.

(ERBIN *goes.*)

MATH. I've had my eye on Erbin for some time.

Now, shipmates, you and I have sailed together

Some long years and understand each other.

What is to stop our taking all this gear?

ODYAR. Why, I suppose he would.

MATH.   How could he, Odyar?

We ar four and he is one. If one of us

Should trip him up, two catch him by both arms,

And then the fourth just run a knife-point in

Between his ribs, then who could stop our taking?

LEAR. Why, I suppose King Arthur would.

MATH.   King Arthur!

302

ODYAR. I don't say that there's anything to stop us,
But one point in your speech I don't quite like,
That about knives' points in between the ribs.
A knife-point leaves a mark which can't be changed
And in these tides a body drifts and drifts.
Sooner or later it always comes ashore
And then it's recognised and there's the mark.
A̶n̶d̶ ̶t̶h̶e̶n̶ ̶m̶e̶n̶ ̶a̶s̶k̶ ̶H̶o̶w̶ ̶d̶i̶d̶ ̶h̶e̶ ̶g̶e̶t̶ ̶t̶h̶e̶ ̶m̶a̶r̶k̶?
And who were the last folks seen with him? Who did it?
Those sailors were the last, people would say.
    WALLT. That's true. The body shouldn't have a mark.
    MATH. Well, why not sew him up in an old sail
And weight him down with ballast or spare anchor?
    LEAR. Captain, you never can depend on sewing.
Besides, captain, corpses can undo the stitches.
I knew a sailor once, who killed his captain,
And said he died of fever in the night
And sewed him up in canvas with some ballast.
But the corpse undid the stitches and followed us
And, when we came to port, denounced the murderer.
    MATH. Well, we'll not knife nor give him burial.
Since we are four and the watch below four more
And he is only one, he shall walk the plank
And then these things will all be ours for ever.
When we reach Camelot we'll tell King Arthur
How when he won the contest at Tintagel
He said he'd stay there till he'd spent the money
But asked us to return to bring the news.
    ODYAR. That is the finest story we could tell.
You could not tell a finer story than that.
    WALLT. But what about these things, captain, this treasure?
    MATH. We will divide them quietly tonight.
But hush, the gentleman is coming on deck.
                    (Enter OWAIN.)
    MATH. Well, sir, you see us well upon our course,
Right in mid-channel with a prosperous wind.
We shall be safe in Camelot by dark.
You are not feeling the motion of the ship?
    OWAIN. No, captain, I am accustomed to the sea.
    MATH. I have been looking at your treasures, sir,

303

Rich treasures richly worthy of a poet.
I hope you are satisfied with our rough sea victuals.
Did my boy attendant serve you as you wished?

    OWAIN. He was a charming lad who served me well.

    MATH. Could I offer you another cup of wine?

    OWAIN. No, no more wine.

    MATH.   A little fruit, perhaps,
Might be wholesome or soothing to the voice?

    OWAIN. Nothing whatever, thank you kindly, captain.

    MATH. You would not like to lie down and rest a little
Before we come to Camelot?

    OWAIN.   No thank you.
I would prefer to stay here where I am.

    MATH. Very good, sir. Will you excuse me, sir,
If I repeat that last remark of yours
To my good crew? Men, did you here his last:
That he would prefer to stay here where he is?

    ODYAR.
    WALLT. Yes, sir; we heard what he said. We heard him, sir.

    MATH. Did it not strike you as a funny remark?

    ODYAR.
    WALLT. Yes, sir, a very funny remark indeed.

    OWAIN. I do not see why it should be funny to you.

    MATH. He does not see why it is funny to us.
Perhaps, sir, you will permit me to explain.
You would prefer to stay here where you are.
We should prefer that you go there and stay there.

    OWAIN. Do you mean down below?

    MATH.   Yes, down below,
Down below into the sea that you're so fond of.
Here is a little pretty gangway, sir,
And a neat plank that leads out to the sea.
And now perhaps you'll go.

    OWAIN.   I understand.
I have heard that sailors joke with landsmen thus
To make them pay their footing. I will pay.
Some of this treasure won this afternoon
Shall now be yours.

    MATH.   Some of the treasure shall.
You speak the truth and nothing but the truth.

304

Only our resolution has been taken
That you shall leave this ship and leave the treasure.
You are a clever man, so people say,
And see that we are four and you are one.
True, you might struggle and hurt one of us,
But you are much too much a gentleman
To force us into such unpleasantness.
There is the gangway, sir; there is the sea,
So wet, so clear, so green, so beautiful,
It makes a man's mouth water just to look at it.
Why linger on base planks with tarry seamen
With all that bubbling freedom at your beck?
Make up your mind to it and go to it,
For, if you can't while I count ten, we'll put you.
One, two, three, four.
    OWAIN.   Yes, you are four and I
Am only one. Remember that the gods
Are always with the weaker.
    MATH.   Well, we'll chance them.
    OWAIN. One against four is not such mighty odds.
    MATH. No, I agree, but we are more than four.
                    (*Enter other* SEAMEN.)
    MATH. Here's five, here's six, here's seven and here's eight,
The watch below, which you forgot to reckon.
You may admit that eight to one is odds.
    OWAIN. Not when the gods are on the one man's side.
    MATH. Well, as I said, we'll risk the help of the gods.
Seize him, you men. Well, did the gods protest?
    OWAIN. The gods are helping more than you suppose.
    MATH. I am glad you are satisfied, for surely we are.
                    (*Enter* GERAINT.)
    GERAINT. Well, wandering poet, you who came from nowhere,
You are soon going back where you belong.
You thought you won our contest, did you not?
The final verdict seems to come to me.
    OWAIN. This is not the final verdict.
    GERAINT.   You think not?
Friend, your last earthly contest is decided.
I have another contest still to try,
When I pay court to the sweet princess Helen

And win the favour that she used to give me
Before your beggarly rags came out of Brittany.
    OWAIN. You do not think that she, who has known me,
Will take any more interest in you?
This incident, I think, is of your planning?
    GERAINT. As you suppose.
    OWAIN.   Well, she will know of it.
    GERAINT. How will she know of it?
    OWAIN.   By the gods,
Who judge of murder and ever make it known.
    GERAINT. This little episode will never be known.
When this ship reaches Camelot we shall say
That you stayed in Tintagel with King Marc.
Nobody knows that you are in this ship,
Nobody knows that I am in this ship,
Except these sailors, who will have your wealth
To bribe them to keep silence, as they will.
Now we will tie you to the gangway rail,
That you may look upon the sea you loved
And make your foolish mind ready for death.
And we will spread this rainment and these purples
Upon the decks and feast on your good things.
      (*The* SAILORS *spread cloths upon the deck. The* BOY *appears.*)
MATH. (*to the* BOY). You dirty young scoundrel, get you down below
And don't come up again until I call.
               [(*The* BOY *goes below.*)]
    MATH. Now sit round, brothers, let us eat and drink.
Since the guest will not sit, being too proud,
He shall have his dinner standing. Take it, poet.
          (*They fling scraps at* OWAIN.)
    MATH. Now let us drink to our good company.
Since Owain will not drink, give him the dregs.
          (*They fling the dregs at* OWAIN.)
MATH. Now Sir Geraint, will you not sing a song
And let us sing the chorus while we feast?
GERAINT. Gladly, good Captain, but my song will be
A scurvy one, about this scurvy songbird.
MATH. Silence, all hands; but join the chorus, boys.
GERAINT [(*singing, to the tune 'Shenandoah'*)].
Owain, I love to see you shaking.

306

CHORUS. Away, you rotten poet.
GERAINT. Your cheeks are white, your knees are quaking.
CHORUS. Away, you're bound to go
Beneath the shining water.
GERAINT. You thought you'd taken all the prizes.
CHORUS. Away, you rotten poet.
GERAINT. But now you've met with some surprises.
CHORUS. Away, you're bound to go
Beneath the shining water.
GERAINT. Soon little herrings will be picking.
CHORUS. Away, you rotten poet.
GERAINT. Unless such carrion makes them sicken.
CHORUS. Away, you're bound to go
Beneath the shining water.
MATH. Geraint will wear your wedding dress
CHORUS. Away, you rotten poet.
MATH. And up and marry your princess.
CHORUS. Away, you're bound to go
Beneath the shining water.
GERAINT. Brothers, since Brother Poet does not join us
Nor entertain us at our simple feast,
Should he stay any longer here?
WALLT.   No, let him swim.
ODYAR. Let the brute swim and go the wet way home.
LEAR. Make him a water spaniel, Captain Math.
WALLT. Overboard with him. Take his lashings off.
MATH. Take off his ropes. We will not waste good rope.
Now, sir, we cannot keep you any longer.
There lies your pleasant path all clear before you.
GERAINT. Any last message to the princess Helen?
OWAIN. Captain, I have a last request to make.
Before I die I would like to speak a poem.
MATH. What do you say, men?
ODYAR.   That sounds reasonable.
LEAR. Refuse him, captain, He'll put a curse on it.
ODYAR. He wouldn't put a curse.
LEAR.   Don't trust him, captain.
A dying man will always put a curse
And a curse sticks.

OWAIN.   But you would hear the poem
And kill me, if it sounded like a curse.
    LEAR.   You never said a truer word than that.
But how should we know if it were a curse
Wrapped up in cunning language?
    OWAIN.   The poet here
Could tell you if a curse were in my poem.
    GERAINT.   That is the truth, I could. In any case,
The curse or curses of so feeble a poet
Would not afflict us much.
    LEAR.   Well, I'm against it.
    MATH.   Are you against it? You're not paid, my son,
To be for or against, but as I say.
Go on, then. Speak your poem.
    GERAINT.   The swan-song of the dying foreign swan.
    WALLT.   You had better fix a time for him to stop,
Else he'll go on till we reach Camelot.
    GERAINT.   Brevity is the soul of poetry.
    MATH.   Well, how long shall we say? An hour or so?
    LEAR.   Five minutes.
    WALLT.   At the most.
    GERAINT.   I say one minute.
    MATH.   One minute is enough in sober conscience.
You, Wallt or Odyar, fetch the minute glass.
Now, poet, watch the minute glass I hold.
The glass is clear, what sailors call Clear Glass.
When I say Turn, and the sand begins to run,
Begin your poem. When the sand has run,
I'll cry 'Clear Glass' and you will stop your poem
And you'll stop, too. Get ready then to start.
    LEAR.   Let us sit down where we can see the glass.
    WALLT.   What will the poet's poem be about?
    GERAINT.   It will be hard for any man to say
What this man's poems are about or not.
    MATH.   Stand up. A Clear Glass; Turn. Begin your poem.
    OWAIN.   O marvellous water, from whom life proceeds,
Make all the tides in me one with your tide,
That I may follow as the moon may guide,
At one with that great urge
Which brims each gully of the land and feeds

308

On the bare granite with the white-tootht surge
And whelms alike man's patience and his pride.
So, being one with you, I shall go on,
Part of an impulse deeper than the ken
Of mortals, at the source,
Deeper than any sunbeam ever shone,
Where Life itself, beginning, draws the force
To grow from rootless lichen into men

MATH. The sands are running out. It is Clear Glass.
GERAINT. Your poetry has troubled its last ears
And sickened its last hearers.
MATH.   It is time.
Is there a ship in sight?
LEAR.   No ship in sight, sir.
MATH. We are far out at sea: but men can swim.
GERAINT. He could not swim to Camelot, I take it.
MATH. No, but when men are forced, they can swim far,
Float, or tread water: they can be picked up.
GERAINT. Not in these northern waters, in the cold.
The cramp destroys them. And, besides, look there.
MATH. Sharks, by the deep; sharks, boys, the very thing.
WALLT. Just like an answer to a prayer, my lord.
ODYAR. Now, since you cannot want your neckerchief
I'll make so bold. (*He takes* OWAIN'S *scarf.*)
MATH.   Stand by, lads; one, two, three
Over he goes. Heave ho.
ALL HANDS.   Heave ho; away.
                (*They heave* OWAIN *over the side.*)
GERAINT. I hope you will enjoy your evening swim.
MATH. He is not swimming, look: but turns to float.
GERAINT. He will soon weary of that in these cold seas.
Could you not sail the ship clean over him?
MATH. No, I'll not do a murder for any man.
GERAINT. It's not murder: it's only making certain.
MATH. It would bring bad luck to the ship: I will not do it.
WALLT. There is no need: the sharks are heading for him.
MATH. Straight for him: see. They are never so far north
Unless with herring-shoals.
GERAINT.   He does not see them.

MATH. They can't see him, nor smell him, nor yet hear him.
But yet they know he is there. Come from the rail
The last scrunch is a nasty sight to see.
    GERAINT. I want to see and hear. There they come, there.
    WALLT. There he rolls over to his back to bite.
    GERAINT. He got him. Yes, the big gray shark has got him.
    MATH. As neat as you could wish: pulled him clean up.
    GERAINT. I wish he had screamed, or shown his terror first.
    MATH. He never knew, he had not time to know
He thought the shark was floating seaweed, likely;
Then, the next instant, he was Abraham's own.
The prettiest neatest thing I ever saw.
[(Enter BOY.)]

    MATH. Hide all these treasures in the after-locker.
And you, you little devil of a boy,
What are you doing here? To keep you quiet
You shall be hidden in the sail-locker.
[And if you squeal before we set you free
Or mention anything to anybody . . .
It will be a scarlet necktie.
    ODYAR.   Made with a knife.
    WALLT. Made with a knife.
    LEAR.   Made with a jagged knife.
    MATH. Made with a battle-axe: get down below.]
Gag him, there, you: and now, to Camelot.
(Curtain.)

[Act III.]

[(The ship's deck. MATH, WALLT, LEAR and ODYAR.)]

    MATH. Here we are safe in Camelot again
And there upon the wharf, waiting for us,
Is good King Arthur and the Christian court.
They want to question with us by their looks.
Boys, answer no man's questions. Let me answer.
Thrust out the gang-plank for our royal king.
Shipmates, long live King Arthur.
    WALLT.
    ODYAR. Long live King Arthur and his noble queen.
    LEAR.

310

(*Enter* ARTHUR, HELEN, *and the* COURTIERS.)

ARTHUR. I thank you, sailors, for your loyal welcome.
I come to hear the story of the contest.
Which poet won?

MATH. The poet Owain, lord.

ARTHUR. Where is he, then?

MATH. He would not come with us, but sent us word
He meant to stay in Cornwall with King Marc.

ARTHUR. He promised that he would return with you.

MATH. Success turns people's heads, they forget promises.

ARTHUR. But he has known success before. Besides,
His head is much too clever to be turned.
I must know more. Speak, tell me all the case.

MATH. Why, my good king, there is not much to tell.
He won the contest, he was given the prize
And all the Cornish folk seemed to go mad
And gave him gifts – I don't know what they were –
But they were many and rich, so people said,
And feasted him with wine till he was flighty
And when he came on board he said to me
Something I wouldn't like to tell your Grace.
What should have not been said should not be told.
He was a young man and he had been dining.

ARTHUR. Dining or not, what did he say to you?

MATH. Lord, it is not for me to say such things
Without a promise that I bear no blame.

ARTHUR. I shall not blame you for repeating words
Spoken by someone else, not by yourself.

MATH. Don't think that he was free to speak such words.
But that my men took hold of me to check me,
I would have torn his teeth out of his mouth
For uttering such-like words about your Grace.
Isn't that true, men? Didn't you have to hold me?

ODYAR. That's true, my lord. We had to hold him down.

WALLT. 'Let me get at him, friends,' he said to us.

LEAR. 'Let me get at him till I smash his teeth
Clean down his brazen throat for speaking so.'

MATH. Those were the very words I used, King Arthur.
I wouldn't pass an insult to your Grace.

311

That is my nature and it always was.
These men will tell you if it isn't my nature.
    ODYAR. It was his nature always, from a child.
    ARTHUR. Well, we will leave your nature as it is.
No doubt it does you credit. Now, come tell me
What was it that this poet said of me?
    MATH. He said, 'I'll come no more to beggerly Camelot,
But stay in good Tintagel, where the king
Knows how to welcome poets like myself.'
He said, 'Go tell your miserly King Arthur,
The beggerly lousy King,' he said, 'King Arthur,
That, if he wants a poet, he must pay him.
But since I know my value, I shall stay
Where others know it, too.' That's what he said.
Now these were rude words full of insolence,
But rude words do not matter to a man,
And to a mighty king they matter less;
But when a man speaks rudeness of a lady
Then my blood boils. Always from a child it did.
And, if, King Arthur, you took your ships of war
And brought that fellow Owain from Tintagel
And had him pulled in two between two ships,
Each going a different way, why even then
You would not give him more than his deserts
For speaking what he spoke of the princess.
    ARTHUR. Omit all that he said of our princess.
    HELEN. I wish to hear all that he said of her.
    ARTHUR. You must not hear.
    HELEN.   Guardian, I must insist.
Words have been spoken publicly about me.
Now let them be repeated, so that I
Can publicly refute them. If he brings charges,
I wish to answer them.
    ARTHUR.   He brought no charges.
    HELEN. From the ship-captain's words it seems he did
And since the reported speaker is my friend
I will examine further.
Now here is Merlin, learned in the law.
Merlin, have I not right to hear the words?
    MERLIN. Absolute right.

HELEN.   Then let me swear these witnesses.
ARTHUR.   No need to swear. This is no law-court, girl.
The captain tells the tale of what was said.
HELEN.   Where truth is sifted in King Arthur's presence
It is a court of law.
ARTHUR.   Well, if you insist,
Let the man swear, then. Will you swear him, Merlin?
MERLIN.   I swear by fire and air and earth and water.
MATH.   I swear by fire and air and earth and water.
MERLIN.   To tell the truth that is demanded of me.
MATH.   To tell the truth that is demanded of me.
MERLIN.   And if I lie in any particle . . .
MATH.   And if I lie in any particle . . .
MERLIN.   May the four elements destroy me utterly.
MATH.   May the four elements destroy me utterly.
ARTHUR.   Begin then, captain. What did Owain say
Against or of the princess Helen here?
MATH.   It wasn't what he said but what he sang.
ARTHUR.   What was it he sang of the princess?
MATH.   He made some verses about the princess' face.
HELEN.   What verses did he make about my face?
MATH.   He began by saying verses about your dress.
HELEN.   What did he say of that?
MATH.   He said you spent
More upon dress than any other lady.
ARTHUR.   No harm in that.
MATH.   'But even so', he said,
'She always looks like a ragbag or a scarecrow.'
HELEN.   What other verses did he make about me?
MATH.   One of his verses said you'd a face like a fish.
Then he said poetry about your hair.
He said it was like to teased-out rope-yarn,
And even at that it wasn't yours, he said,
And changed its colour according to the princes
Who happened to be staying at the court.
One of his verses was about your skin.
He said that it was like a dog-fish skin
And could be used for cleaning rusty metal
Or might be used so, if it weren't so painted.
And one of his verses . . . but I won't repeat that.

313

HELEN. You are sworn to. Speak.

MATH.   No, lady, no, forgive me.
But luckily we had on board a man,
Who answered the foul slander of the drunkard
In the only way such ruffians understand.
A man on board dared to defend you, lady.
That man is here, the king's poet Geraint.
                    [(*Enter* GERAINT.)]

MATH. This is the man, King Arthur and Princess.
While we, poor men, awed by the poet's rank,
Could only gnash our teeth in impotent fury,
He leaped upon your dear ward's foul traducer
And gave him the thorough thrashing he deserved.

ARTHUR. Geraint on board? What brought you in the ship?

GERAINT. I as a poet, although deemed unworthy,
Wished to be present at the contest, lord.
Owain spoke beautifully and movingly.
I am his rival, but I see his merit.
He well deserved the prize. It is not talent
That he is lacking in, but character.
After his victory, being flown with wine
And talking foully, as he often does,
It was my privilege, great lord and king,
To defend the fame of this most sweet princess.

ARTHUR. Give me your hand, Geraint. I thank you for it.
You well deserve reward for what you did,
A great reward, the greatest in my power.

MATH. He deserves the hand of your princess, oh king.

ODYAR. Yes, king, he deserves the hand of your princess.

WALLT. The princess Helen and our good Geraint.

LEAR. Noble Geraint and the princess for ever.

GERAINT. Your Majesty, these simple men, my friends,
Have claimed for me what I, a humble poet,
Should never have presumed to ask you for,
But now that they have spoken for me, king,
I humbly dare petition for myself.
I kneeling ask for the princess's hand.
                    (*Enter* ERBIN.)

ERBIN. Your Majesty, don't be deceived by scoundrels.
You have been listening to lies, your Majesty.

314

These men are murderers, they murdered Owain.
This kneeling dog, Geraint, was the ringleader.
Question him, King: Arrest him.
    ARTHUR.   What man is this?
Who dares to interrupt us in our session?
    MATH. Seize him there, starboard watch, before he starts.
He's a poor madman, lord, religious-mad,
Gone totty in the poll — collar him, follows
From hearing sermons. Mind he doesn't bite.
    WALLT. Bite, would you? Bite?
    LEAR.   Trip him up, quickly.
    ODYAR.   Down.
I've got him down.
    ERBIN.   I am not mad, King Arthur.
They murdered him for gold.
    ODYAR.   I've gagged him, lord.
    MATH. Did he bite any of you?
    LEAR.   No, sir: no.
    MATH. Let me see your hands: better sure than sorry.
No: there's no mark of teeth, I thank my stars.
And you thank yours –
He bit a calf in Camelot market once
And three weeks afterwards the calf went mad
And bit a flock of sheep and the sheep went mad.
Lord, there was hell to pay all over Mendip
With those sheep foaming at the mouth and biting.
One of them met my wife on a Sunday evening . . .
Is he secure? Carry him down below.
                  (ERBIN *is removed*.)
    MATH. I took him from the madhouse out of pity
For his poor mother. We lock him up below
In port, because he scares folk, but today
He managed to break loose. I'm sorry, lord.
I'm truly grieved for such a scene to happen,
Before this fair young lady and yourself.
A painful sight, to see what men become.
    GERAINT. Perhaps this purse might pay for surgeons for him.
    MATH. Thank you, sir, truly.
    ARTHUR [(*to* HELEN)]. Come aside while I speak with you.
Helen, this worthy poet, proven our friend,

Having defended you from evil speakers,
Asks for the honour of your hand in marriage.
What do you answer to his suit?
    HELEN.   I? Nothing.
Not even the honour of a denial.
    ARTHUR.   These are hard words. Not many months ago
You gave Geraint your favour, did you not?
Then Owain, I suppose, altered the case.
You have now heard how Owain mocks at you.
So put him from your thought.
    HELEN.   My thought's myself
I cannot put it from me if I would.
    ARTHUR.   Girl, was there ever any talk of love
Between yourself and Owain?
    HELEN.   Never, my lord,
[He is my friend, and I defend him here
Against all who attack him in his absence.]
    ARTHUR.   Still; you were often with him. There's a proverb:–
One of each two companions falls in love.
I do not blame you, but I blame myself
For having let you be so much with Owain.
These tales are the result.
    HELEN.   You don't believe them?
    ARTHUR.   Whether these stories are the truth or not
Your name and through yours ours is dragged through mud.
I should be glad to silence evil tongues
By marrying you forthwith to one who loves you.
That is my attitude. Now, what is yours?
You do not like Geraint. Give me some reason.
    HELEN.   His face and touch and then the thought of him.
Besides, he is a treacherous jealous rival
Of Owain.
    ARTHUR.   Let us examine both your epithets.
Where is his jealousy, where his treachery?
You heard this good sea-captain on his oath
Tell a plain tale: Geraint told a plain tale:
And I am grieved to say a likely tale
That Owain, drunk with wine, foully traduced us
Till Geraint checked him. If the tale be false,
Why has not Owain kept his plighted word,

Returned to me, and to yourself, moreover,
His friend, whose vote gave him the victory?
Explain his absence. Why is he not here?
    HELEN. My lord, I do not know but Geraint knows.
    ARTHUR. Geraint has told us.
    HELEN.   He has told you lies.
    ARTHUR. One like Geraint would never commit perjury.
    HELEN. He was not sworn.
    ARTHUR.   It's true, he was not sworn.
    HELEN. Then swear him, my lord, let him make his oath
That what he says is true.
    ARTHUR.   That is absurd.
I know Geraint. I cannot so insult him
As to suspect his word in such a case.
Remember that he uttered nothing willingly.
He did not speak save to confirm the captain.
    HELEN. Then at the least do not believe the captain,
Till you have made enquiries in Tintagel.
    ARTHUR. That is a difficult thing for me to do.
Owain is not my subject but a stranger.
I know not what to think. Long before this,
Very strange tales were told me about Owain,
Whom no-one knows, remember. These last tales,
They might be false . . .
    HELEN.   They are.
    ARTHUR.   I hope so, Helen,
But coming as they do, vouched for and sworn to,
You being our princess and I the King,
I cannot stoop to question what is sworn.
    HELEN. Then you believe these lies?
    ARTHUR.   Gently, my daughter.
I think that poets often have two sides,
One more profound than ours and one less good.
That may be so with Owain.
    HELEN.   And Geraint.
    ARTHUR. Geraint is waiting for an answer here.
Like him or not, he offers all he has
And needs an answer from you.
    HELEN. I will not answer him, because I know
Deep down within me that the man is false.

317

ARTHUR. Girl, what you call your knowledge may be prejudice.
You cannot slight a good man's love for nothing.
    HELEN. Good, my lord? He is evil to the bone.
    ARTHUR. You speak from the vexation of the moment.
    HELEN. I speak out of the wisdom of my grief.
    ARTHUR. Helen, there is a law which I as king
Am sworn to keep enforced. Rebellious wards
May be imprisoned within nunneries.
    HELEN. Very well, my lord, send me to a nunnery.
    ARTHUR. No, Helen, no. A nunnery will not serve.
Let Merlin who is gentler than myself
Reason with you. Come, Merlin, plead with her.
Geraint offers his hand.
    HELEN.   Which I refuse.
    MERLIN. For reasons?
    HELEN.   No, for deeper cause; for instincts.
I will not listen to your reasons, Merlin,
I know them all, that he is rich, accomplisht,
Well-thought-of, handsome, and King Arthur's favourite.
    [MERLIN. Dowered with poetry, which some call God's gift] . . .
    HELEN. All that is nothing to me; less than nothing. . .
My heart is given to another man.
Even if he strike me in the face, as now . . .
I shall not love another, while I live.
    MERLIN. My lord and King, wisdom herself is helpless
Against three things: love, youth, sincerity.
Give up all hope, my lord: you, too, Geraint.
    [GERAINT. Your majesty, I see well how it is.
The princess has been shaken by the news.]
    ARTHUR. Geraint, I will not tell you 'Give up hope'.
But rather, for the moment, 'Give up trying'.
This is not now the time to press your suit,
So leave it till a more propitious time.
But in the meantime, friends, there is a matter
To be decided by ourselves and you.
We have a post about our court at Camelot,
Paid but by glory and a ton of wine,
I mean the Poet Laureateship. This post
Is vacant at the moment, as you know.
I meant to keep it vacant till tonight

318

And offer it to Owain – no, not offer,
Confer it, as a right. He is not here
Nor any word from him,
In spite of solemn promise to myself.
Geraint, as you have heard, has earned our thanks.
His poetry has not less worth than Owain's
And his reward this evening has been scant.
Now therefore, I suggest to all of you
That the proud office of the Laureateship
Should be conferred upon Geraint. What say you?

MATH. Geraint, Geraint for Poet Laureate!

WALLT. A wise choice!

ODYAR. Let Geraint be Laureate!

LEAR. Long live the noble Laureate, Geraint!

ARTHUR. Merlin, you have the crown of poet's bay
With which we crown our Laureates on election.

MERLIN. This is the crown and worthy to be worn.
The green bay, whence it sprang, grows on the tomb
Of Constans, called the sweet-tongued from his poems.
Upon that fragrant tomb of the great dead
Young poets kneel to pray that the sweet power
May fall on them.

ARTHUR. Come forward then, Geraint,
Kneel down before us while we crown you Laureate
According to the rite made centuries since.

GERAINT. I thank you, lord, and you whose friendly voices
Confer this crown, earth's mightiest prize, upon me.
All of my life's ambitions and deep dreams
Have been but this – to win a crown of poesy.

MERLIN. Take the crown, King. The King confers the crown.

ARTHUR. Hear, all my lords and commons gathered round;
We are about to consecrate this poet
The Laureate of this realm.

MATH *and* SAILORS. Long live Geraint!

ARTHUR. Bend down your head, Geraint,
That I may crown you. I here pronounce
According to the rite –

(*Enter* SOOTHSAYER *hurriedly.*)

SOOTHSAYER. Stay, good King Arthur, stay.

MERLIN. Who bids King Arthur stay?

319

ARTHUR.   Who are you, fellow?
SOOTHSAYER. I am a soothsayer with a message for you.
[ARTHUR. Utter your message when I have conferred the crown.
SOOTHSAYER. My message must be said before you do so.]
MATH. Here's a high-stomached one, with 'must be said'.
GERAINT. Lord, shall we lay him under an arrest?
MATH. Let us heave him off the ship, my lord.
Come, you, get off the ship, where you belong.
SOOTHSAYER. My lord, first let me speak, let me convince you
That I am worth the hearing. Stand aside.
[ARTHUR. You are interrupting us in performing a rite.]
SOOTHSAYER. Nothing but holy and important matter
Would make a man dare interrupt a king.
ARTHUR. That is well answered, stranger: but a stranger
Should not be heard in public until bidden.
MERLIN. My lord, a stranger should be always heard,
Because the gods have always come as strangers.
ARTHUR. I am corrected: well remembered, Merlin.
Stranger, begin. I give you leave to speak.
SOOTHSAYER. My lord, will you first bid this sea-farer
To come a little forward into sight?
ARTHUR. Stand forward, captain. Let us look at you.
SOOTHSAYER. Will you observe the kind of cloak he wears?
ARTHUR. I see the kind of cloak. What of it, man?
SOOTHSAYER. It is a cloak of splendour and rich woof,
Too splendid for a mere sea-captain's cloak.
MATH. Of course it is. It is a cloak of ceremony.
I put it on to wear before the king.
SOOTHSAYER. Is there a little mark within the cloak?
MATH. I dare say there are many little marks.
SOOTHSAYER. I say there is one mark, one mark only.
MATH. I dare say there is one. I have not looked.
This cloak is one I very seldom wear.
It is above my place as a sea-captain.
I keep it for the days of festival.
SOOTHSAYER. Would you mind saying where you got the cloak?
MATH. No, not at all.
SOOTHSAYER.   Then tell us where you got it.
MATH. Among the eastern islands five years past.
Five years it was, fellows, or was it six?

LEAR. Six, I think, captain.

WALLT.   Six or was it seven?

ODYAR. It was that Cretan voyage, six years past.

MATH. Odyar is right. It was that Cretan voyage
Six years ago.

SOOTHSAYER. Then, if it comes from Crete,
The mark it bears should be a Cretan mark.
You Merlin, who are said to know all mischon,
What is the Cretan symbol, can you tell us?

MERLIN. Of old, it was a double-headed axe,
Now, five red crosses and two gold lilies.

SOOTHSAYER. What is the mark of Marc, the king of Cornwall?

MERLIN. A white disc with three flecks of ermine's tails.

SOOTHSAYER. I say the captain's cloak bears King Marc's mark,
Not any mark of Crete.

MATH.   Maybe it does.
I do not know what mark it has, nor care.
What's all this talk of marks and double axes?

ARTHUR. Take off your cloak, captain. Let's see the mark.

MERLIN. It is the Cornish symbol, not the Cretan.

ARTHUR. It is, indeed, the Cornish sign.

MATH.   What then?
Cloaks go to Crete from Cornwall every day.
Besides a juggler carries marks in's sleeve
And sticks them where he will.

ARTHUR.   The mark proves nothing.

SOOTHSAYER. King, having prophesied about the mark
May I but hold the cloak a little moment?
It may suggest more things to be revealed.

ARTHUR. I do not like this matter, Soothsayer.
It seems unholy to me.

MERLIN.   No, King Arthur.
He does this by some sense unknown to us,
Not by unlawful means or evil spirits.
Let him proceed. He has a wondrous gift.

ARTHUR. Soothsayer, take the cloak. Ship's captain, give it.
              (The SOOTHSAYER *takes the cloak.*)

SOOTHSAYER. I press this noble rainment to my head.
A perfume rises from it as of spices.
I see strange things, rich things, most costly things.

Spices and costly rainment and rich armour,
Jewels and shoulder knots and rings and chains
And precious stones from half the shining world
And gold and silver, both in coins and bars.
Captain, it is a lucky thing for you
All of these things are hidden in the ship.

    MATH. Well, Soothsayer, you lie. There is no treasure.
This is a coastwise trader: ask the men.

    LEAR. Treasure indeed. There's none.

    ODYAR. We've nothing precious save our pound and pint.

    WALLT. Go down and search. A precious stink of bilge
Is all the precious treasure we've aboard.

    LEAR. A stink that you can cure consumption with.

    SOOTHSAYER. Oh king, I say again that there is treasure
Within the captain's cabin in a locker
This side the stern post. And the locker's key,
Where is the locker's key? A brief while since
It lay within the pocket of the cloak.
Now it is in the captain's clenched right hand.

    ARTHUR. Open your hand, captain. What is that key?

    MATH. It is my mother's kitchen cupboard key.
She lost it months ago and could not find it.
I found it in the cloak pocket just now.

    ARTHUR. Is there a locker in your cabin, captain?

    MATH. There is a locker, yes.

    ARTHUR.   And is it empty?

    MATH. Yes. It was empty when I last opened it.

    ARTHUR. But was it empty when you closed it, captain?

    MATH. As empty as my hand, upon my oath.

    ARTHUR. Merlin, take these two men. Go to the cabin.
See if this key will fit the cupboard lock.
Bring what is in the cupboard to the deck.

            (*They go out and soon reappear with the treasure.*)

    MERLIN. These things and many more were in the cupboard,
Even as this man foretold. He surely is
The greatest soothsayer that ever lived.

    SOOTHSAYER. I say that all these things, now brought to light,
Come from Tintagel and are stamped and marked
With the black flecks upon a ground of white,
Which shows that they are from the Cornish court.

MERLIN.   They are. They are Cornish things, all stamped in
    Cornwall.
MATH.   This wizard put them there and stamped them, then.
One moment, let me ask my men about them.
Did any of you men bring these aboard?
    WALLT.   They never came on board while we were here.
    MATH.   You never put them in the cabin locker?
    I███   No, sir, ███ ██████ put them in the locker.
    MATH.   Or did some Cornish merchant ship them with us?
    ODYAR.   No, sir, no merchant shipped them: reason why.
This is a wizard, who makes people see
What really is not there and all these things
Aren't really real, but things he makes us see.
Being a wizard, he should have his thumbs
Bound tight with cord and then he should be burned.
    WALLT.   Burning's the best for wizards; burn him, King.
    MERLIN.   I, too, have been a wizard in my time.
This is no wizardry nor magic practice,
But strangeness for the King's enquiry.
Proceed, King Arthur: make the captain answer.
    ARTHUR.   Well, captain, how did these things reach the locker?
    MATH.   I do not know . . . I cannot tell . . . unless . . .
I know, King Arthur, how they reached the locker.
That little devil, my black-hearted boy,
Whose liver should be cut out with a whip,
Idle, young, thievish, knavish, sluttish skulker,
Has stolen them on shore and put them there.
    WALLT.   That's it. Depend upon it, it was he.
    LEAR.   He always was a dirty little thief.
    ODYAR.   Of course it was the boy: well thought of, captain.
    ARTHUR.   Where is this boy?
    MATH.   He crept ashore, my lord,
As soon as we made fast beside the pier.
    ARTHUR.   Had he a key? Could he unlock the cupboard?
    MATH.   Why, very likely, lord. I do not know.
You see, my mother's key unlocked the cupboard.
    ARTHUR.   Where is the proper key?
    MATH.   It had no key.
We are simple sailor men and trust each other.
We have no need of keys, on board my ship.

Leave keys and locks to landsmen, not to sailors.
I and my comrades share and share alike.
I see the whole case clearly as a pike-staff.
That little devil stole the things in Cornwall,
Hid them on board, while we were at the contest,
Then ran away, directly we reached port,
To get a hand-cart or a wheelbarrow,
Intending to come back at dead of night
And take these things away. That's how it is.

WALLT.   That's how it is, indeed.

ODYAR.   And that accounts for all the things we've missed
Ever since you took him with you out of pity.

MATH.   Bide with me, Majesty, if I drop a tear.
All through my life I've tried to do good turns.
I've trusted human nature and been deceived
And now this boy, who was like a son to me,
A little blue-eyed boy with flaxen hair,
Whom I was training up to be a man,
Has blasted all my trust in human nature.

WALLT.   Now do not weep, good captain, he is unworthy.
These blue-eyed people always were the devil.
Now at this moment, while you shed these tears,
These manly drops that are a credit to you,
That little devil is drinking with his mates
In some low ruffian's den down by the river,
Thinking how he deceived his good kind master.

LEAR.   Well, the gods help him, if I come across him.

ODYAR.   King Arthur, would you call your men-at-arms
And search the city for the runaway?

WALLT.   Yes, good King Arthur, have him routed out
From where he sits carousing: drag him here
And torture him till he confesses all.

ARTHUR.   We will arrest this boy as you desire.
Give word for seven archers of the guard
To beat the inns and bring him here to me.

ODYAR.   There's good King Arthur taking up the case.
Bear up, good captain; he will find the boy.

                    (A wailing is heard below.)

ARTHUR.   What is that noise that seems to be below?

MATH.   I expect the cat has caught a rat, my lord.

324

ARTHUR. No rat on earth could make a noise like that.

MATH. No, lord, perhaps the rat has caught the cat.

[(ERBIN *rushes on from below.*)]

ERBIN. I'll tell you what it is. It's the ship's boy
Locked up in the other locker by the stern post.

ODYAR. Locked up in the other locker: shut your head.

MATH. Don't let that lunatic begin again.

WALLT. Don't let him bite our lord's anointed leg

LEAR. Collar him, Wallt: don't leave it all to me.
I've got him, good King Arthur, have no fear.

ARTHUR. I have no fear. Stand, you, away from him.
You say the boy is prisoner in the locker?

ERBIN. Yes, good King Arthur, bound and gagged and locked.

ARTHUR. Merlin, go down and see: if that be so,
Break in the door and bring the boy to us.

(MERLIN *goes down and reappears with the ship's* BOY.)

MERLIN. It was as this man had foretold, my lord.
The boy was there, locked up and almost stifled.

MATH. Now you young villain, down upon your knees.
Confess you stole the things and hid them there.
You stole them at Tintagel, did you not?
It's no good you denying. We know you did it.

ARTHUR. Now captain, leave the boy alone. Come here, boy.
Do not be scared. Who shut you in the locker?
I am the king. Answer, no one shall harm you.
Did you go into the locker to sleep or hide?

MERLIN. He could not have gone in of his free will.
He was tied hand and foot and had been gagged.

ARTHUR. Who tied you hand and foot and put you there?

BOY. It was the captain, if you please, my lord.

HELEN. What sort of locker was it where he was?

MERLIN. A locker used for storing sails and ropes.
You could lie down but not stand up in it.

ARTHUR. Why did the captain put you in the locker?

BOY. He said that, if he put me in the locker,
I should not be about to answer questions.

ARTHUR. What questions?

BOY.   Of how the treasure came here?

ARTHUR. The treasure, eh? How did the treasure come here?

MATH. My lord, this is the dirtiest little liar
That ever made a good man's heart to grieve.
    ARTHUR. Let the truth-teller hold his peace awhile,
His turn shall come. How did the treasure come here?
    BOY. The people at Tintagel brought it here.
They came with trumpets and with flowers and treasure.
They left the treasure here and then we sailed.
    ARTHUR. Why did they bring the treasure? Was it freight?
    BOY. No, lord. They were the prizes in the contest,
The prizes which the poet Owain won.
    MATH. A likely tale with Owain in Tintagel.
    ARTHUR. Now when these people at Tintagel left
This treasure in the ship, who took the treasure?
    BOY. It was on the deck, lord, with the poet, Owain.
He left it on the deck while he had supper.
I served him supper when we left Tintagel
And then he went on deck and presently
I heard him speak a poem and men laughed
And running up on deck I found him gone.
Then the captain said the treasure must be hidden
And I must be kept quiet, so they seized me,
Bound me and flung me in the other locker
And said that that would stop me telling tales.
    ARTHUR. Captain and crew, you hear what the boy says,
That Owain started from Tintagel with you.
What do you say to that?
    MATH. Well, lord, it is an evil day for Britain
When eight good able-bodied mariners
Are disbelieved before a boy like this.
The only answer honest men can make
Is – come straight to Tintagel in the ship.
The truth can all be known there in three minutes.
    WALLT. Yes, king, come to Tintagel and enquire.
    LEAR. This mad young liar ought to have the whip.
Come to Tintagel, king, and learn the truth.
    GERAINT. Really, my lord, I think we need not pay
Any attention to this ship's boy's tale.
I add my word to that of the ship's captain.
The boy has uttered falsehood first and last.

Give him a little tasting of the whip,
He will confess his falsehood and his theft.
    SOOTHSAYER. Have I convinced you of my right to speak?
    ARTHUR. I had forgotten you, good soothsayer.
Yes, you, who told where the things would be,
Should tell us how they got there.
    MERLIN.   I agree.
    GERAINT. My lord, is there not danger of injustice,
When you displace men's reason in a question
And judge by anything than the proved facts?
This is a vagabond and market conjurer.
    ARTHUR. Grant that he be, he is a very good one.
    SOOTHSAYER. I am a conjurer and worth the watching.
Since you have called me conjurer, I will conjure.
I will conjure up what person you may name.
Not you, oh king, not you, Merlin, nor you.
Princess, what person would you have appear?
    MERLIN. I do not like this kind of conjuring.
It seems to me unholy. Bid it stop.
    ARTHUR. Stop this, man, if your methods are unholy.
    SOOTHSAYER. They are lawful.
    ARTHUR.   Then proceed. Answer him, girl.
Whom would you that the conjurer conjure here?
    HELEN. The poet Owain.
    SOOTHSAYER.   And he is here, princess,
For here I strip off my disguise, oh king.
Secure these villains: listen to my story.
    MATH. By all the gods it is his ghost come back.
    WALLT. I told you from the first that ghosts come back.
    LEAR. I told you not to do it, but you would do it.
And now he comes and what he wants is blood.
    GERAINT. What are you that come back thus out of the sea?
    OWAIN. I am restored to life by a miracle.
I charge all here, this poet and these sailors,
With theft of goods and an attempt at murder.
    GERAINT. Murder? A likely charge to bring against me.
    ARTHUR. Wait. Did you leave Tintagel in this ship?
    OWAIN. I did and these men, prompted by Geraint,
Made up their minds to fling me overboard
And seize my prizes. This they promptly did.

327

They flung me into the sea and left me there,
Thinking that I should drown.
    ERBIN.   They did not, poet.
They thought the sharks would eat you.
    WALLT.   My good poet,
I was always dead against their killing you.
I knew no good could come of it. I told them.
You bear in mind I told them not to do it.
    ARTHUR.   Silence that man there.

(WALLT is silenced.)

    ARTHUR.   Proceed then, Owain.
How came it that you were not drowned or eaten?
Were you picked up?
    OWAIN.   I called upon the creatures of the sea,
And lo, they helped; [dolphins came flying up
Before the sharks;] a dolphin buoyed me up
And bore me to the shore invisibly.
Landing, I put on this disguise, and came
To learn what tale my murderers might tell.

(The SAILORS *fling themselves upon their knees.)*

    WALLT.   Oh good King Arthur, we confess we did it.
    LEAR.   We are poor labouring men, poor sailors, lord . . .
    ODYAR.   Forced by harsh laws to obey a wicked captain.
    ARTHUR.   And, wicked captain, what have you to say?
    MATH.   I would have scorned the act but for temptation.
The wicked poet promised me a farm.
Sailors go wandering through the world, my lord,
One beacon guides them on, through fair and foul,
The hope of calm old age upon a farm.
That snake in human form, knowing my weakness,
Tempted me with the one bait that might move me.
    ARTHUR.   And you, Geraint, most impudent of scoundrels,
You have no voice even if you have some shame.
But you are not so brazen that you dare
Deny this charge.
    GERAINT.   Deny it? No, my lord.
I did it and I'll do it again better,
If ever there's the chance.
    ARTHUR.   You will not do it again. Remove him, guards,
While we deliberate upon your sentence.

(GERAINT *is removed.*)

ARTHUR.   Captain and crew, you deserve instant death,
Breaking my orders to bring Owain back,
Attempting murder and theft of a man's goods,
Slighting a poet dowered by the gods
And uttering perjury before my face.

OWAIN.   Lord, let them live to do you seamen's service.

ARTHUR.   I do not relish service from such hands.

OWAIN.   They were rough men tempted beyond their strength,
But, in the main, their service is worth having.

ARTHUR.   Do you hear, sailors? Your victim pleads for you.
I was minded to have sewn you in a sail
And drowned you all, like kittens in a bag.
At his request I spare your lives.

MATH.
WALLT.
LEAR.   We thank you.
ODYAR.

ARTHUR.   But you shall serve me five years as I choose
And for the first year, this, your cabin boy,
Shall be your captain. Boy there, take a rope.
You are the captain now. Give them the orders
That once were given to you. Say, 'Down, you dogs'
And 'Sweep the cabin out.'

BOY.   You dirty scoundrels, when did you wash your hands?
Now down, you dogs, and sweep the cabin out.

ARTHUR.   Put more authority in your command.

BOY.   Get down, you dogs, and sweep the cabin out.
(*They get down.*)

ARTHUR.   Helen, a moment since, when I was blind,
I spoke most harshly and I ask your pardon,
I, who am law-giver, was most unjust.
Take here my sceptre and judge the unjust king.

HELEN.   There is no thought of anything like that.

OWAIN.   King, when I sailed this morning to the contest,
I was determined that, if I were victor,
I would demand the hand of your princess.
I am not worthy her, she may not love me.
At least I offer her the crown I won
There at Tintagel from the assembled poets.

329

I also offer her the crown of Brittany,
Since I am prince of Brittany, no upstart
As some have said.

    ARTHUR. Ask the princess.
    HELEN.   The princess grants your suit.
    MERLIN. Come, let me join your hands and pledge your troth.
    ARTHUR. And now we will to the palace to a feast.
Tomorrow we will celebrate the marriage.
Music, strike up. You, Merlin, lead the way.
                      (They move off.)
    OWAIN *([singing, to the] tune 'John's Gone to Hilo').*
For many hours no comfort shone
    CHORUS. Away . . . to Ireland
    OWAIN. But now the bitterness is gone
    CHORUS. Gone away to Ireland.
    OWAIN. From this let all good people know
    CHORUS. Away . . . to Ireland
    OWAIN. That sorrows will not stay but go
    CHORUS. Go away to Ireland.
                      (Curtain.)

Part III

UNPUBLISHED DRAFTS FOR POEMS

The Old Tale of the Breaking of the Links

Drafts

Soon as the colour-giving dawn was seen,
Arthur bade call
His Court, to judge the sinning of his Queen
There in the hall:
Himself, in scarlet, sat upon his throne
To hear her plead
She, with her beauty only, stood alone,
Alone indeed

Then uprose Mullet of the Bitter Word
And told the tale
How Modred's trappers died as ye have heard
For all their mail
For all that all their party fought but one
The man they fought
Was Lancelot the traitor who had won
The Queen to naught.

'I, who was with them on the wall,' he said,
'During the fight
Saw her behind him watching, as we played,
By taper-light.
I knew her by her red-gold hair and by
The rings she wears . . .
The death her sinning made my fellows die
See that she shares.'

Then Modred told 'I followed when she passt. . .
I saw her meet
This friend whose treacheries you know at last
This cockled wheat.
Then I with warrant went with Agravaine
But doom so shaped

333

That by this felon were my fellows slain
While he escaped.

Doubtless this felon has bewitcht your Queen.
Seeing her there
So lovely, with such majesty of mien,
So proud, so fair,
One cannot doubt that it was Lancelot
Whose arts beguiled
Her beauty to the ruin of this blot
Of bonds defiled.

Therefore King Arthur, pardon her, and slay
Your traitor knight
Let the court-marshal bring him to a bay
And bind him tight
And fetch him to his judgment, setting free
This fair, wronged thing
Blinded (it may be) but by sorcery
Be just, O King.'

Then Arthur spoke, 'You bid me to be just.
Justice decrees
Death for the petty treason of a lust
And brooks no pleas . . .
Death for the wife by burning at the stake
The law is clear
No shadow of exception will I make
It is death here . . .

Unless the one accused can bring defence,
Of such a king
That we be certain of her innocence.
Justice is blind
Blind, truly, to the rank of those accused
But else most keen
To see the truth lest virtue be abused.
Speak, therefore, Queen.'

Then the Queen answered 'You are tender, lord,
To grant this grace

To let me answer as you sit at board
To try the case
A few short hours ago you ordered men
To kill unheard
My friend and me: not having prospered then
Law is preferred –

Moon yrom mould must the low tremoler me
Tell by what right
You sent a dozen men in secrecy
In the dark night
To kill untried two subjects, one your Queen
Because they met.
Whatever our indebtedness has been
That pays the debt.

As for the charges brought by these your spies
The knights most mean
Such as the very scullions would despise
I, as the Queen,
Deserve more credit at a husband's hands
Than to be cast
Because two scourings from your killers' bands
Wish sentence passt –

What have they proven? Nothing, save that I
Met Lancelot.
They tried to murder us but got thereby
The thank ye wot
Now in revenge for such discomfiture
They turn the King
To make their else aborted murder sure.
A marvellous thing.

What are these two who came intent to kill
In darkness, armed,
And fled, their dozen comrades lying still
Themselves unharmed
They scurried screaming without scratch to show
Mad with their fear

335

I who am speaking heard and saw them go.
Now they stand here.

They were thirteen against a man and me
These two remain
Unwounded cowards in their infamy
The things unslain
The curs who fled now witness for the crown
In the King's cause
The murderers who toppled justice down
Applying laws.

Truly I wonder that you stoop so low
As to give heed
To mongrels of your meyny whom you know
Traitors indeed.'
'Ay,' Arthur said, 'Alas that Gwenivere
My Queen and mate
Should stoop so low as to be questioned here
And faced with Fate.

These are not all who witness, but the last.
Full many swear
How you have had your lover in the past
I unaware
Too many prove it showing time and place
Besides these two . . .
You say you met the person in this case . . .
Why? What to do?

Why go disguised, in darkness, and alone
To the gate-tower?
Why take such trouble not to have it known
Why choose that hour?
Why bolt the door, why, when my summons came,
If all were well,
Did you not open, why? if not from shame?
I charge you tell.'

'Why?' the Queen said, 'these cowards with their gang
Shouted aloud

(Beating the door until the quarter rang)
That they had vowed
To you, to murder us, if we un-did
Or else break in
To cut our throats: if hearing this we hid
It were no sin . . .

But lord we did not hide: we issued out
Against their odds
Surely the issue cannot leve a doubt
Which cause was God's . . .
We opened and in self-defence repaid
Good blows for blows.
You have not yet explained in what you said
Your sending those.'

'No,' Arthur answered, 'I will make it clear:–
Lancelot is
Swift as a stag and sturdy as a steer
Because of this
And because felons caught in guilt will fight
I thought it best
To send a strong detachment yesternight
To break your rest.

Now you explain your going in the dark
Unknown to all
Alone in ardent hope that none might mark
There to the wall
To meet a man whom many people prove
To have been long
Linked with you lady in unlawful love
You went for wrong.

Ay, and were interrupted in your sin
Confess the truth . . .
Lancelot, traitor, has contrived to win
Your faith, your youth,
Your honour as a woman and a Queen
Your love as wife.

337

My joy is as a summer that has been
Here ends my life.

You cannot any longer time deny
The charges brought
You have been Lancelot's in harlotry
Of act and thought
You cannot answer to a truth declared
You see the end
Shame . . . and a dozen captains better spared
Killed by your friend.

Now therefore since the ancient law is plain
For sin like this
And you refuse to plead or plead in vain
Your sentence is
That you be burned within the public ring
Outside the wall
Before this noon, thus sentences the King
Bear witness all.'

Then Gawaine said, 'King Arthur this appears
More force than sense
This lady should have trial before peers
Time for defence
Time to assemble friends and test the tales
Told by her foes.'
Then Arthur said, 'She shall not, naught avails,
To stake she goes.'

Then Gawaine said, 'The world goes upside down
When youth rules age
Arthur you tear the sapphire from your crown
Being thus in rage.
This young man Modred's hatreds sway you so
That for his sake'
'Silence,' the King said, 'Gwenivere shall go
Straight to the stake . . .

And you, Gawaine, for your impertinence
To me the King

338

Shall call the bodyguard and take her hence
Out to the Ring
And there see sentence done as I command.'
Gawaine gave word
'I am no hangman, Arthur, understand
But a knight spurred.

Que you a hangman for a hangman's work
I, a King's son,
Refuse it, whether you command or ask.'
Then everyone
There in the hall began to shout or cry
'Down with Gawaine.
Drag out the royal harlot: let her die
Let both be slain.'

And those the widows of the captains killed
Came pressing hard
With hands that clutched and cruelty that shrilled
About the guard
Snatching and spitting at the Queen as prize,
Their long red nails
Stretched for the Queen's apparel or her eyes
Over the rails.

Then Arthur bade his trumpeters to blow
To still the roar
Then in the hush he bade Sir Gareth go
With twenty more
As bodyguard to see the lady burned
Without delay
Then, never looking on the Queen, he turned
And went his way.

Gareth was but a boy of twenty years
He called aloud
'Let twenty of the guard fall in with spears
And clear the crowd
Make gangway to the door': then to the Queen
He cried 'Alas

That I should ever look on such a scene
And bring't to pass.

But still these brawlers shall be husht at least
Be silent all.'
But at his cry the rioting increast
Throughout the hall
The women thronged their victim much as curs
In the green wood
Surround the dying lion who not stirs
But knows death good.

They screamed 'This golden harlot once so proud
Shall now be tame.
Come to the fire, malkin, in your shroud
And feed the flame.
You who were hot shall now be hotter still
We will attend
To watch the fire make your singing shrill
Until you end.'

Then, suddenly, while all the building rang
From those who curst
The bronze doors were forct open with a clang
And in there burst
Lancelot and his meyny with Sir Bors
Ector and Urre
Cutting aside the keepers of the doors
To rescue her.

Then, while the women shrieked, the bodyguard
To stem the tide
Formed, till the passage to the Queen was barred
And there they died
For Lancelot with all his meyny broke
Their weak array
There Lancelot killed Gareth with a stroke
And Ector Kai

And Bors killed Gauter of the Barren Pass;
And Bel the Proud

Was killed by Urre, a sudden fight it was
A startled crowd
Lancelot reached the Queen and cleared a ring
With his great sword
And cried 'I take this lady from the King
No more our lord.'

Then, with his arm about her, he returned
Facing his foes:
Women and men who would have seen her burned
Shrank from his blows
They quailed, but, quailing, snarled, as he returned
To the bronze doors
Sir Ector of hte Marsh his left hand squired
His right hand, Bors.

Then as they issued into the great court
To mount and ride
Modred from shelter shouted 'Bar the port . . .
Man the Usk side
Close the approaches to the bridge: and blow
The saddling call
Come all you horsemen, never let them go
Capture them all.'

Then, as some ran to horses, Lancelot
Mounted and rode
For the great gate across the Usk at trot
Sir Bors abode
With Ector and a dozen more to check
The King's pursuit
Modred cried 'Hurry. Scatter them to wreck
Shoot, archers, shoot!'

Then the great bell within the castle tower
Boomed men to arm
But Lancelot brought safe his golden flower
From hurt and harm
He crossed the Usk and saw Sir Ector come
Keeping his rear

341

The hoofs beat like the thudding of a drum
The sun shone clear.

The last five stanzas of this full draft are almost identical with those of the poem as published: the most significant difference is that the draft has 'In which the rooks went slowly in black broods' where the published poem has 'They saw white Venus star the solitudes' in the fourth-last stanza.

Midsummer Night

Selections from the Dialogue Drafts

IDDOC.

I am King Iddoc of the realm of Kent,
I played in danger at a triple game,
First with the pirate kings
Many of whom I welcomed when they came;
Next with King Arthur; next, with false intent
With Modred whom I fashioned to my bent.
The end of all my plots and counsellings
Was to be master and command the springs
And see my subjects tremble at my name.

[LANCELOT?:]

I would have welcomed Arthur's mis-born son
Had but that son been upright, loyal, true.
Modred was friend to every evil one
Within the royal household and without
Ev'n from the day he came.
He joined with traitors at the secret game
Gwenivere's sister joined her to the crew
Small cause for Gwenivere to bless, I doubt.

[GWENIVERE to GWENIVACH:]

One week before you told me of your troth
Modred had been detected sending word
Against all loyalty and knightly oath
To Kol the pirate, killer of my son.
All other should have died
For treachery so gross, as soon as tried.
That was the moment when yourself preferred
Your suit to him, expecting benison.

MODRED.

Kol was my trusted friend, for when a man
Is taunted and neglected and denied

343

He turns to such companions as he can
So I to Kol: I also tell you this
I told Kol hour and day
Of Lacheu's riding, so that he might slay
And slay Kol did at dawn by Channel side
My father lost that lawful son of his.

Later, you say, men caught me sending news
To Kol who held the Channel in his ship
Queen, the occasion was too good to lose
There was a chance that he might swoop and seize
You and my father King
And either kill or hold to ransoming
While I myself with my companionship
Took order for the kingdom at our ease.

An alternate version of this stanza:

Later, you say, men caught me sending news
To Kol . . . alas, they did, and wreckt a chance
A rare occasion harrowing to lose . . .
An opportunity to swoop and seize
You and my father King
And put an end to you by murdering
So that myself might have inheritance
Of father's kingdom, crown and royal fees.

Still, as your spies were clever, it mis-went. . .
You triumpht for a while, but not for long . . .
You called me wicked, but your own intent
Was, to meet secretly with Lancelot
The which we soon perceived. No very holy thought
Which, having learned, another web we wrought
To catch your footsteps tripping into wrong
Your sister wove, I, Modred, drew the knot.

GWENIVACH.

Our purpose, sister, was to make the throne
Assured to Modred when King Arthur died
You purposed it for Lancelot alone
King Arthur's cousin, whom you loved in sin

Yet still, for peace's sake
There was a bargain that we tried to make
This, that if Modred's claim were satisfied

An alternate version of Gwenivach's speech:

GWENIVACH.

Yet thinking that perhaps a lost respect
Might win you to support us in our claim
We frankly came to you and pled our best
Simply that Arthur's son should be his heir.
You primmed a virtuous face
That my beloved Modred's birth was base
That Britain's King should have unspotted name
Such as your holy self and Arthur bare.

We knew, untold, the inmost of your plan,
That, after Arthur's death, the crown should go
To Arthur's cousin, Lancelot, your man,
Your midnight lover in the secret tower.
I asked this: you replied,
'That virtuous you and Arthur would decide.'
Thereon I struck your harlot's lips a blow
Joy of it paid for many a bitter hour.

No need thereafter for pretence of love
Betwixt us sisters, no, but war declared
The dagger drawn, the hand without a glove
Spirit and body offered up to Hate
As dwelling and as tool
To bring about the downfall of your rule. . .
To have the treason of your loving bared. . .
And to your Check of malice answer Mate.

Another alternate version, including Gwenivere's response:

GWENIVACH.

And you, my elder sister, Queen of Grace,
So beautiful, my lady golden-red,
You, who despised my Modred as too base

345

Yes, you, who used to dread
Lest he should touch your skirts too widely spread
Or speak, your husband's son
To you, the pure, the perfect married one
He lived to take the colour from your face.

I lived to see it, too, I thank my lot
I Gwenivach the little, had a share
In that which purged my Modred from the blot
That fate had made him bear.
God sees the scorned one suffer: unaware
He makes the tide to turn
I helped, and by the helping made you learn
How despised Modred outweighed Lancelot.

You were in happy state: the wars were done
Your lover Lancelot was close at hand,
Arthur, who never sinned, suspected none,
I, as your sister, kept within my place . . .
Snubbed and kept under, I . . .
Then Modred dawned upon that quiet sky
Like the red planet on a summer land
To change your fortune and the kingdom's case.

His story also came: the tale was known
How Modred's mother was his father's aunt
Visibly royal was he, blood and bone,
It was a joy to note his sudden brain
So serpent-swift and keen
After your son's, your Lacheu's, that had been
Modred declared himself a royal plant
Yes, but you righteous only saw the stain.

So when your party triumpht and forbade
That Modred should be heir when Arthur died
Modred and I our lover's compact made
And I, your sister, coming straight to you
Within your blue-hung bower
In Camelot in the Augusta tower*

---

* *In a variant draft:* 'within the Sunset Tower'.

Told how I loved him and would be allied.
Scant blessing then my soul's confession drew.

GWENIVERE.

No, for whatever beauty love might add
To you, in your confession, hate was still
Prime mover in whatever plans you had
Hatred of me, of Arthur, hate that longed
To bring all order down
Into the dust together, king and crown
That was your spirit, sister, lust to kill
All that restrained you, as you termed it, wronged

LANCELOT.

I, who am Lancelot, the son of Ban,
King Arthur's cousin, dealt the land the blow
That brought him to his fall.
My sinful loving caused the overthrow
My love of Gwenivere from which began
The slaying of full many a noble man
The burning of the pillars of the hall
The ruin and the scattering of all
That else had stood for distant Times to mow.

GAWAINE.

I am Gawaine, whom men call Silver-Tongue,
Cousin of Arthur and of Lancelot
Upholder of the throne
Hater of Modred's plot and counterplot
Till my beloved Gareth's soul was flung
Deathward by Lancelot to madness stung
Saving his lady when she stood alone
Damned to the burning stake at Caerleon
Then I withdrew and after meddled not.

GWENIVERE.

Not any sin of yours but wicked mine
Loving Sir Lancelot destroyed the realm
That, and the midnight battle on the wall,
Made the proud kingdom fall.

347

That was the lightning flash that gave the sign
Of deep division at the nation's heart
Thence all the evils held so long apart
Gat unison and came to overwhelm.

The Sailing of Hell Race

Outline and Drafts

Outline (Second Notebook)

When Arthur had fought the Pentland war, and had made for himself a name throughout Britain, he determined to go west, in the ship Prydwen, in search of the unknown, or of the Underworld.

He sailed from the Severn in the Prydwen, and reacht the land of diseases, he and his 27. Here the Queen, Death, propounds her conundrum, what upholds my kingdom? Seven die before he can answer, that the kingdom is maintained by flies.

On leaving the kingdom of disease, he comes to the land of cruelty, where the King propounds again, what sustains my kingdom? Seven die before he can answer, that the kingdom is sustained by vanity.

Sailing on, he comes to the land of cities, where the king also propounds, what maintains my kingdom. Seven die before he can answer, that the realm is maintained by stupidity.

Sailing thence, with only seven men he comes to the island of Wisdom and talks with the Queen.

From this talk, he learns, that the old way is to come to an end, and that a sign will be given to him. Sailing home, he sees a chariot race on the sands of the Dee mouth, where Gwenivere, her sister Gwenivach and other princesses are racing for a gold torque given by the King. Gwenivere wins. Arthur loves her. Gwenivach is jealous

Upon this, there follows his betrothal, and the poem of the Ring.

After this, there comes the great invasion

First Draft (Second Notebook)

So having fought the Pentland War and won
A name through Britain and a peace secure
He felt the red horizon cast her lure
To set him hunting of the setting sun
To take a ship and sail
West through the grassless pastures of the whale
West to the wilderness of nothing sure
But unseen countries and the deeds undone

He took his ship, the Prydwen, and his crew
Of twenty seven seamen from the west
Sand-raddled Severn glittered at her breast
As first her set sail wrinkled and then drew
She dropped down with the tide
Past Wye, past Usk, then leaned upon her side
And smote the spindrift from the billow crest
And strode from raddled waters into blue.

And after heading west for many days
Lo, in the darkness on ahead, a light,
A beacon, as he thought, upon a height,
To guide ships safely through the channel's maze
But drawing nearer shore
Spied by the fitful bonfire flame a score
Of men with tridents busy at a rite
Consuming dead men's bodies in the blaze.

And landing at the city's rotting pier
Thr grim guards of the ruler of the land
Brought them to prison with the heavy hand
Through avenues of death and streets of fear
For all that kingdom thrilled
With fell diseases by which men are killed
The million-stabbing dagger never scanned
The murderers whose steps men cannot hear.

There the diseases ruled among their slaves
There King Disease upon his fatal throne

Said to that crew 'I take you for my own,
A man each day, a doom which nothing saves,
Nothing prevents, unless
One of your number have the wit to guess
How the triumphant murder-seed is sown
Whose harvest fills the city-streets with graves.'

There, in the prison, one by one they died
By secret horror smiting in the dark
In ways unguesst at, they could only mark
The stricken comrade turning on his side
They felt the flusht flesh burn
The life grow fainter but they could not learn
What unseen power struck the hero stark
Nor on what cleavage life and death divide

Till, presently, when seven men had gone
Out of the certain into the unguesst,
The death bells rang the city to its rest
And on the walls again the corpse fires shone
Then Arthur in his thought
Stirred by distress the hidden secret caught
And won release, and stood into the west
Over the fruitless heaving striding on

And as he sailed, behold another shore
Red from much devilry, by devils manned
The grim guards of the ruler of the land
Thrust them to bitter prison as before.
That country's savage trade
Was war unending, bloody warfare made
On what the spirit hoped or wisdom planned
Or righteousness of soul had striven for.

There the Red King pronounced the second doom
'Rot within prison, bleeding day by day
Or guess what is my bloody country's stay
This bringer down of youth into the tomb'
Each day the killers smote
One of King Arthur's seamen through the throat

Seven in all their fellows saw them slay
By bale fire light within the prison gloom.

Then Arthur guesst the secret and was freed
He and his crew (now halved) and sailing thence
He saw a city stretching so immense
That all a land seemed eaten by its greed
Small comfort was therein
But hurrying thousands in unceasing din
Ceaselessly seeking for sufficient pence
To render tribute to the god of speed.

There the Gray King pronounced upon them thus
'Each day in prison one of you shall die
Until you guess what gives me empery
Over these sufferers and these covetous.'
Each day, as he had sworn,
One of the crew was carried thence and torn
Till seven more lay dead beneath the sky
There in the town of lifeblood gluttonous.

And there, when hope was dying, lo the Queen
His Helper from of old, the Ever Kind,
Sent, in a dream, the answer to his mind
The explanation of that tragic scene.
And he declaring then
The rune, was licenced by those city men
To sail where'er his will went, or the wind,
So home he turned across the gray seas and green.

And as he sailed, he pondered much the things
That had so wreckt his purpose as he sailed
And learned how hard the knowledge that availed
Against the power of the triple kings
But as he sailed, behold
The Queen of Wisdom in her crown of gold
Strode to him over billow-crests that quailed
And blesst his head and shadowed him with wings.

'Arthur', she said, 'Now you have seen the foes
Of body, mind and soul that break a realm

You have beheld how they can overwhelm
And seen their props and you can conquer those.
Within these few weeks hence
A New Way will be opened to your sense
A way to help you as you stand at helm
Against those Kings and make their gates unclose.'

So sailing thence, much pondering on her speech
He and his seven came to British lands
And there beheld a crowd upon the sands
Watching a chariot race upon the beach
Three chariots brazen-poled
Drawn each by stallions bright with beaten gold
Each urged and ordered by princesses' hands
Two glorious princesses stood in each

And at the turning, leading to the straight
He saw how two white stallions and two black
Raced for the vantage at the curving track
And saw the driver of the whites elate
With streaming red gold hair
And eyes like stars illumined and aware
Crouched watchful, to the grippt reins straining back
Urging those foamers thundering like spate

And as she swung, the black team, edging near
Urged by a darker lady to collide,
So nearly smote them that the people cried
But yet too soon, because the whites drew clear
And passt the post ahead
'Who is the lovely Queen so golden red?'
King Arthur asked. A stander-by replied
'That is the western princess, Gwenivere.'

A Later Draft (First Notebook)

When Arthur came from warring, having won
A name in Britain and a peace secure
He felt the red horizon cast her lure
To set him hunting of the setting sun,

To take a ship and sail
West, through the grassless pastures of the whale,
West, to the wilderness of nothing sure
But tests for manhood in the deeds undone.

He manned his ship, the Britain, with a crew
Of twenty seven seamen from the west
The Severn glittered at the Britain's breast
As first her set sail wrinkled and then drew;
She dropped down with the tide
Then, ere the changing, leaned upon her side
And smote the spindrift from the billow-crest
And strode from raddled waters into blue.

Then, having wandered west for many days
Lo, in the darkness before dawn, a light
A beacon, Arthur thought, upon a height
To guide ships safely through a channel's maze
But coming nearer shore
He spied about a bonfire flame a score
Of men with tridents busy at a rite:
Consuming dead men's bodies in a blaze.

Nor had he long to wonder at the scene,
Because by dawn the keepers of the land
Struck all those Britons with the heavy hand
And bore them to the palace of the Queen:
Through evil streets they went
Where rats with yellow teeth were well content
In rot that brought the waters to a stand
And lapped the dwellings in a stew obscene.

All things within that land were in decay
The broken column served to mend the sty
Moss greened the roofs, the windows hung awry,
The marble mansion had been patcht with clay.
From huts of sodden wood
Gaunt children, savage from the want of food,
Glared as they passt: the aqueduct was dry
Within its black recess the lepers lay.

Within the ruined shrine the murrained beast
Disputed for the shelter with the sick;
The water dropped with melancholy tick
In stinking aisles forgotten by the priest
If sunlight ever gleamed
Upon that ['city'>] temple, all its alleys steamed
With fog of poison floating stealthy thick
Incense of death where living thought had ceast

And in the marsh and in the blowing dust
Within that city's limits, sounds of fear
Whined with the threat of death in Arthur's ear
Of manhood brought to rot and swords to rust;
Of red blood withering pale;
Beauty defiled, wisdom of no avail;
Of murderers whom none could see nor hear
Who served all living to their mistress' lust.

There the pale fevers issued from the fen
To yellow the sick cheek and cloud the mind
There tetters changed the child's skin into rind
Or scored the forehead with an angry pen
There palsies twitcht the lips
Or hamstrung men with anguish in the hips
Or with their blearing blinkers made them blind
Or with their madness left them no more men

And, as the soldiers dragged them, Arthur saw
In all the streets, in cracking bronze or paint,
Records of glories gone of king and saint,
Who once had made that city without flaw
Spent was their spirit's tilth
Boys daubed the portraits of the kings with filth,
Disease had made the spirit's effort faint
The doing hand was stricken into claw.

So, being dragged, they reached the palace gates
Where wretches deckt with bones burned precious gum
Praying the goddess fever not to come,
Hoping with mumblings to arrest the fates

355

The haggard sentinel
Muttered 'More come to perish: it is well.'
The clanging bronze behind them struck them numb
A guard cried 'Drive them in: our ruler waits.'

Then they were forct before that country's Queen
The winged and browless fierceness on the throne
Bright-mailed and gleaming in her hall of bone

Then they were forct before that country's Queen
Within her hall of desert-beaten bone
Browless and winged she sat upon her throne
Fanged, stinged and mailed in metal gleaming green
No thought was in her eyes
In where her victim's blood lay she was wise
Her death-flies filled the palace with their drone
Her darts of death out-glittered and were keen.

'Arthur', she said, 'And you whom he commands,
I and my minions took this realm of old
And crumbled down its glory into mould
And filled its treasure-rooms with drifted sands

'Arthur', she said, 'And you whom he commands,
I and my minions took this realm of old
We made her guiding captains lose their hold
We filled her thinkers' skulls with drifted sands
Your hands and skulls, like theirs,
Shall also bleach beneath the fretting airs,
A man a day until your tale is told
Shall die in prison at my killer's hands.

Unless, until, you have the wit to guess
The secret of our power, how it spreads,
How even the healing air our murder sheds
And the clean sea asists us hardly less.
Now, as you face me here,
My unseen murderers are very near.
To prison with you; and, to save your heads
Use them, before you drop to nothingness.'

Then, at her nod, the killers made them fast
Within the prison, and at dusk each day
One of their crew was surely made away;
A secret poison made him breathe his last,
But how, they could not learn . . .
Within the flesh they felt the fever burn
Blood, mind and spirit into disarray
But guesst not how, nor how the seeds were cast.

Till on the eighth day, seven having died,
As all were sitting in their prison-house,
Arthur beheld a bird among the boughs
Of planes that grew along the prison side,
A little shining bird;
Precise and sudden as a thought it stirred
Undaunted in that den of death and drowse
A glittering swiftness bright and eager-eyed.

It roved the leopard patches in the bark
It cruised the air, here, there, till Arthur thought
This creature braves the poisons undistraught . . .
Death's arrows flying never touch this mark . . .
The Death is in the air . . .
This bird defies it, therefore it is fair
To think that in the air the evil wrought
Is brought by flies, though how it deals is dark.

Having declared this answer they were freed
Seven men less; again they wandered on
For many days, till red before them shone
The castle kingdom of a warrior-breed
Who, as they came ashore,
Seized them and led to prison as before
Through angry streets from which the peace had gone
These many years, through bitterness decreed.

All red that city shone from bale-fires' light
Glowing in iron baskets on the towers;
The bronze-shod feet had worn away the flowers
From all that city's gardens of delight;

357

War had become her trade
Armourers' hammers on the anvil brayed
In every street the trumpets called the hours
And shouting sergeants drove the boys to fight

And all night long men stood upon the walls
Watching for foes, and all day long they drilled
Striplings, to take the places of the killed
Whose deaths scarce earned them any funerals
The ploughshare ceased to ply
The sergeants beat the ploughboys out to die
There in the mud where raged the never stilled
Battle that roared like many waterfalls.

Why they were fighting was forgotten now;
So many years had fed the fires of rage
That the beginnings in the gentler age
Were overlaid; what mattered why and how?
The quarrel was; it flamed;
Ev'n if they died their neighbour must be shamed
Wisdom was treason: to be sane or sage
Was instant death with branding on the brow.

So in that country all the women wrought
At tools of death, and all the old men wrote
What joy it was to grip a foeman's throat
And all else languisht while the manhood fought
The children starved to feed
The men who bled that other men might bleed
Man's spirit there was partly wolf part stoat
Teeth, with intent to bite, no other thought.

And there the marching to the thrilling fife,
The comradeship of arms, the something new,
Honoured and dangerous together, drew
Seven of Arthur's men to join the strife.
They joined the fighting men
They marcht beneath strange banners out of ken
To where the holders of a line were few
And yards of mud were bought by human life

358

So, loosing thence, he stood away, away
Over the waters of that sullen sea

*With the next page, the draft effectively begins again, and constitutes
another draft: its first twenty-four stanzas correspond quite closely to
stanzas 3–5 and 9–26 of the published version, except that there are also
variant drafts corresponding to stanzas 17 and 27, and opposite to the
stanza corresponding to stanza 24 is:*

He left astern those towers toppt with fire;
He sailed the seas of hell, along hell's coast
Where the salt satyr wandered like a ghost
By Sodom's columns and the wrecks of Tyre;
Past ruins sown with salt,
Dwelt in by leper devils maimed and halt;
By countries blasted to the uttermost;
Till heaven reddened o'er him as with ire.

*Following the drafts corresponding to stanza 27, after the excision of most
of a leaf, are:*

Mars was that circle's King
Mars (and his lady Vanity) controlled
That frantic hell where children starved to feed
The men who bled that other men might bleed.
Splendid he was in loot and borrowed gold
He watched, enthroned on high,
The sergeants beat the ploughboys out to die
A vulture pill-skulled from his carrion greed
Percht on his bridle-arm with horny hold.

Mars and his lady Vanity controlled
That hell with law, that all should starve to feed
The men who bled that other men might bleed;
Splendid the couple sat in borrowed gold
To watch, enthroned on high,
The sergeants beat the ploughboys out to die
Among the carrion on the blasted mead
Where shredded flesh war-mangled made the mould.

359

A stanza corresponding to stanza 29 follows, and two drafts corresponding to stanza 30, then, after the stubs of two excised leaves and before the excision of a stanza, comes:

> All things within that land were in decay
> Though not deserted, it was still the sty
> For all the deaths that kill and cannot die,
> Driving the shrinking ghost out of the clay
> As Arthur trod the street
> The rat looked at him from his nightmare meat;
> The alleys steamed, the aqueduct was dry,
> Within its chill recess the lepers lay.

A final page bearing three stanzas concludes the draft:

> Evil had reacht the city as the dust
> Settles upon the bronze or on the paint
> Little by little, upon king or saint
> Till plasters crackle and the metals rust.
> In that still city sick
> The water dropped with melancholy tick;
> There the strengths triumpht that make mortals faint,
> Too foul for glory and too weak for lust.
>
> And everywhere King Arthur saw the wreck
> Of what was first a city, then had swelled
> Into a vastness as the force impelled
> Until the devils entered and called check
> Man there had turned away
> From Earth's robustness and the light of day
> Man with his ingenuity was quelled
> For asps to nest in and for daws to peck.
>
> And even as he walkt, King Arthur knew
> The death-seed mingle in his blood with chill,
> As with their death-notes ever whining shrill
> The devils thronged him in the air that blew
> By every swinging gate
> Those murderers of mortals lay in wait
> They seized him, for the Empress Devil's will
> Was to destroy both Arthur and his crew.

360

The Aftermath

Drafts and Outline

From the second notebook:

> But when the news of Uther's death was brought
> To Iddoc, sworn his brother, Iddoc launcht
> His ship for vengeance and the waves were blancht
> With foam until he reacht Tintagel bay
> And landing there he caught
> King Merchyon in his hold and bore him thence
> To show him in the city cage for pence
> As one who killed a sleeper where he lay,
> Till Death the ender his releasing wrought
>
> And when King Bran of Benwick heard the news
> He, too, set sail for vengeance, but arrived
> A too late bee, to find the honey hived
> King Merchyon gone and in his stead a worse
> The black usurper Breuse
> Him King Bran slew and

On the back of this page of the notebook comes the outline:

When the news of Uther's death was brought to Iddoc, he sailed to avenge his blood-brother. Landing at Tintagel, he seized Merchyon and carried him off to the East, where he was prisoned in cage till death.

As soon as Breuse who was away at the time of the raid knew of Merchyon's capture, he seized the Cornish crown; M's son being then in the south.

Bran, hearing of the murder of Uther, sails to the west, finds Breuse in charge and kills him, crowns Merchyon the Second, and marries Elaine: he also sends Ygerna to Sarum, to be with Ector, Kol and Guy. Elaine presently bears Lancelot.

361

Lastly Lot hears of the murder; he goes to the west, finds all things settled, but bears off Morgause.

Beginning on the page opposite the outline are further draft stanzas:

> But when the news of Uther's murder came
> To Iddoc in the East, King Iddoc swore
> To let his brother's blood cry out no more
> From that green valley where his body died,
> But to avenge the shame;
> So sailing to the west, he took the King
> The evil-doer of the murdering,
> And caged him prisoned in the rampart's side
> Where death the changer swiftly made him tame.
>
> But Breuse, who, when King Merchyon was seized,
> Was in the southern isles, with Merchyon's son,
> Seeing a chance that power might be won,
> Seized the boy Merchyon and the Cornish throne,
> And governed as he pleased
> All Cornwall rich in tin, and let his hand,
> Red with men's blood, lie heavy on the land,
> He swore that bright Elaine should be his own
> That so men's   appeased.
>
> When Bran
> When Ban of Benwick heard how Uther died
> He, too, set forth to bring the killers down,
> And finding Breuse had seized the Cornish crown
> He fought him in Tintagel man to man
> And thrust him through the side
> Killing him dead, and crowned young Merchyon King
> And wed Elaine the golden with a ring
> (A Queen well fitted to the golden Ban)
> Then home to Benwick with his bride
>
> But for Ygern, King Uther's steadfast knights
> Kol, Guy, and Ector, took her to the Plain,
> In Sarum there they helped her in her reign,

362

Over King Uther's fief of windy grass
There Arthur's childhood she and Arthur dwelled
On the wide downland soared o'er by the kites
And there in time the happy news was brought
That Elaine's son was beautiful past thought
Surely the noblest boy that ever was
Being Lancelot (the peerless as men held).

Kol brought the news of Uther's murdering
To Iddoc in the East within few days
He, the blood-brother, suffered no delays
But manned his dragon ships and sailed and took
[King Merchyon] the murderous
Back to Augusta
Tintagel and her King

Kol brought the news of Uther's murdering
To Iddoc in the East within few days
He, the blood-brother, suffered no delays
But manned his dragon-ships and sailed and brought
Merchyon the Cornish King
East, into Kent, and hung him till he died
Caged in a cresset on the rampart side
But Breuse whose traitorous hand the killing wrought
Breuse was still scatheless, having taken wing.

Breuse was on foray with King Merchyon's son
There in the south when Merchyon was made prize
And at the news he thought in heartless wise
'This boy being prisoned, I might have the crown.'
No sooner said than done
He seized the youth, usurped the Cornish throne
Swore that the girl Elaine should be his own
And thought that all the barriers were down
Twixt him and Kingship and the struggle won

But meanwhile Guy had brought the bloody news
Of Uther's murder to his comrade Ban
The Benwick King, the mould of glorious man,
Who would not leave his vengeance long delayed

363

But sailed in quest of Breuse
Sailed to Tintagel, landed, killed him there
Set free Elaine that princess golden hair
Loved, wooed and wedded with that royal maid
And bore her home as booty from the cruise.

On the back of this page comes the stanza:

Lastly, tne news of Uther's death was brought
To Lot of Orkney, who arrived too late
For any vengeance, since he followed fate
After King Merchyon and Breuse were dead
One deed that pirate wrought
Seeing the little Morgause on the shore
He snatched her up to be his prize, and bore
Her north to Orkney where in time he wed
(She being grown) that fairy mischief fraught

Beginning opposite this are further draft stanzas which follow on from those on the front of the page:

And there, the next year, in the Keep of Joy
Their son was born, prince Lancelot the Bright
Known in his manhood as the peerless knight:
There by the sea he gathered manliness.
Ygerna for her boy
Ruled Uther's downland and beside her stood
Kol, Guy, and Ector, helpers wise and good,
Who taught the child the ways of knightliness
That stands against all powers which destroy.

To bit, to saddle, and to shoe the horse

And there the next year, in the Keep of Joy
Their son was born, Prince Lancelot the bright,
Known in his manhood as the peerless knight:
'The fairest manchild ever seen by men'
They called that glorious boy.

364

And at his birth a shining one of those
Who dwell within the changing seas arose
And signed him with a blessing beyond ken
That no man's steel should maim him or destroy.

But at the birthfeast held for Lancelot
Young Merchyon the Second wooed and wed
Ban's sister Helen in that Joyous steral
And bore her home to high Tintagel keep
That lovely pair begot
Olwen, whom Tallorc married, and King Marc
To whom the portioned destiny was dark
Queen Isolt's sinning made his spirit weep
In ways his happy childhood reckoned not

And meanwhile Queen Ygerna bred her son
In white-walled Sarum in the downland wide
O'er which, all day, the singing larks abide,
And wind makes ripples gleam along the slopes
There Arthur was begun
By Kol and Guy in every manly play
Of gentle dealing: there he learned the way
Of horse and battle – there he raised the hopes
Of those who taught him, as a likely one.

There, too, when he had grown, he came to know
An older man, Sir Ector of the Marsh,
There where the sea makes Parret water harsh
Often with Ector he would sail that fief
The brown sail loitering slow
Through thickets of dense reeds, and pools, and ways
By islands fortified in ancient days,
To spear the pike beneath the lily leaf
Or drop the flying heron with the bow.

There Ector taught him war as practised then
By Roman soldiers, there he grew apace,
Dark haired, immense of bone and calm of face
When he was hardly twenty he was sent
To rule his western men

Beyond Caerleon, for the country seethed
Destruction poisoned all the air men breathed
Destruction of all stable government
Down to the roots that man might start agen.

So, in Caerleon town he made his seat
Keeping his father's league with other Kings;
Wales and the islands hummed with mutterings
Of some great storm of pirates soon to break:
When they had reaped the wheat
Of that hot summer, lo the pirates came
Throughout the west the farms went up in flame
Into each haven thrust the fiery drake
Up to each wall the wolves came seeking meat.

And in that foraying of many packs
Though Arthur kept the coasts of southern Wales
The heathen reddened ocean with their sails
And held their course beyond him to the south
King Kolbein, Bloody Axe
A chief among them stormed Tintagel tower
Killed Merchyon, took his kingdom for his dower
And settled there and ruled to Helford mouth
Making men slaves with loads upon their backs.

When Kol brought the news of the killing of Uther to
        Iddoc
His blood-brother sworn, in his city Augusta by Thames
King Iddoc at once manned his dragons to sail to Tintagel
For vengeance on those who had killed and to rescue
        Ygern.
So he sailed for Tintagel and landed and captured the
        King
And bearing him home hung him up in a cage on the wall
Where he died

Lastly, the news of Uther's death was brought
To Lot of Orkney, who arrived too late
For any vengeance, since he followed Fate,
Breuse had been killed and Merchyon was dead

366

One pirate's deed he wrought:
Finding the infant Morgause on the strand
He took her as his prize to Orkney-land
There in his pirate's haven she was bred
To womanhood, that fairy mischief-fraught.

She grew to beauty, dark, lithe, supple, small,
With fierce black brows and sudden eager ways
A solace in the pirate's idle days,
And more than that, when she was seventeen

And though she was a small, dark, bustling

She grew up to be black-browed, eager, small,
Supple, with bright skin and decisive ways
Soon, thought of her filled all the pirate's days;
In time, he wed her, making her his Queen.
She ruled that pirate hall.
She bore him sons, the Silver tongued Gawaine,
Gaheris, Swiftfoot, Bitter Agravaine;
Two followed these, and better had it been
For Britain, had those two not been at all.

The final stanza in the notebook is clearly intended to follow that immediately before Masefield's experiment with alternating fifteen- and fourteen-syllabled lines:

King Merchyon's daughter would have been his slave
Had not King Tallorc come and borne her forth
To be his Queen in Pictland in the North
Where she soon died in giving Tristan birth,
Soon like a broken wave
The furies of the heathen onslaught slackt
Their ships drew homewards leaving much unsackt
'When next they came,' they said, 'they would leave
    dearth
From Tyne to Wight one desecrated grave.'

Three further draft stanzas survive in typescript:

367

So Uther died, but, when men brought the news
To Iddoc, pledged as brother to the dead,
He swore never to rest till Merchyon's head
Was bleached upon a spike,
Where nesting birds his withered locks might use.
Therefore he gathered all his bodyguard
And westward on the tossing sea he sped,
His seething galley straining at the yard,
Like a great sea-beast launching to the strike.

And, coming round the grim rocks of the west,
He sailed at noon beneath Tintagel crag,
That sea-mews' nest, the mansion of the shag,
And armed and came to land
And scaled the great rock's stairway to the crest,
Burst in the gates and took that traitor king,
Cutting away the white horse from his flag,
Then bore him east to pay for murdering
A sleeper with no weapon in his hand.

And, coming round the grim rocks of the west,
He sailed at noon beneath Tintagel crag,
That sea-mew's nest, that mansion of the shag,
And, landing with his men,
He scaled the castle stairway to the crest,
Burst in the postern, took that traitor king,
Trod under foot his scutcheon and his flag
And bore him off to pay for murdering
Uther as he lay sleeping in the glen.

Part IV

UNPUBLISHED PROSE

Notes 1

An ancient Welsh archaeology gives the second fatal blow of Britain as that given by Mordred to Arthur.

Gwenhwyvar was the daughter of Gogyrvan Gawr. Camp Gogyr van is a mile to the north of Oswestry.

Arthur's sword in the Welsh is Kaledvwlch, which means either hard to cut or harsh in cutting.

Gwenhwyvar means white fairy. There is a Welsh proverb about her,

> Gwenhwyvar, girl of Gawr the bold,
> Was bad when young and worse when old.

The battle of Kamlan was one of the three foolish battles.

Iudoc was one of the three secret traitors of the isle of Britain. He joined Mordred and became one of the causes of the three fatal battles. He was then a young man and, when Arthur sent him to Mordred to ask for peace, Arthur told him to use to him the most winning words that he could, but, instead of doing this, he spoke as though Arthur had said nothing but insults and this brought about the battle of Kamlan. Regretting what he had done, he withdrew before the end of the battle of Kamlan and went apparently into the Picts' kingdom to do penitence.

Mordred is called by some the son of Lleu, the son of Kwynvarch. Kwynvarch was apparently a brother of King Marc of Cornwall.

Mordred divided his troops into three corps at the battle of Kamlan. Kamlan is shown with Arthur's tomb in Cornwall at Camelford, not far from Tintagel.

Mordred was one of the three royal knights of the court of Arthur. He was the second of the three and the three were so charming and so winning and such beautiful speakers that it was difficult to refuse what they asked.

The three men who escaped from the battle of Kamlan were the ugly man, the lovely man and the very strong man.

Kamlan may quite well be some place near Queens Camel in Somerset. The earthwork, Cadbury Banks, was known as Camelot until the sixteenth century.

371

Of the three treacherous interviews of the isle of Britain the third was the interview of Mordred and Iudoc, when they came to an understanding to betray Arthur, from which the Saxons obtained power. Arthur was betrayed by Iudoc, who made public his secrets.

Among the three traitors in their souls Mordred is the second, because he made friends with the Saxons, so that he might have the monarchy from Arthur. This made a large part of eastern England Saxon.

The second of the three evil discoveries of the island of Britain was Arthur's carrying away the head of Bendigeit Vran from the white hill, which is supposed by some to be London. The head of Bendigeit Vran, that is Bran the blessed, son of King Lear, had its face turned towards France and as long as it stayed in that way the Saxons could not oppress this island. Arthur dug it up, because he thought it wrong that this island should be guarded by any strength other than its own. It was Owen, the son of the emperor Maximilian, who hid the head of Bran.

Arthur was an inferior kind of bard.

Notes 2

Arthur married Gwenhwyvar, whose sister was Gwenhwyvach. Mordred or Medrawt was the son of Arthur.

Mordred was born on a May-day. He was Gawain's brother or half-brother, Gawain's father being King Lot and his mother Morgause. Agravaine, Gaheris and Gareth were all Gawain's brothers. Lot was king of Lothian and of Orkney and was killed by King Pelenor. He was buried in the church of St Stephen in Camelot.

Sir Mordred throughout has a bad name for treachery, stabbing people in the back and other unfair dealings. He was one of the chief fomentors of the trouble in the court against Sir Lancelot. He was with Arthur in his disputes with Lancelot.

King Arthur was at Caerleon. King Lot's wife, Morgause, was Arthur's sister or perhaps his half-sister, but the relationship was quite unknown to Arthur himself. She was sent to Caerleon with her four sons as a spy upon her brother. She was a lady of great beauty, Arthur loved her and Mordred was the child of their love.

Merlin told Arthur that he had committed incest and that the child of the incest would destroy him. When Arthur learned that the child, who should destroy him, would be born on a May-day, he ordered that all the children born on May-day of lords and ladies should be sent to him. Mordred, among many others, was sent. The ship, in which the child travelled, was wrecked and Mordred was found and nourished by a good man till he was fourteen years old, when he was brought to the court.

When Arthur went out of England to attack Lancelot, Mordred seized the kingdom. He plundered Arthur's kingdom in Cornwall and threw Gwenhwyvar from the throne and struck her.

Another story is that he loved and married Gwenhwyvar's sister, Gwenhwyvach and that the two sisters quarrelled upon some matter and struck each other and that this quarrel of the wives brought about the battle of Kamlan. This quarrel was known as one of the three furious ear-boxes of the isle of Britain.

Mordred is among the three men of dishonour of the isle of Britain. He comes third and is counted the worst of all.

373

Old versions of the name are Modred and Modrot.

The Welsh sotry is that Arthur was bidden by the Romans to pay the tribute, which Britain had paid Rome for centuries. Arthur refused the tribute and made war beyond the sea against the Romans and lost many of his men abroad. Mordred seized the kingdom in his absence. Arthur returned and fought at Kamlan. Arthur killed Mordred and was mortally wounded and died. The Welsh annals under the date 537 say that the battle of Kamlan took place. It was a year of great mortality in Britain and in Ireland. The Welsh annals say that the battle was caused by a blow, which Gwenhwyvach gave to Gwenhwyvar. Kamlan seems to mean 'the bent bank'. There are Kamlans in various parts of Wales. The Welsh say that the cause of the comparative failure of Arthur at Kamlan was that he divided his army into nine divisions instead of into only three. Three men are supposed to have survived the battle – Morvran, who was so ugly that people mistook him for a devil, Sandde, angel-face, because people mistook him for an angel, and Kynnwyl, who was the last to ride away from Arthur.

Prospectus

Prologue

Arthur, the king, is married to Gwenivere, who is childless

At the moment of the opening of the play he is threatened with a judgement or disaster, because he carried away the head of Bran the blessed, the son of King Lear, from where it lay on the white hill looking towards France. While it was there the Saxons could not land, but Arthur had removed it, thinking it wrong that Britain should be guarded by other strength than her own. Owen, the son of Maximilian the emperor, had hidden the head of Bran.

It is revealed to Gwenivere that Arthur has no heir, because of a sin committed by him in the far past, when he committed incest with his sister, Morgause, wife of King Lot of the Orkneys and mother of Gawain, Agravaine, Gareth and Gaheris.

Through this incest Modred was born.

On her death-bed Morgause declared that Modred was Arthur's son and Arthur has brought him up as his heir. He has recently married Gwenivere's sister, Gwenivach, and has brought his wife to court.

Act I

The meeting of the two sisters, Gwenivach very much younger than Gwenivere and ambitious for her husband. In their train is Modred's friend, Iudoc, a young man with a winning manner. Iudoc was in league with some of the Saxon pirates and quite ready to bring about their supremacy by any means. In the course of the act the two sisters quarrel and Gwenivach strikes Gwenivere with one of the three furious ear-boxes of the isle of Britain.

Act II

Modred, being egged on to vengeance by his wife and needing little spur, having plentiful ambitions of his own, contrives through Iudoc to persuade the warring factions in Gaul, revolting under some half-emperor, to claim tribute from Arthur with personal defiance

375

and also by raiding of some of the coastal strong-holds. Arthur, on hearing the news, sends a defiance to the claimers of tribute and goes in person after the raiders, leaving Gwenivere and a council to govern in his stead. As soon as he has gone Modred assails the queen, who temporises with him. Her sister, Gwenivach, thinking that she has beguiled her husband, attempts to poison her, but inadvertently drinks the poison herself.

Act III

Arthur returns to England hurriedly. Modred since his wife's death has lost his nerve and is quite eager to treat for peace on such terms as he can get. He sends Iudoc to treat. Iudoc distorts all the terms in such a way that each side thinks the other implacable. The battle of Kamlan ensues, in which Modred and Arthur destroy each other.

Sketch

Arthur was the son of Queen Ygern by Uther her enemy, who obtained access to her through the device of Merlin, who put upon him the shape and appearance of her husband. Arthur was brought up in the court at Tintagel, entered the service of the Romano-Britons and was stationed as a young man at Caerleon on Usk. As a young man he rose to the command of this garrison and there begat Modred incestuously. His half-sister, the queen Morgause of Orkney, a lady married to one of the many Scandinavian pirates raiding the outer islands, had been sent to his court as a spy. Not knowing the relationship, she beguiled Arthur and Modred was the result of the love-affair. She brought up Modred with her other sons, Gawaine, Agravaine, Gareth and Gaheris. At the time of Modred's birth Arthur was twenty-two. (We suggest the year 500 for the birth of Modred).

Ocrevan, a king in northern Shropshire, calls a great horse-show for all the kings of Britain. All the horse-breeders and lovers among the kings come to this under the Wrekin in the year 500. Arthur there first meets Gwenivere, the daughter of Ocrevan. Gwenivere was then eighteen and her sister, Gwenivach, a child of nine.

Arthur falls in love with Gwenivere, whom he marries that year, and has a son, Lacheu, in the next year, 501.

In the next years there are continual raidings of the heathen, in which Arthur shows genius as a soldier. He is given command of the Romano-British army and fights a long and successful campaign in Scotland, partly on the Clyde, partly on the Firth of Forth and in the Lammermoor.

In 518 the heathen make a great attack and are destroyed by Arthur at Badon Hill. This crowning success made Arthur the most important man in the island. All the kings who had served under him unanimously make him their overlord. He has, for the time, regained even the Kentish and eastern provinces and is king of Britain as far as Dumbarton.

He celebrates his victory and crowning by ordering the removal of the relics of the blessed Bran from Ludgate Hill, where they lie under the destroyed temple built over them before the legions left the island. He says that the island will not be defended by the relics of a dead man, however good, but by living good men. On his scattering the ashes of Bran, he is cursed by the last of Bran's followers.

It is at this time that Modred comes to court, full of ambitions and of bitterness. He finds a kindred soul in Gwenivach, who hates Gwenivere as much as he hates Arthur. Modred finds an ally in Yudoc, a Briton allied by marriage and by sympathy with the heathen in Kent and the east. Yudoc assures Modred of his help and tells him that large bodies of the Kentish and Essex heathen, furious at Arthur's triumph over them, are resolved to go warring over the seas against the British settlers in Brittany. It is at this time that Gwenivere and Lancelot become involved in love.

During one of the campaigns Gwenivere had been carried off by the heathen horsemen, but had been pursued and recaptured by Lancelot. This was the beginning of their love.

Modred, now married to Gwenivach, who is some years older than himself, determines to make use of this love affair for his own ends. There is a scene between the two sisters. Gwenivach strikes Gwenivere and swears to ruin her. Soon after this she and Modred find that Gwenivere is visiting Lancelot. They cause the lovers to be beset, but Lancelot routs them and saves the queen, when she is brought to trial the next morning.

It is at this point, when the court is in tumult with Lancelot and all his followers away, that a messenger comes from Brittany with the news of an appalling raid and an appeal for help.

Modred is, for the moment, triumphant, thinking that all his plans are succeeding beyond his hopes, when Lancelot returns with the queen, saying that this is no time for civil wars or disputes and that he has come to be reconciled both to Arthur and to Gawaine and to go with the army into Brittany. Gwenivere is made regent, while Arthur and his army sail for Brittany. As soon as they are gone Modred besieges Gwenivere and takes the kingdom for his own, being supported in the east by Yudoc and the heathen. Arthur hears of Modred's treachery and hurries back. On the way back Gawaine and Lancelot break into a quarrel over the death of Gareth and remain behind to fight their duel. Arthur proceeds alone, breaks through the first array which Modred sends against him and pushes into the west to save the queen. At Kamlan he sends to parley with Modred. Modred sends Yudoc, who hears all

Arthur's terms, but distorts them in his report, so that the battle takes place. Arthur is sorely wounded in the head and Modred is killed. Queens row in a barge to the shore and carry Arthur away into the island of Avalon.

Chronology

476 Uther, the king over what is now Wiltshire, Berkshire and parts of Dorset, Somerset and Hampshire, or roughly that land between the Thames and the Bristol Channel, excepting Kent, Surrey, Sussex, Devon and Cornwall, succeeds the great Ambrosius and Pendragon or chief of the British kings. He endeavours to make the Pendragonship effective against the heathen raiders.

He makes treaty with Iddoc, King of Kent, Ban, King of Benwick and then by chance with the Orkney pirate, King Lot.

477 While seeking alliance with Merchyon, King of Cornwall, he takes Ygern, Merchyon's eldest daughter, begets Arthur and is killed. The news of his killing is brought at once to King Iddoc, who, being by much the nearest of the allied kings, at once takes up the blood feud, sails to Tintagel and carries King Merchyon away, meaning to try him before the assembled kings in Augusta, but Merchyon dies before the trial.

King Ban of Benwick hears of Uther's killing and comes to Cornwall, where Breuse the Heartless, has seized the power. He kills Breuse, releases Merchyon's son, whom Breuse has imprisoned, and sets him on the throne of Cornwall as Merchyon II. Having done this, he married Elaine, old Merchyon's second daughter, and goes home to Benwick

Merchyon II, in alliance with Iddoc, administer's Uther's kingdom in trust for Arthur.

478 While Merchyon is away at Sarum about the end of March, he marries Helen.

On the same day Arthur is born at Tintagel.

A week later King Lot of Orkney, who has been wintering after a piratical cruise on the Irish coast, hears for the first time that Uther has been killed. Lot is a savage desperado specially bound to Uther by ties of devotion and gratitude. He at once sails for Tintagel, finds the blood feud at an end, but takes Morgause, Merchyon's youngest daughter, as a spoil. When she becomes seventeen (490) he marries her and has sons, Gawaine, Agravaine, Gareth and Gaheris. Merchyon returns, finds Morgause gone, but has no knowledge of who has taken her. The taking of children was then too common an occurrence.

Arthur and Ygern are brought up partly at Merchyon's court in Tintagel and partly under the three chief men at Sarum, Uther's trusted friends, Kol, Guy and Ector, sometimes called Ector of the Marsh, whose fief lay at Glastonbury and at Camelot close to it. Arthur grew up and was trained as a soldier in the Roman discipline and, while still a young man, made his name.

479   Lancelot is born at Bamborough.

480   Olwen, the daughter of King Merchyon II, is born.

489   Marc, the son of King Merchyon II, is born.

490   King Lot of Orkney marries Morgause.

496   A great raid of pirates all down the west coast. They are driven back, but not defeated. They go into winter quarters at the Orkneys and Lot sends Morgause to the camp at Caerleon on Usk to act as a spy and discover what steps are being concerted among the British. Arthur is with the legion at Caerleon engaged in keeping the south Welsh coast and the Severn, Usk and Wye from the raiders. Morgause tempts him, in order to get information from him. She fails in this, but is left with child by him.

497   The pirates make a great attempt as soon as the spring weather comes. Merchyon II is killed by Kolbein Blood-Axe; King Tallorc, coming to the rescue just too late to help Merchyon, takes away Merchyon's daughter, Olwen, (born in 480), but King Marc remains Kolbein's captive.
Kolbein settles as the ruler of Damnonia and is, for the moment, left in control there.

Modred is born.
This marks the beginning of the power of the heathen raiders.

498 Arthur, while engaged in northern Shropshire and the Tee, meets Gwenivere, daughter of one of the Shropshire kings.

499 Arthur and Lancelot first meet in repulsing a raid in what are now the Chilterns. Arthur (aged twenty-one) marries Gwenivere, but shortly after the marriage the heathen have a triumphant success and force the British to the south within the limits of the Wansdyke. While Arthur is away at Caerleon the raiders break across the Wansdyke and carry off Gwenivere, but Lancelot recovers her. This is the beginning of the love between Gwenivere and Lancelot.

517 Arthur is called in by the Pictish kingdoms to deal with a great invasion on the Firth of Forth. He overcomes this invasion and returns.

518 The defeated raiders come in great numbers to the eastern coast, are joined by the Kentish king and by the heathen settled in the eastern counties. A really great invasion takes place from the direction of Reading, going towards the Wansdyke and Arthur's kingdom of Sarum and Somerset. Arthur, inspired by a vision, attacks the heathen at Badon Hill and destroys them utterly.

520 Modred comes to court.

525 Arthur goes in his ship Pridwen to the underworld and returns with only seven of the heroes who went with him.

477 Uther goes to Merchyon, takes Ygern, begets Arthur and is killed.
Iddoc takes Merchyon to Augusta.
Merchyon II (born about 459) succeeds to the Cornish crown.
Merchyon II has been hitherto kept in subjection in the extreme south-west.

478   Merchyon II marries.
Just after his marriage, when Arthur is a little baby, Lot of
Orkney seizes Morgause from Tintagel and carries her away.

497   Merchyon is killed by Kolbein. His daughter Olwen (born 480)
is carried away by Tallorc. Marc (born 489) is kept by Kolbein.

Unpublished Lecture

When I was seventeen years of age I thought that I must at all costs strive to be less ignorant of life, past and present. Even now, seventy years later, I am the most ignorant man in the societies to which I come, but my ignorance now has some patches that it had not then received.

I was in New York City, working in the Hotel of one Luke O'Connor of whom I can never think without deep thoughts of gratitude. Among the books that the nearest bookshop offered was a modern reprint of the Morte d'Arthur of Sir Thomas Malory, which I read as history, or as closely based on history.

This reading turned me to the study of King Arthur in books and magazines for some months, when it was my fortune to meet every day a young Welsh chemist who knew another kind of Arthurian history [–] the memory of the Welsh for whatever had occurred in Wales since Rome ceased to be a power here. He knew; as the Welsh [seemed] to know instinctively what king had ruled in each small throne.

From this man I learned this Arthur was not a king, only a clever soldier employed by allied kings against marauding pirates, and that at some time in his career he had won a great victory over the pirates at a place called Badon Hill.

After this victory, he said, the war ceased, for a full generation, and Britain knew a little quiet.

This was my first hearing of Badon Hill [.]

I see, now, that such a man must have been chosen by a great body of rulers who controlled a large part of Roman Britain not yet swamped by piratical settlers, + that this area could still be held with success, by certain types of defence, and that these types of defence demanded instant signalling of attack and swiftness of counter attack.

The swiftness of the signalling of the attack could be made by [visible] signals from height to height, and would have been necessary only in those months of the year when navigation of the Channel and Irish Sea was reasonably safe with tolerable weather for small squadrons of wooden primitive shipping.

384

[The sign] could be given by fire-signal or by local telegraph, from small hill stations using the great arms of such primitive telegraphs as gave warnings during the French wars 14 centuries later.

The arms set in motion were also primitive and swiftly set moving.

May not the tradition of the banded Knights of the Round Table have existed as special trained horsemen, allotted to dealing swiftly at all threatened points of the coast. Their possible danger some landing-places could be swiftly guarded, and the attackers quelled by the horsemen and their members killed.

Few attacks at first, however many they may have seemed, could have been manned by many men.

The destruction of many small parties of pirates must have tended to attempts by larger groups of allies.

Presently, somewhere in the coveted lowlands of central Britain, in the first quarter of the Fifth Century A.D. the defenders were attacked by a strong allied body of raiders, and after a long and doubtful struggle were beaten and destroyed to a man.

We know nothing more of this attack save that it was mostly claimed to have been North of the Scottish border, or somewhere in Shropshire, or in Berkshire[,] Hampshire, Wiltshire and elsewhere, but that it ended the attacks by raids, in the victory at Badon Hill.

NOTES

1   Constance Babington Smith, *John Masefield: A Life* [hereafter cited as CBS] (OUP, 1978), p. 180.
2   Jennifer R. Goodman, *The Legend of Arthur in British and American Literature* (Boston: G.K. Hall [Twayne], 1988), pp. 94–95.
3   John Masefield, *So Long to Learn: Chapters of an Autobiography* [hereafter cited as *SLL*] (London: Heinemann, 1952), pp. 10, 12, 90.
4   John Masefield, *In the Mill* [hereafter cited as *IM*] (London: Heinemann, 1941), p. 44. Indeed, as late as 1966, Masefield could write to a friend, 'It was bliss to come to Browning after a nightmare of Idylls by Alfred T.': *Letters to Reyna* [hereafter cited as *LR*], edited by William Buchan (London: Buchan and Enright, 1983), p. 486.
5   *SLL*, p. 11.
6   CBS, pp. 9, 16–21; *SLL*, pp. 72–73.
7   CBS, pp. 22–33.
8   *IM*, p. 44.
9   *SLL*, p. 90: the account included here was first published in 'The Joy of Story-Telling' in the April 1951 issue of *Atlantic*.
10 John Masefield, 'In a New York Saloon', in *A Mainsail Haul* (London: Elkin Matthews, 1905), p. 94.
11 CBS, p. 35; *IM*, p. 44.
12 See *LR*, p. 380, and Judith Masefield, 'Introduction' to Corliss Lamont, *Remembering John Masefield* [hereafter cited as *RJM*] (New York: Frederick Ungar / The Crossroad / Continuum Publishing Group, 1991), p. 7.
13 *IM*, pp. 47–48.
14 Punctuation and a probable reading supplied in square brackets: see *Unpublished Lecture* in Part IV for the full text; by 1965, Masefield had already imaginatively realized a number of the historical speculations in these notes in his novel *Badon Parchments* (1947).
15 See *LR*, pp. 235–36, and Dame Muriel Spark, who noted after her visit with Masefield in 1950, that he had spoken of his admiration for Peacock's poetry, especially mentioning the 'War Song' from *Elphin*: 'Visiting the Laureate', *The New Yorker*, 26 August 1991, p. 66 (also incorporated into the latest edition of her *John Masefield*).

16 *SLL*, p. 92 (and note p. 13), 112–14; CBS, pp. 41–43, 46, 49–50.

17 Letter of '[6 Nov 1930]' in *Letters of John Masefield to Florence Lamont* [hereafter cited as *LFL*], edited by Corliss Lamont and Lansing Lamont (London: Macmillan, 1979), p. 187.

18 LR, pp. 107, 116–17 (with paraphrase from Malory XXI, 13).

19 CBS, pp. 53, 234: could this be Masefield's version of the story of Taliesin? – given his acquaintance with both the *Mabinogion* and *The Misfortunes of Elphin*, it is a tantalizing possibility, though he might simply have used 'Elphin' freely, as he does other Arthurian names in his later works: unfortunately, the current location of the notebook is uncertain.

20 Masefield had become acquainted with Yeats's *Poems* in 1899, and was one of his circle of friends by late 1900; it was in this context that a close friendship developed between Masefield and that other Arthurian, Laurence Binyon: CBS, pp. 59–67, 72.

21 I thank Professor Francis Berry for drawing my attention to this reference; I quote *Animula* from *Collected Poems* [hereafter cited as *CP*] (London: Heinemann, Oct. 1941 rpt. of 1938 'New and Enlarged Edition'), pp. 663–68.

22 John Masefield, 'Introduction' to R.C. Phillimore, *Poems* (London: Sidgwick and Jackson, 1913), p. x.

23 Poems: *The Everlasting Mercy* (1911), *The Widow in the Bye Street* (1912), *Dauber* (1913), *The Daffodil Fields* (1913), *Rosas* (1918), *Reynard the Fox* (1919), *Enslaved* (1920), *Right Royal* (1920), *King Cole* (1921); verse dramas: *Philip the King* (1914), *Good Friday* (1916), *A King's Daughter* (1923).

24 Letter of 28 June 1966 and 'Introduction' in *RJM*, pp. 95, 8.

25 CBS, pp. 77–79, 186–92; and see Kenneth W. Pickering, *Drama in the Cathedral: The Canterbury Festival Plays 1928–1948* (Worthing, W. Sussex: Churchman Publishing Ltd, 1985).

26 Further possible illumination must await the examination of Masefield's extant unpublished correspondence and other papers; the surviving archives of William Heinemann Ltd unfortunately seem to include nothing relevant from this period.

27 *SLL*, pp. 227–29.

28 'The Fight on the Beach or The Passing', stanza 2.

29 Among the manuscripts of *When Good King Arthur*; it is very close to the published version: those who, like Norris Lacy, find 'Uther saw Ygrain the Bright, / His heart went pit-pat at the sight' to be 'genuinely terrible lines' may prefer the original reading – 'black heart lusted' – revised here in Masefield's hand to 'heart went pit-pat' (see Norris J. Lacy and Geoffrey Ashe, *The Arthurian Handbook* (New York: Garland, 1988), p. 190).

30 In 'Midsummer Night', Modred describes himself to Arthur as 'your bastard by your aunt', which is in keeping with the *Chronology* and 'The Begetting of Arthur' – but in the next stanza calls himself 'son and nephew'!

31 For example, in both, Marc is 29 years old in the year of the battle of Badon, which is 20 years after Kolbein's killing of Meirchyon, and Tallorc's rescue of Olwen, allowing Tristan to be 'about twenty years' old in A.D. 518.

32 Letters of '[1920]' and '[2 Apr 1927]' in *LFL*, pp. 162–63, 165–66.

33 John Masefield, *I Want! I Want!* (London: National Book Council, 1944), p. 20.

34 As far as the draft goes – it extends to the stanza corresponding to stanza 25 – it is quite close to the published version, on the whole.

35 Events still presupposed in both 'The Aftermath' and 'Midsummer Night' dialogue drafts.

36 Letters of '[Sep 1927]' and '[16 Sept 1927]', *LFL*, pp. 169–70. Two years later, writing of an article 'about K Arthur's twelve battles' in which the author 'makes no shot at the whereabouts of Badon', Masefield says 'so my two sites, especially the better of them, still hold the field with me' – without naming them (see *LFL*, p. 178). However, Miss Audrey Napier-Smith has kindly transcribed for me a passage not included in *LR*, from Masefield's letter to her of 26 September 1962, in which he says of 'Baydon', 'in the heart of the Berkshire Downs', 'which has the highest-up church in England', 'I think that it is the Badon Hill where K Arthur scuppered the Pagans [. . .] but there are many other candidates for the site. (I have been to them all now, + I stick to Baydon)'. (Note also *LR*, pp. 169–70.)

37 See the letter of 'September 1970' from Mrs Willard Connely, 'whose stage name is Agnes Lauchlin', to Corliss Lamont, quoted in *RJM*, p. 76.

38 Anne Ridler, 'Introduction' to Charles Williams, *The Image of the City and Other Essays* (London: OUP, 1958), p. lxiv.

39 Modred's apparent age in 'The Fight on the Beach' is another factor requiring consideration here.

40 There is no clear final draft of 'The Aftermath': Part III includes the text of all that is extant (incorporating final emendations), from which, for Part II, I have extracted from the notebook the sequence of what seem the latest drafts of each section, though omitting those concerned with the same matter as 'Brother Lot' and 'The Taking of Morgause', ignoring an experiment in a different stanza-form, and selecting an earlier stanza on Ban because it seemed superior to its successor.

41 Might 'The Hunt is Up' hold the key: that, following its rejection,

389

Masefield developed 'Breuse' independently in both 'The Fight on the Beach' and 'The Begetting of Arthur' (etc.)?

42 Quoted in *RJM*, p. 82.

43 *I Want! I Want!*, p. 20.

44 Fraser Drew, *John Masefield's England: A Study of the National Themes in His Work* (Rutherford: Fairleigh Dickinson UP / Cranbury, NJ: Associated University Presses, 1973), p. 40.

45 CBS, pp. 189–91.

46 *SLL*, p. 216.

47 While it would be interesting to identify Modred's follower 'Math' in 'The Fight on the Beach' with 'Captain Math' here, I know of no evidence to support this.

48 See CBS, pp. 187, 205: the second cast list includes the note '1 copy + 1 carbon to Masefield Boars Hill Oxford'; the reference to Lear could indicate that the play followed the 'Hill Players' first production, *King Lear*, on 6 April 1922' (CBS, p. 187); otherwise, (1) the draft of 'The Old Tale of the Begetting' could have been written for Act I of the play, or reused at any time in it (Masefield has revised Math's line 'All about mewing and spewing and weathercocks' to 'All about dukes and pukes and would I were dead', which would suggest that his later intention was to use 'The Old Tale' draft as Owain's song – an extraordinary choice to sing before Arthur!: I have included Math's line in its unrevised form, and retained the previously unpublished 'Pendragon Ruthercock' as Owain's song); (2) the attention to women voting need not be more pertinent before 2 July 1928, when an act of Parliament extended the franchise, than after that date; (3) similarly, allusion to the Laureateship need not be less likely before 10 May 1930 than after; (4) Lewis Masefield (born 1910) may have acted at an early age; (5) Leslie Davey appears in both the cast list of *A King's Daughter* (1923) and the acknowledgements of *Minnie Maylow's Story* (1931); (6) only one date, difficult to decipher, occurs among the MSS – July 14 (or '24'?) 1931 (or '1932', or '1933'?) – and it comes in the notebook, with apparent reference to the draft of a poem unconnected with *When Good King Arthur*, only after everything relating to the play: while this may mean that the play must have been drafted before this date (whatever it is), it need not tell us anything more exact about when the play was written, as the additions might have been made to the notebook at any time thereafter.

49 Cf. the details concerning Arthur's sword in 'The Fight on the Beach'; in 'An Art Worker', the imagined plan for a painting of 'Arthur's and Modred's bands / In fight on Camlan Sands'

includes, 'in the rocks, the Past, / Claiming her sword at last' (*Gautama the Enlightened and other verse* (NY: Macmillan, 1941), pp. 43–44).

50 *SLL*, p. 90.

51 For example, in *I Want! I Want!* (p. 28), Masefield says 'Think what remains to be done in clearing-up the Dark Ages, in solving all the problems of the Wansdyke, Bokerley Dyke, Offa's Dyke, and, perhaps, identifying Badon Hill beyond any possibility of error.' (In a passage of Letter 893, from 1963, which Miss Napier-Smith has transcribed, Masefield refers to 'a line of the Wansdyke' which 'runs from Inkpen west to near Bath' as 'a great barrier made by K Arthur (I wd say)'.)

52 See Drew, pp. 22–24, 52, for an introduction to Masefield's interest in (non-Arthurian) Roman Britain, and note *SLL*, pp. 152–53, 230–31; Miss Napier-Smith has transcribed for me, from 'Letter 872' (1963), an example of the kind of anachronistic play both Jones and Williams also enjoyed: Masefield responds to her reference to what was reputedly the oldest surviving pillar-box (in Buxton), 'Was it King Arthur's pillar-box or did / the Druids frame it, hollow, mouth and lid?'

53 On Masefield and midsummer more generally, note Drew, pp. 75, 77 – and the early poem also entitled 'Midsummer Night'.

54 It is my understanding of the conclusion of the poem that the boy did not reach his mother before she died (which precludes any concern with her enjoying, or suffering, life within the world ever since); the remembered sorrows which move Marc to help the boy may relate to his being orphaned, as in *Tristan and Isolt* – a fate shared with Masefield, who was also about the boy's age when his own mother died; in 'An Art Worker' (p. 44), the summary of the tale says, of 'The Fruit, Eternal Life,' that Marc 'went out into the dark / And gave it to a poor / Sick woman at his door.'

55 Contrast the end of 'Tristan's Singing' where either some kind of bodily assumption is intended, or Tristan and Isolt's 'rags and robes' include, by metaphor, their bodies, which, as 'relics' on a bier, 'lie there still within the holy shrine' in 'the Dun'.

56 John Masefield, *The Midnight Folk: A Novel* (London: Heinemann, 1927), p. 231; it is noteworthy that they are in general fellow-workers with the Saxon 'St. Alpig' (p. 226: presumably Ælfheah, Archbishop of Canterbury, martyred in 1012, whose body was found to be incorrupt in 1105), and help Kay to restore, to active use in a cathedral, treasures including images of such 'Bringers of Blessings' as 'Saint Augustine' and 'King Alfred of Wessex' (p. 316).

57 I have not attempted to compare the versions of Fordun in his *Scotichronicon*, or of Roger of Wendover in his *Flowers of History*, and for Vincent (who specifies 'ubi quatuor viae conveniunt') I have relied on the extract provided in Appendix B of Sabine Baring-Gould's *Curious Myths of the Middle Ages* (London: Longmans, 1892): see pp. 224–27, 641–42; I am indebted to Mr Andrew Smith for informing me of these sources in this account.

58 Masefield had already completed at least a partial draft of this poem (c.4–5 Mar. 1927), when he wrote the first draft of 'The Sailing of Hell Race' (finished 'Feb 25. [. . .] 192[8]'), in which Arthur's Helper is described as 'The Queen of Wisdom'.

59 I have not given separate attention to reincarnation, which seems an element of the retelling (in *Tristan and Isolt* and in 'The Begetting' and 'The Birth of Arthur'), since – as Masefield's poem, 'A Creed', makes clear – though it entails practical complications, it does not affect the need to submit to purification in accordance with a transcendent good; note also Drew's discussion of Masefield's beliefs about the persistent effects of actions (pp. 51–54).

60 *SLL*, p. 12.

61 Whatever misgivings one may have about some of Masefield's accounts of purification, such as that of Rosamund in 'The Rose of the World', in *Minnie Maylow's Story* – where we are blithely told 'the White Sisters prayed her into Heaven' and more importantly 'wrought / A white-rose tomb for her from loving thought / So that none thought of her, nor ever will / Save as a lovely thing that suffer'd ill' (CP, p. 994) – or that of Isolt and Tristan in 'Tristan's Singing', with its inattention to Marc.

62 Charles Williams, 'John Masefield' in *Poetry at Present* (Oxford: Clarendon Press, 1930), p. 119: curiously, Williams includes neither *Tristan and Isolt* nor *Midsummer Night* in his bibliographical note, and I am unaware of any reference by him, published or unpublished, to any of Masefield's Arthurian works; while Masefield might seem to follow Williams in connecting Arthur and Byzantium – first in *Basilissa: A Tale of the Emperor Theodora* (1940) and subsequently in *Badon Parchments* (1947) – I have not encountered any reference by Masefield to Williams or his Arthurian works.

63 Cf. what Peacock does in chapter 2 of *The Misfortunes of Elphin*.

64 In *RJM*, p. 4. *The Midnight Folk* was written – and published (November 1927) – while Masefield was working on his Arthurian cycle. In the first notebook, between the drafts of 'Arthur and His Ring' (4–5 March 1927) and 'The Hunt is Up' (25 June 1927) occurs an untitled five-page plot summary of the novel (with

additional notes on facing pages and following the summary), which differs in many details from the finished work – and includes no reference to Arthur and his court. While this need not be significant in such a summary, it is also possible that the novel did not originally have any such element, and that its addition was an effect of the Arthurian context in which the book was written. Notable in *The Midnight Folk* are Kay's flying with the Bat in 'a suit of wings' while wearing 'fox-eye spectacles', and swimming with the Otter 'wearing otter-skin', and, in chapter 4 of its dream-sequel, *The Box of Delights or When the Wolves were Running* (1935), his transformations, courtesy of Herne, into stag, duck, and fish – to which Jennifer Goodman (pp. 95–96) points, as a likely source for Arthur's similar transformations in T.H. White's *The Sword in the Stone*. It seems possible that such details (including the transformations of Cole's 'play' with cubes in *The Box of Delights*, ch. 2), together with Kay's flight from his witch-governess and his fortuitously obtaining knowledge magically prepared by the witches and not intended for him, in *The Midnight Folk*, represent a deliberate play with elements from 'The Story of Taliesin' in the *Mabinogion*.

393

SOURCES AND ACKNOWLEDGEMENTS

Sources

This volume reproduces the English first-edition texts of all of the works previously published in books, with any typographical errors silently corrected. 'The Ballad of Sir Bors' is from *Ballads* (London: Elkin Mathews, 1903). All the other books were published by William Heinemann Ltd (London): *Tristan and Isolt: A Play in Verse* (1927); *Midsummer Night and other Tales in Verse* (1928): all the poems in this book except the non-Arthurian 'Fulfilment' are reprinted here; 'The Love Gift', 'Tristan's Singing', and 'Simkin, Tomkin and Jack' from *Minnie Maylow's Story and Other Tales and Scenes* (1931); 'Tristan and Isolt' from *On the Hill* (1949); 'Caer Ocvran' from *In Glad Thanksgiving* ('First published 1966' / copyright 1967). 'My Library: Volume One' is reproduced from *The Saturday Review of Literature* (20 May 1950) 16.

Among the previously unpublished works, only *When Good King Arthur* has an authorial title: I have, for convenience of reference, given titles to the rest.

MS Eng. 811.8(11) in the Houghton Library, Harvard University, is the source for both *When Good King Arthur* (written under the pseudonym 'Alfred Jones') and 'All Hallow Night' (a one-page TS). The editions presented here are from a microfilm copy.

The sources for all the other previously unpublished poetry and prose are in the Harry Ransom Humanities Research Center (HRHRC), the University of Texas at Austin. The following are TSS: 'Arthur's Youth' (3 pp.), three stanzas of 'The Aftermath' drafts (2pp.), *Notes 1* (3 pp.), *Notes 2* (3 pp.), *Prospectus* (4 pp.), *Sketch* (4 pp.), and *Chronology* (6 pp.: the main sequence occupies five pages, with the three entries which I have placed at the end, on a separate page). The rest are in MS, with the *Unpublished Lecture* filling '[6pp. in notebook]', the 'Midsummer Night' dialogue drafts occurring on loose sheets, and all the others in two notebooks. In the HRHRC, what I call the first notebook is described as 'Arthurian poems work book' and what I call the second notebook as '[Notebook 8]'. Some details concerning these notebooks are included in the *Introduction*.

In his verse, Masefield tends to punctuate fairly lightly, and his publishers have respected this. While not fair copies, most of the MSS of the unpublished works presented here are in Masefield's hand. I have not, however, made a concerted attempt to identify all the hands represented, and have been unsuccessful in such attempts as I have made (Masefield's amanuenses were apparently numerous and varied). On the whole, I have been conservative in my editing, even where accidentals are concerned – for example, changing very little of the punctuation found in typescripts or holographs, and not attempting to standardize it.

Where *When Good King Arthur* is concerned, I have, however, to some extent followed the conventions used in *Tristan and Isolt*. I have also added some stage directions, placing these in square brackets. Because no fair copy of a final version survives among these manuscripts (nor, so far as I know, anywhere else), the text I present is necessarily a composite one, and in arriving at it, I have not always felt certain what Masefield himself finally intended. I have taken the liberty of including some lines which it is not clear that Masefield intended to retain in a final version. All such lines are also in square brackets. In Act III, for the sake of consistency with Masefield's late intentions, whenever Helen addresses Arthur as 'father' I have silently altered this to 'my lord', and in one instance altered 'my father's' to 'King Arthur's', while in Math's speech after the entrance of Geraint I have altered 'daughter's' to 'dear ward's'. Where Masefield has revised the end of Arthur's line 'By marrying you forthwith to this your lover' to 'this who loves you' I have altered 'this' to 'one'. Six other alterations, all within square brackets, must be noted. Act I: (1) Helen's first speech: 'The judges may prefer him before Owain' > 'Those judging [. . .]'. (2) Helen's line at the end of her exchange with Geraint (inserted from an earlier version): 'Here is my father. Tell him if you dare.' > 'Then tell the king, my guardian, if you dare.' (3) I have replaced Merlin's lines – 'King Arthur, vote: that's well: now I myself, / Howel, now Kynon, captain Math and crew.' – with a stage direction. In Act III, the only text which survives for the end of the scene preceding the appearance of the Soothsayer is from the version referred to in the *Introduction*, in which Arthur is about to 'utter judgement in this case', namely 'In Geraint's suit for the princess's hand.' In consequence, some lines are inapt to the revised scene in which Arthur is about to crown Geraint Laureate. (4) and (5): in one exchange, Arthur: 'Utter your message when I have given sentence' > 'Utter your message when I have conferred the crown', and the Soothsayer: 'My message must be said before you sentence' > 'My message must be said before you do so'. (6) Where Masefield has revised the line 'You are interrupting us in uttering sentence' to 'You are interrupting Arthur in his court', transferring it from Arthur to Merlin, I have restored it to Arthur and altered the last words to 'us in performing a rite'.

Acknowledgements

I am very grateful to the Society of Authors, as the literary representative of the Estate of John Masefield, for permission to reprint the published works and to publish the previously unpublished works included in this volume, and to quote from further works in the *Introduction*. I am also indebted to William Heinemann Ltd for permission to reprint the published works. The works published here for the first time appear variously (so far as the rights of those libraries extend) by permission of the Houghton Library, Harvard University, and of the Harry Ranson Humanities Research Center, the University of Texas at Austin: I am most grateful to those institutions for allowing me to examine (in photo-reproduction) the manuscripts of Arthurian works by Masefield in their care.

John Masefield's England by Fraser Drew is a *sine qua non* of the present volume, having first introduced me to Masefield as an Arthurian poet, and now directed me to all of Masefield's major critical references to the Arthurian material, and all but the last of the Arthurian works in verse, published during his lifetime. I am also grateful to Professor Drew for responding to my queries and for his kind encouragement. Similar thanks are due to other 'Masefield people' as well: to Dr Corliss Lamont and Mr Crocker Wight (both of whom also generously gave me copies of the latest editions of their works on Masefield), Professor Francis Berry, Miss Audrey Napier-Smith (who in her immense kindness reread all 1285 of Masefield's letters to her, to see if she could discover any Arthurian references not included in the published selection, *Letters to Reyna*), and most especially to Mr Geoffrey Handley-Taylor, whom it would be difficult to thank adequately, for all the valuable information and suggestions he has proffered so courteously and with such promptness and thoroughness. I am pleased to thank Mr Andrew Smith, Dr Arthur Kincaid, and my father, for variously giving me the benefits of their learning and industry.

My unsuccessful search for the manuscript of 'The Tale of Elphin' incurred many debts of gratitude: to Mr Stephen Crook of the Berg Collection, New York Public Library, Miss H.M. Young of the University of London Library, Mrs A.S. Paice of the Ledbury Library, Ms Sandra Cromey of the New College Library, and most notably to Mrs Mary Desborough, who searched through the papers of her late husband, Vincent R. d'A. Desborough, for it, and to Miss Constance Babington Smith – whose suggestion that I consult the HRHRC led to my acquaintance with the unpublished works there. I am grateful to Ms Cathy Henderson and Ms Heather Moore of the HRHRC for all of their assistance in first informing me, and later supplying me with photocopies, of all the Arthurian works in the John Masefield Collection. I am similarly grateful to Ms Jennie Rathbun of the Houghton Library for sending me details of their Masefield holdings, and supplying me with a microfilm of MS Eng. 811.8(11). I am gratefully indebted, in Oxford, to the County, English Faculty, and Bodleian Libraries, for giving me ready access to the works by Masefield in their collections – and especially to Dr Judith Priestman of the Bodleian for all her help, and also to the staff of the Gemeentearchief Barneveld and to Mr J. Richard Abell and the staff of the History Department at the Main Branch of the Public Library of Cincinnati and Hamilton County, for their assistance with microfilm readers.

I am very thankful for the encouragement and support of Dr Richard Barber and Boydell & Brewer, who have done so much to make the volume possible in its present form. John Masefield regularly dedicated his books 'To my Wife' – even the second Arthurian notebook bears an informal equivalent: 'For Con from Jan'. If an edition could have a dedication, I too would write, 'To my Wife', or 'For Tilly': I can at least thank her, whose support and help made the completion of this volume possible.

ARTHURIAN STUDIES